THE UFO FILES

THE UFO FILES

THE INSIDE STORY OF REAL-LIFE SIGHTINGS

DAVID CLARKE

The National Archives

First published in 2009 by
The National Archives
Kew, Richmond, Surrey TW9 4DU
United Kingdom

www.national archives.gov.uk

The National Archives brings together
the Public Records Office,
Historic Manuscripts Commission,
Office of Public Sector Information,
and Her Majesty's Stationery Office.

A catalogue card for this book is available
from the British Library.

ISBN 978 1 905615 50 6

Jacket design by
Goldust Design

Book design and typesetting by
Ken Wilson | point918

Printed in Malta by
Gutenberg Press

Cover Illustration
UFO Over a Lake, Getty images

The author and publishers would like to thank
the following for permission to reproduce their
material in this edition:
Punch Ltd, 1; Mary Evans, 6, 11, 13;
Robert Jones, 7; Ronald Claridge, 10;
Stan Hubbard, 14; Contact International UFO
Research, 19; Alex Birch, 25; Don Moreland, 39;
David Hastings, 47. Figs. 4, 12 and 16 feature head-
lines from the *Scarborough Daily Post* (20 February,
1913), the *Sheffield Telegraph* (9 July, 1947) and the
Yorkshire Evening Press (20 September, 1952)
respectively. Figs. 36 and 37 are taken from
Hansard, 18 January 1979, which is Crown
Copyright. All of the other images are taken from
the files at the National Archives. See picture
captions for file references.

CONTENTS

INTRODUCTION 7

ONE **STRANGE LIGHTS IN THE SKIES** 11

TWO **THE FLYING SAUCER AGE** 32

THREE **COLD WAR UFOs** 56

FOUR **CLOSE ENCOUNTERS** 79

FIVE **CROP CIRCLES AND ALIEN ABDUCTIONS** 102

SIX **TURN OF THE CENTURY UFOs** 125

AFTERWORD 148

NOTES ON THE TEXT 152

RESOURCES 154

INDEX 156

ACKNOWLEDGEMENTS 160

INTRODUCTION

THROUGHOUT recorded history people have observed objects in the heavens that they have been unable to identify. Until relatively recently celestial phenomena such as comets, the aurorae and eclipses of the sun and moon were regarded with superstitious awe and terror. Today most people have a basic understanding of an eclipse and the origins of comets and meteors, but there remain many less readily recognizable things in the sky. Together such things fall into the category of Unidentified Flying Objects, or UFOs, a term that covers anything in the heavens that cannot be readily identified but carries the heavy implication of an extraterrestrial origin.

This book is largely based upon the real-life accounts of UFO experiences recorded in files collected by Britain's Ministry of Defence (MoD), many of which are today held by the National Archives, based in Kew, Richmond. This is a repository of key documents covering a thousand years of British history. The National Archives has made many of the most popular documents available in digital form via its website (*www.nationalarchives.gov.uk*). These, however, currently represent a relatively small percentage of the dazzling array held by the National Archives, the vast majority of which, from MI5 records to trench maps and census returns, can be ordered up and consulted onsite for free by anyone who is in possession of a reader's ticket (see www.nationalarchives.gov.uk/visit/whattobring.htm).

The sightings described in this book were mostly made by ordinary people, from all walks of life, who felt they should report their experiences to the authorities. They range from strange sightings made in the early

1900s and during the First and Second World Wars, through the first sightings of 'flying saucers' in the late 1940s and 1950s, right up to the present day. There are a great variety of stories recorded in official files and some are far more credible than others. Some describe lights and shapes in the sky, others involve close encounters with strange flying objects and their crews and even contacts with 'alien occupants'. Where substantial quotes are taken from documents in National Archives files, document references are given in the text at the end of the quote.

The most recent of these files, covering the period 1978–2007 and popularly described as 'Britain's X-Files', were opened to the public in digital form only in 2008, three years after the arrival of the UK's Freedom of Information Act (FOIA). Released with personal information obscured, this collection, which otherwise would have remained closed for the standard 30-year period, contains some 160 files. It is being transferred to the National Archives in chronological order in a process scheduled to end in 2010. Podcasts and records guides can be accessed with PDFs of the files themselves at *www.nationalarchives.gov.uk/ufos/*. The complete original files, where these have survived, will eventually be opened when the normal 30-year closure period has ended.

The release of the files led to unprecedented media interest across the world and serious coverage by most national and regional newspapers and TV news in Britain. During the days that followed the opening of the first collection in May 2008, the National Archives UFO page — set up to provide access to the files — received more than 1.7 million visitors, more than double that of previous campaigns such as the launch of the Domesday Survey online. Statistics showed internet searches on UFOs tripled overnight across the globe and it was reported that the bookmakers William Hill had lowered the odds of finding extraterrestrial life from 100/1 to 80/1.

The MoD's decision to release these files early was taken, so they said, to counter what they described as 'the maze of rumour and frequently ill-informed speculation' surrounding their alleged involvement in UFO research and investigation. But why has the government kept these documents under lock and key for so many years?

Secrecy and Freedom of Information

In the aftermath of the Second World War some countries, such as the United States, Canada and Great Britain, established official projects to collect and scrutinize reports for any clues that might suggest UFOs could be a threat to national security. In Britain reports were collected and, on occasions, investigated by the Air Ministry and Ministry of Defence (MoD). The MoD states that it examines UFO reports solely to establish if what was seen has any 'defence significance'. This is normally taken to mean a threat such as that posed by an enemy aircraft or missile, but the MoD says that to date no UFO report has revealed any such evidence.

Nevertheless, great secrecy surrounded many aspects of military operations and intelligence during the Cold War and the MoD's interest in UFOs was no exception. At the same time the fact that many official papers on UFOs have been withheld for half a century, and destroyed in others, has increased speculation about what the remaining files contain and provided a steady supply of fuel for conspiracy theorists.

Before the arrival of Freedom of Information the British public had no *automatic* right to examine any government papers. Things began to change in 1994. Before then files containing information on UFO sightings were treated in the same way as all other government records: they were retained for a minimum of 30 years before they were reviewed for preservation at the National Archives (then known as the Public Record Office). Any material deemed 'sensitive' could be withheld for longer periods and, in the case of intelligence records, this could be 50 years or more. Furthermore, the Grigg Committee of 1957 recommended that some 95 per cent of government records could be destroyed at first review stage. As a result many papers on subjects that the reviewers arbitrarily decided were of no historical importance—as UFOs were categorized until 1967—were lost before they reached a public archive.

In 1994, John Major's government introduced a limited right of access to records younger than 30 years. This legislation was known as 'The Code of Practice for Access to Government Information' and was a precursor to the full Freedom of Information Act that became part of the Labour Party manifesto in the General Election of 1997. By 2007, when the decision was made to transfer the remaining documents, more than 200 UFO files had already been opened at the National Archives.

The chronological spread of the documents begins before the First World War and, when the transfer process is complete, the National Archives will hold a complete collection of official UFO files up to the present day. For the period 1962 to 2007 this includes details of around 10,000 sightings reported to the Ministry of Defence. While some more traditional historians may not regard UFOs as a serious topic, the subject is undeniably an important part of the social history of the twentieth century and this is reflected in the intense public interest in the content of the UFO files. This book is based upon a selection of the more fascinating examples and charts how the government, scientific establishment and media have reacted to experiences that defy attempts to explain them.

ONE *'What is the explanation of the strange mystery of this goblin airship? Does it really exist or is it a figment of an excited imagination?'* Daily Mirror, 27 February 1913

STRANGE LIGHTS IN THE SKIES

T HE TERMS 'Unidentified Flying Object' and 'flying saucer' were first coined in the aftermath of the Second World War. In the years that followed, the Ministry of Defence would go on to receive and file away thousands of reports from ordinary members of the public, while the idea of alien visitation became a mainstay of science fiction books, films and TV series.

This does not mean that there were no strange things in our skies before then. If you know where to look history is full of accounts that seem spookily similar to modern UFO sightings, although contemporary explanations were often very different. A good example comes from late nineteenth-century America where a flood of sightings of flying machines were attributed to a lone inventor who had perfected a design and was testing it in secrecy. These sightings, however, took place more than five years before the Wright brothers' flimsy aeroplane took to the air at Kitty Hawk. Intriguingly they also included many themes that would later turn up in UFO 'flaps', including landings in remote areas, crashes that left behind strange pieces of metal inscribed with hieroglyphs, and even encounters with crews.

Airships and scareships

In Britain one of the earliest examples dates from just over a hundred years ago, in the spring of 1909, when news began to trickle in of weird lights and cigar-shaped objects seen lurking in the heavens at night. Startling accounts soon appeared in the press. Among these was one volunteered by Fred

Harrison from King's Lynn, Norfolk, which was published in the *Daily Express* on 14 May 1909:

> 'I heard a whirring noise overhead, and when I looked up I saw that the fields round were lit up by a bright light. The light came from a long, dark object which was travelling swiftly overhead. It was low down—only a little way above the trees—so I could see it plainly... The searchlight lit up the road, the farm buildings, the trees and everything it touched, so that it was like day.'

Some reports came from respectable sources. One of the first was made by a serving officer of the Peterborough police force who was pounding the beat in the early hours of 23 March 1909. According to a story published in the *Daily Mail* two days later, PC Kettle heard 'the steady buzz of a high-powered engine' and on looking up saw a powerful light high up in the dawn sky and 'a dark body, oblong and narrow in shape, outlined against the stars.'

If these accounts had appeared today they might well have made headlines as the latest UFO or flying saucer sightings. In 1909 they were interpreted not as evidence of alien craft that had crossed vast interplanetary distances, but of enemy airships that had travelled to Britain across the North Sea. The monstrous German Zeppelin was less than a decade old but had in its various incarnations come to symbolize German technical superiority in the air. With rivalry between the two countries growing, these sightings were taken by some as incontrovertible evidence that Germany was spying on Britain from the air.

AN EARLY SILLY SEASON.

The Sea-Serpent. "WELL, IF THIS SORT OF THING KEEPS ON, IT'LL MEAN A DULL AUGUST FOR ME."

FIG. 1 A *Punch* cartoon by Bernard Partridge published at the height of the 'phantom airship' scare in 1909.

As with the late nineteenth-century American sightings there were even allegations of 'contact', as found in the tale of the Cardiff man who encountered what he thought to be a landed airship on a remote hillside in South Wales. Mr Lethbridge, a Punch-and-Judy showman, was riding across Caerphilly Mountain late at night in May 1909 when he turned a bend and saw 'a long-tube-shaped affair lying on the roadside'. Two men dressed in heavy fur-coats and caps were busy at work on their flying machine. As he approached they jumped up and 'jabbered furiously to each other' in a language he didn't understand. Before he could say anything, the men (whom he assumed were German spies) jumped into a cabin beneath the airship, which then 'rose into the air in a zig-zag fashion'. It disappeared towards Cardiff, showing two brilliant lights as it rose into the sky.[1]

As headlines questioned 'Whose is the airship?' some members of the press used these alarming stories to pressurize the British government to increase spending on aircraft. Others asked 'does it really exist or is it a figment of our imagination?' It was, as many recognized at the time, highly unlikely that any extant German airships would have been capable of such a journey. After all, it was only in July 1909 that French aeronaut Louis Blériot completed his famous aeroplane crossing of the English Channel, a feat that led the newspaper magnate Lord Northcliffe to proclaim 'England is no longer an island'.

Sceptical journalists dubbed the nocturnal visitors scareships and phantom airships and asked why they seemed to vanish at dawn. At some 500 miles each way, the round trip from the Zeppelin hangars at Friedrichshafen in Germany to the east coast of Britain would also have been impossible to complete under cover of darkness and would have taken the giant airship over parts of Belgium and France in daylight, where it would have been seen by thousands of people.

The Sheerness incident

Although the 1909 airship scare came to an end after a couple of months, more sightings would follow. In 1912 Winston Churchill, then First Lord of the Admiralty, presided over what could be called the first government inquiry into a UFO sighting over a sensitive military base. The future Prime Minister's interest in this subject would resurface again when UFOs made headlines during the 1950s (see p.46).

On 13 October 1912 a new naval Zeppelin, the L-l, set out on a 30-hour endurance flight from its base at Friedrichshafen in Germany. The airship made slow and steady progress out over the North Sea; it then turned towards Berlin, where it landed at 3.45 pm on the following day. Just after sunset that afternoon, something was seen and heard flying above the port of Sheerness in Kent. The dockyards here were an important part of Britain's defences and home to a Royal Navy torpedo school and naval flying station at Eastchurch.

As the days passed news of the Zeppelin flight over the North Sea reached the British government and the incident assumed a more sinister aspect for officials. On 25 October the director of the Admiralty Air Department, Murray F. Sueter, asked the Captain of the Royal Navy torpedo school to 'make

FIG. 2 Winston Churchill in 1910. Two years later, as First Lord of the Admiralty, he ordered the first British government inquiry into a UFO sighting over the Sheerness naval base in Essex. This UFO was suspected to be the German Zeppelin, the L1.
COPY 1/543

private enquiries' to discover whether a Zeppelin had visited Sheerness. Questioned in the House of Commons on 21 November, Churchill wrote: 'I caused enquiries to be made and have ascertained that an unknown aircraft was heard over Sheerness about 7 pm… Flares were lighted at Eastchurch, but the aircraft did not make a landing.'[2] Questioned further as to whether he knew 'where our own airships were on that night', Churchill replied: 'I know it was not one of our airships.'[3]

The outcry that followed publication of this story led Count Zeppelin to telegram the editor of the *Daily Mail*: 'None of my airships approached the English coast on the night of October 14th.' This was also the conclusion reached by airship historians. The Eastchurch sighting was followed by hundreds of others, but no evidence has been found that any of the German airship fleet actually visited the English coast during the winter of 1912–13. We are therefore left to wonder what was seen and heard above the torpedo school at Eastchurch and elsewhere as Britain found itself gripped by 'airship mania'. Were people simply imagining things?

Dangerous rumours

In some cases it certainly seems that people might have been. One dramatic and slightly comic example, which can be found among the old Air Historical Branch files at the National Archives, happened near the Vickers shipyard at Barrow-in-Furness just days after the outbreak of the First World War. Although the first real German air raid against England by Zeppelins did not occur until January 1915, the War Office was inundated with reports before then; with widespread fear of imminent attack from the air, every light in the sky was transformed into an enemy airship.

The Vickers shipyard in Barrow-in-Furness, Cumbria, like Sheerness, was of great military importance and was guarded by the only anti-aircraft gun on the west coast. Sentries were posted around the dockyard with orders to open fire on anyone who did not answer their challenge. Late on the night of 10–11 August, Major Becke, Commander of

FIG. 3 Alarmed by reports of an airship, soldiers opened fire on the night sky on 10 August 1914. The first real Zeppelin air-raid on Britain took place five months later, in January 1915. AIR 1/561/16/15/62

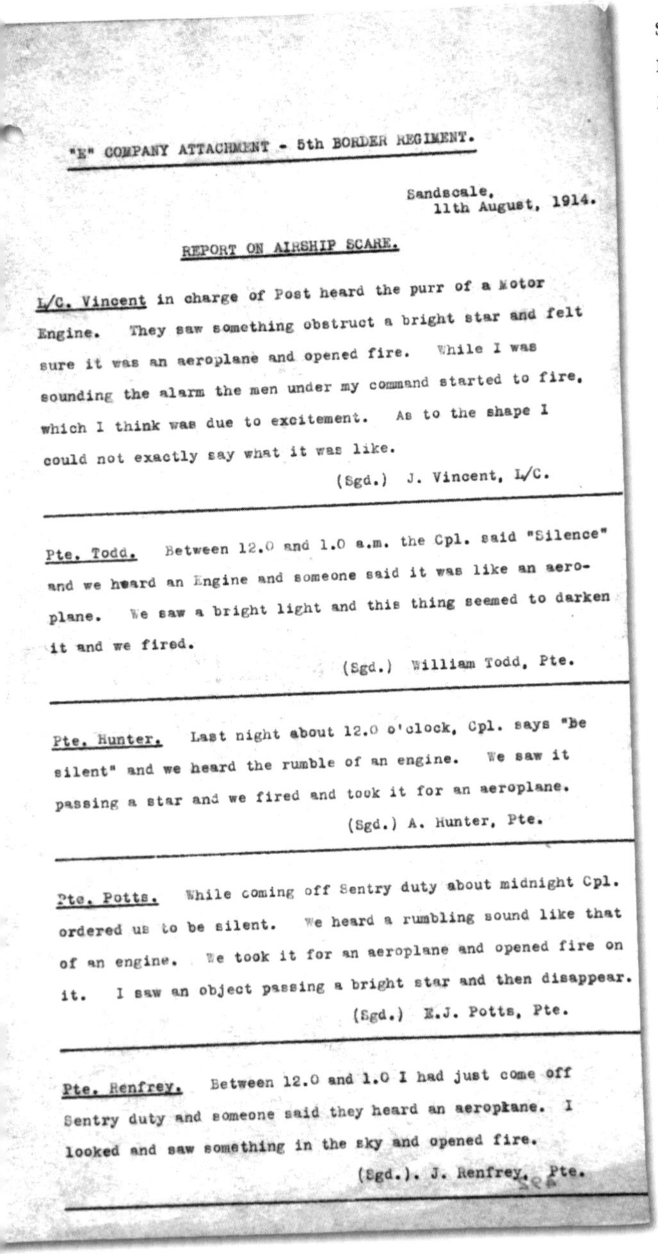

"E" COMPANY ATTACHMENT - 5th BORDER REGIMENT.

Sandscale,
11th August, 1914.

REPORT ON AIRSHIP SCARE.

L/C. Vincent in charge of Post heard the purr of a Motor Engine. They saw something obstruct a bright star and felt sure it was an aeroplane and opened fire. While I was sounding the alarm the men under my command started to fire, which I think was due to excitement. As to the shape I could not exactly say what it was like.

(Sgd.) J. Vincent, L/C.

Pte. Todd. Between 12.0 and 1.0 a.m. the Cpl. said "Silence" and we heard an Engine and someone said it was like an aeroplane. We saw a bright light and this thing seemed to darken it and we fired.

(Sgd.) William Todd, Pte.

Pte. Hunter. Last night about 12.0 o'clock, Cpl. says "be silent" and we heard the rumble of an engine. We saw it passing a star and we fired and took it for an aeroplane.

(Sgd.) A. Hunter, Pte.

Pte. Potts. While coming off Sentry duty about midnight Cpl. ordered us to be silent. We heard a rumbling sound like that of an engine. We took it for an aeroplane and opened fire on it. I saw an object passing a bright star and then disappear.

(Sgd.) E.J. Potts, Pte.

Pte. Renfrey. Between 12.0 and 1.0 I had just come off Sentry duty and someone said they heard an aeroplane. I looked and saw something in the sky and opened fire.

(Sgd.) J. Renfrey, Pte.

the Barrow Defences, stated that two, or possibly three, airships had been seen during the night flying over the Vickers yards and had been fired upon by the anti-aircraft gun without effect.

In a detailed description of events, Lieutenant W. Adair of the 5th Border Regiment based at nearby Sowerby Lodge tells how his men had seen two cigar-shaped craft travelling at great height in a northerly direction, their shapes lit up by the glare from the ironworks. At midnight sentries at Sandscale spotted another light and opened fire with their machine guns. Alongside the enthusiastic statements from those who saw something or fired into the night sky was one from the men's commanding officer who, having heard shots found them

'gazing at a bright star; small clouds were flitting over this star and darkened it to some extent. I thought my self, that the men had been deceived, as I could see nothing in the shape of an aircraft.' (AIR 1/565 16/15/89)

Elsewhere in the same Air Historical Branch file is a more troublesome account from the end of 1914, which was recorded by the crew of a Hull trawler—the SS *Ape*—the night before the German High Seas fleet bombarded the east coast ports of Scarborough and Whitby. In a statement to an intelligence officer, the ship's master described how his ship was steaming towards Yarmouth at 4.10 pm on 15 December when the crew sighted 'a black object astern which gradually drew nearer'. They saw the airship turn and head towards the Lincolnshire coast, where it vanished in the haze and fog.

Alone among the many reports of airships from the first year of the war this was recorded in the official history as 'proved to be founded on fact'. However, we now know that a German airship could not have been responsible for this sighting. Airship war diaries examined by historian Douglas Robinson show that weather conditions were so atrocious on 15 December 1914 that none of the German naval airships were able to leave their sheds on the Continent. And as with earlier sightings, any German airship making its way to these shores would surely have been seen somewhere by someone as it crossed mainland Europe.

Whatever visited England in darkness during the first months of the war, it could not have been a Zeppelin. So what was being seen? During the 1909 wave it emerged that jokers had successfully fooled at least some witnesses with lighted box-kites and fire-balloons. Indeed, as recently as 2009, fleets of Chinese lanterns—lit by tiny candles—have tricked people into thinking they were seeing UFOs. Could the same be said in 1912 and 1914? Were these strange sightings just balloons and bright stars transformed by fear and anxiety into something more threatening? Whether or not this was the explanation, these early sightings are undoubtedly direct precursors of the UFO scares that would follow in the modern era.

Encounters over London

The most important 'phantom airship' sighting recorded in the official history of German air raids stands apart from others made at this date and also counts as the first encounter with a UFO reported by a British military pilot. On the night of 31 January 1916, the crews of nine German Navy Zeppelins left their sheds on the Continent with orders to attack Liverpool, with London as a secondary target. In the event, the plan was thrown into chaos by poor weather conditions of freezing rain, snow and thick ground mist. This hid much of the countryside from the air and made accurate navigation impossible. In the confusion that followed, several towns in the Midlands were bombed leaving 71 people dead and 113 injured.

During the raid, the War Office was able to plot the course of all nine raiding airships. From the maps they produced it appears that none of the raiders reached London or the southeast of England, but at least one of the raiders initially turned south after crossing the East Anglian coastline at 7.00 pm. The War Office calculated that if that course was held the Zeppelin would be over London within one hour and aircraft defending the capital were ordered to intercept them.

Shortly before 8.30 pm two Royal Flying Corps pilots flying B.E.2C biplanes reported pursuing moving lights at 10,000 ft above central London. Both lost their targets in cloud, and it seems possible they had actually spotted lights on each other's planes without realizing it. But another sighting by a Royal Navy pilot is much more difficult to explain.

At 8.45 pm Flight Sub-Lieutenant Eric Morgan took off from the Royal Naval Air Service station at Rochford in Essex and began to patrol at 6,400 ft when his engine started misfiring. At this point he saw a little above his own altitude and slightly ahead to his right, about 100 ft away from his plane, 'a row of what appeared to be lighted windows which looked something like a railway carriage with the blinds drawn.' Assuming he had come face to face with a Zeppelin preparing an attack upon central London, Morgan drew his Webley Scott pistol and fired. Immediately, 'the lights alongside rose rapidly' and disappeared into the inky blackness, so rapidly in fact that Morgan believed his own aircraft had gone into a dive. He battled to bring his plane under control and was forced to make an emergency landing on the Thameshaven Marshes.

An account of Morgan's sighting, described as 'an encounter with a phantom airship', appears in Captain Joseph Morris's official history *The German Air Raids on Great Britain 1914–18*, published in 1925 and based upon then classified records. Morris refers directly to the airman's report filed with the Admiralty, but this report is not mentioned in the official account of the 31 January 1916 raid published by the War Office which charts the flight paths of the Zeppelins and the attempts by British fighters to intercept them. As a result, historians have been left with the impression that the authorities gave no credence to it.

There was in fact a story from a fourth pilot, Flight Sub-Lieutenant H. McClelland, who reported seeing what he described as 'a Zeppelin' caught briefly in the glare of searchlights above London at 9.00 pm, 15 minutes after Morgan's encounter. It disappeared as he closed the distance. His report was forwarded to the Admiralty where the Third Sea Lord, Rear-Admiral F.C.T. Tudor, dismissed it with the comment: 'night flying must be difficult and dangerous, and require considerable nerve and pluck, but this airman seems to have been gifted with a more than usually vivid imagination.'[4]

The light on the moors

Phantom Zeppelins were not the only phenomena that authorities struggled to explain during the First World War. Given the widespread belief that German spies were active in Britain in large numbers, they found themselves carrying out a number of investigations into things that might have been ignored during peacetime. Most obvious of these are the stories of moving lights that began to reach the War Office and which, it was feared, could reveal attempts to communicate with German ships or aircraft from the ground via sophisticated flares.

During the period 1915–16, for example, the Royal Navy base at Devonport began to receive accounts of mysterious lights seen on Dartmoor. Among the Admiralty records at the National Archives is a statement signed by Lieutenant Montague Elliott, Commander-in-Chief, Royal Naval Reserve, Devonport, which mentions 'countless reports' describing a ball of light that 'is seen to rise perpendicularly from the ground to a height of

FIG. 4 Like many others, this article from the *Scarborough Daily Post*, published 20 February 1913, explained the airship sightings by suggesting Britain was under 'systematic surveillance from the skies by the aerial spies of a foreign Power'.

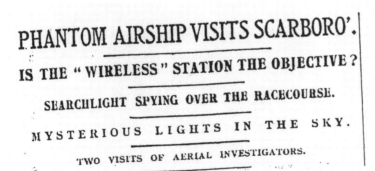

PHANTOM AIRSHIP VISITS SCARBORO'.

IS THE "WIRELESS" STATION THE OBJECTIVE?

SEARCHLIGHT SPYING OVER THE RACECOURSE.

MYSTERIOUS LIGHTS IN THE SKY.

TWO VISITS OF AERIAL INVESTIGATORS.

Scarborough people will learn with the deepest surprise that the Queen of Watering-Places has been visited on at least two occasions by what has come to be known as the "Phantom Airship."

It will be recalled how immense sensation was caused some weeks ago at Sheerness, where a number of people reported that they had seen a mysterious nocturnal aerial visitor passing over the naval dockyards there in the night.

At first their statements were received with derision, then with mild scepticism,

MISS HOLLINGS' STORY.

The first and the more sensational flight over the town was witnessed by several people on the night of Sunday, February 2nd, though up to the present we know of only two who have come forward with their story.

Probably the very first to notice something unusual was Miss Hollings, the daughter of Dr. Hollings, of Scarborough. This lady was on Stepney-road some time after nightfall, and heard "a noise as of machinery" in the air, in the direction of the Racecourse ahead. Looking up, she

inhuman as to force a quarrel upon England.

FOUR NIGHTS LATER.

The incident which we have described does not stand by itself. Our investigations into the above story have elicited the information that on Thursday night, Feb. 6th, the lights of an airship were seen over the Castle Hill, proceeding in the direction of Throxenby Mere, which is only a stone's-throw from the position in which the lights had been seen on the previous Sunday night.

A youth named Ross Tyson, of Dyson's

anything from 30 to 60 feet.'[5] These sightings caused great concern and attempts were made by intelligence officers to capture those responsible for the 'floating light' by staking out parts of bleak Dartmoor late at night.

An extraordinary account of one such operation is contained in the same file. Lieutenant-Colonel W.P. Drury was the garrison intelligence officer at Devonport and in late December 1915 he questioned a number of civilians living in the Ashburton area who had seen mysterious lights moving over Dartmoor in the early hours. One of these was a Mrs Cave-Penny who lived in an isolated farm that commanded an excellent view of the moors around Hexworthy Mine. She and her daughter reported seeing on several occasions 'a bright white light rise from a point a few hundred yards to the East of the mine', which swung across the valley and disappeared. 'The light sometimes rose above the skyline, at others it showed against the loom of Down Ridge on which the mine is situated', Drury's report stated. 'On each occasion it rose from the same spot and followed the same course.'

> 'We observed a bright white light, considerably larger in appearance than a planet, steadily ascend from the meadow to an approximate height of 50 or 60 feet...'

Alerted to this regular occurrence Drury obtained permission to stake out three locations where the lights had been sighted. After several night-time visits he saw the phenomenon himself. At 9.30 pm on 4 September 1915 Drury and another intelligence officer began watching Dartmoor from a hiding place opposite the main Totnes–Newton Abbot road. His report describes how suddenly,

> 'we observed a bright white light, considerably larger in appearance than a planet, steadily ascend from the meadow to an approximate height of 50 or 60 feet. It then swung for a hundred yards or so to the left, and suddenly vanished. Its course was clearly visible against the dark background of wood and hill, though, the night being dark it was not easy to determine whether it was a little above or beneath the skyline. We were within a mile of the light and both saw its ascension and transit distinctly.' (ADM 131/119)

Unfortunately for their operation, the River Dart lay between the two men and the mysterious light and there was no bridge or ford where they could cross to reach the meadow from which it appeared to rise. Unable to solve the mystery, Drury completed his report on a note of disappointment:

> 'I have watched Down Ridge, Dartington Manor, and Barton Pines by night on several occasions before and since September 4th, but that date is the only time I personally have seen this "floating light" which has so often been reported by other and reliable witnesses...' (ADM 131/119)

Three months later GHQ Home Forces issued a 16-page confidential report on the outcome of their investigations into hundreds of similar reports of lights in the sky that had been widely attributed to German spies. This concluded there was 'no evidence on which to base a suspicion that this class of enemy activity ever existed' and said around 89 per cent of the reports had been explained. In the section dealing with 'moving lights in the air' the report states:

> 'These lights are often difficult to explain satisfactorily. The planets and very bright stars have frequently given rise to these reports ... [and] in one case there are grounds for believing that these lights have been based on the hitherto improperly observed phenomena of marsh gas or "ignis fatuus".' (WO 158/989)

This conclusion is less than convincing. It seems highly unlikely that this rare phenomenon, known in English folklore as the 'Will-o'-the-Wisp' and 'Jack-o'-Lantern', could have been responsible. At that time, chemists believed that methane produced by rotting organic matter could spontan-eously ignite to create incandescent lights that, after dark, might appear to rise into the air. More recent studies, such as that published in 1980 by chemist Dr Alan Mills from Leicester University, have concluded that any bubbles of marsh gas that did ignite would create a dim glow at ground level and would be short-lived. This would not explain sightings of brilliant lights that rise into the sky or follow a regular flight path, such as those described by the observers on Dartmoor during the First World War.

Great balls of fire

The mysterious floating lights reported to naval intelligence during the First World War were never satisfactorily explained, but official interest in reports of this kind largely came to an end after the war. One quite surpris-ing group did, though, continue to collect accounts of unusual lights in the sky: scientists working for the Meteorological Office who were trying to understand ball lightning.

Ball lightning is often described as an incandescent sphere and is usu-ally, but not always, seen in the sky during thunderstorms. Unlike fork or sheet lightning, which lasts for seconds only, those who have experienced ball lightning sometimes claim it is visible for minutes.

It was first recognized as a distinctive phenomenon in 1886, but stories describing lightning balls of considerable size and power can be traced back many centuries. One of the best-known historical accounts comes from Widdecombe-in-the-Moor, on Dartmoor. During a great thunderstorm there in October 1638, an 8-inch ball of fire entered the church and split into two. One fireball escaped through a window while the other vanished, leav-ing behind it a foul odour of sulphur and thick smoke. The building was partly destroyed by the blast and four parishioners were killed and 60 injured.

In 1921 the Meteorological Office, at that time part of the Air Ministry, received a spectacular account of ball lightning seen over St John's Wood, North London, during a severe storm on the evening of 26 June. A lady letter-writer said she was watching the thunderstorm from her window, which faced southeast. Without warning, at 2 am, she suddenly saw a fireball in the sky. Her account read: 'It appeared as an incandescent mass floating in the atmosphere below the clouds. It was pear-shaped, the greatest width being equivalent to three moons, the height to four or five.'[6] She was unable to say how far away the fireball was, but her account suggests it could have been of enormous size. This light in the sky was visible for at least two minutes, because she had time to walk to a friend's room and rouse her before it vanished.

'It appeared as an incandescent mass floating in the atmosphere below the clouds. It was pear-shaped, the greatest width being equivalent to three moons, the height to four or five'

Her account fascinated meteorologists at the Air Ministry and they decided to launch an inquiry. Within days a press release was sent out to the national newspapers appealing to anyone who had seen ball lightning 'and related phenomena' to contact the Meteorological Office. The results of this inquiry survive in an extraordinary file at the National Archives containing over one hundred letters and questionnaires completed by members of the public who responded to the appeal. One of those who filled in a questionnaire was Mrs Phillis Coe from Enfield, Middlesex, who appeared to have seen the same fireball. She wrote:

> 'I observed in an easterly direction a long, incandescent mass apparently floating just beneath the clouds and to all appearances stationary. This mass seemed to dilate and contract as it floated during the 10 or 15 minutes I watched it. The sight was so extraordinary that I awoke my husband and drew his attention to it, but we were both unable to account for the phenomenon and although we questioned several people afterwards we could not trace anyone who had seen it.' (AIR 2/205)

While some correspondents described seeing the fireball over London on 26 June, the Meteorological Office also received descriptions from people who had seen similar things at different times. And this is where the file becomes particularly intriguing. Annie Baker, for example, of East Southsea, Portsmouth, had read of the 'strange ball of fire' seen over London and wrote to tell what she had seen during another thunderstorm in the last week of July 1921. In her letter she described how:

> 'in the early hours … about 2 o'clock [I saw] a strange-looking bladder-like monster the shape of an airship only much wider. It quite startled me. I called to my husband to look at it, but knowing I am a bit nervous about thunderstorms, he did not get up. Well, it flickered very much, it was certainly [on] fire inside it, and looked as if it were going to burst. It

was quite stationary for a few minutes, but thank goodness it passed away and disappeared quickly…' (AIR 2/205)

More dramatically, a woman from Waterford in Ireland wrote to say that while she had not seen the fireball in St John's Wood she thought she might have seen one back in 1912. At the time she had been out on a night-time winter's walk when 'without any warning, a huge ball of light appeared through the clouds.' According to her letter it remained stationary for about a minute before going up into the clouds again. About five minutes afterwards she heard a loud explosion out at sea. Echoing the contents of letters that would later be sent to the Ministry of Defence by many UFO witnesses, she asked: 'This has often puzzled me and I would be glad if you could tell me what it was.'

Of the 115 letters and questionnaires received by the Air Ministry in 1921, just 65 appeared to describe the phenomenon of ball lightning. The remaining accounts included some truly bizarre examples that appeared when no thunderstorms were present. One story in this category was submitted by a man in Scotland who described something that had happened to him as a child in 1898. 'I remember to this day,' he wrote,

> 'whilst coming home from school I saw a great ball of lightning about the size of a football, only it was flat as a coin and white. It would have put you in mind of a full moon high up in the heavens. But what made me write to tell you about this was that it was so low I could have thrown my cap and hit it. I ran after it and followed it for about 10 yards. Then, travelling very fast, it vanished.' (AIR 2/205)

The results of the inquiry were published by Harold Jeffreys in *The Meteorological Magazine* during September 1921. In his paper Jeffreys describes how he tried and failed to find a common denominator in the reports he surveyed. As we have seen, 50 of those who responded to the questionnaire had seen lights in

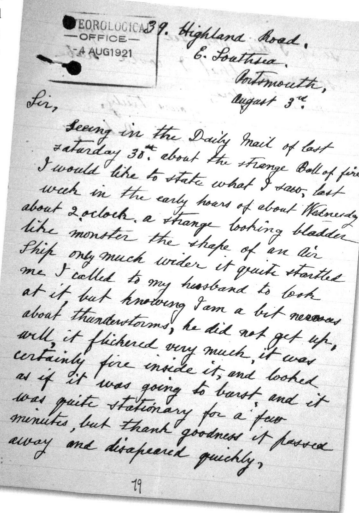

FIG. 5 A letter sent to the Air Ministry Meteorological Office in 1921 by a woman who saw 'a strange looking bladderlike monster' in the sky during a thunderstorm. AIR 2/205

the sky at different dates and times, and were possibly not ball lightning at all. Even among those who described seeing what the Meteorological Office did categorize as ball lightning there was little agreement on its size or the length of time that it was visible. Some said the fireball they saw was between 3 in and 1 ft in size. Others described a light high in the clouds that they compared with the disc of the full moon. Jeffreys recognized this meant the diameter of ball lightning could be as small as a few inches, or as large as 60 ft, but few observers were qualified to make such precise judgements.

Similarly diverse and contradictory were the time estimates. Some ranged from less than 10 seconds to between 1 and 5 minutes. Likewise, colours described by observers ran from bluish-white to deep red, but the great majority were reddish or yellowish. Shapes described were usually spheres, but several described pear-shaped and elongated objects resembling Zeppelins, similar to the reports of 'phantom airships' seen during the First World War. Most reported seeing single objects but one described 'the appearance of three balls simultaneously, coming from a church spire at a point where it had been struck by an ordinary flash.' When it disappeared, ball lightning was usually silent. Sometimes the phenomenon faded gradually, while others burst and vanished suddenly.

Surveying the evidence, Jeffreys pondered the extraordinarily varied descriptions, noting that it seemed impossible that any two correspondents had seen the same phenomenon.[7] Similar conclusions have been reached in official investigations of UFOs in later decades, which suggests that observers are actually reporting many different types of phenomena, all of which could have different origins. During the Second World War more sightings were reported, including many by pilots flying combat missions over Europe and the Pacific. UFOs and flying saucers were still unheard of, but American pilots had another phrase to describe them: foo-fighters.

Where there's foo there's fire!

On the evening of 26 April 1944 Flight Lieutenant Arthur Horton taxied his Lancaster bomber onto the runway at RAF Mildenhall, Suffolk, in preparation for a raid on Essen, deep in the steel-making German Ruhr valley. It was, he thought, just another routine, if terrifying, mission for 622 Squadron crews.

The raid went exactly as planned despite the potentially fatal distractions of Luftwaffe night-fighters and the flak that sought them out amongst the searchlight beams. Bombs dropped, Horton's Lancaster turned for home. Then, shortly after leaving the target, his intercom crackled into life with a warning from the rear-gunner. Some odd lights had appeared out of the darkness and were following the plane. Horton asked the gunner if he was certain. Yes he replied, four orange balls of light were tailing them, two on each side of the aircraft, accelerating in short powerful spurts. According to the worried gunner they were about the size of large footballs and had a fiery glow to them. Another thought he could see small, stubby wings and possibly an exhaust glow from the rear of the objects. Now Horton was getting worried. Some 43 years after the event Arthur Horton clearly recalled exactly what he did next:

> 'I immediately dropped the aircraft out of the sky. My gunners didn't know what they were. Should they fire? By this time I was standing the aircraft on its tail and beginning a series of corkscrews and turns with the things following everything I did—but making no move to attack us. By this time we had the throttles "through the gate", the gunners still asking what they should do. Apart from flying the thing I had to try and answer them. But were they some form of flying contraption that would explode at some specific distance from us, or on contact? Did they want us to fire at them to cause an explosion? Out of the kaleidoscope of thought the only answer was "If they are leaving us alone, leave them alone".'[8]

'By this time I was standing the aircraft on its tail and beginning a series of corkscrews and turns with the things following everything I did ...'

Horton's term 'through the gate' refers to a technique by which Lancaster pilots could move the throttle sideways and forwards, breaking a wire, 'the gate', in the process. This would give considerable extra power, but put an immense additional strain on the engines. Horton continued evasive action for 10 minutes, during which time all the crew except him and the bomb aimer could see the pursuing balls of light. Whatever the objects were they stayed close to the Lancaster, duplicating its every move, until they reached the Dutch coast when, in the words of one of the gunners, 'they seemed to burn themselves out'.

Exhausted but relieved, Horton flew the Lancaster safely back to England. His attempts at evasive action had caused a serious mechanical fault that forced the crew to land at a different airfield. Horton and his crew were baffled by the experience, and could only presume they had been chased by a German secret weapon, perhaps a radio-controlled anti-aircraft rocket. Upon reporting their experience to the intelligence officers at debriefing they were met not with interest but ridicule. Nevertheless, Horton stuck to his account and would not be persuaded that he and his crew had imagined the experience.

Although Horton has stated that he had never heard of any similar stories at the time, his description is entirely consistent with those of aircrews of other nationalities during the Second World War. American bomber crews coined the phrase 'foo-fighters' in or around 1943 to describe the strange moving balls of fire that pursued their aircraft during night-time raids over Germany. No one is certain where it came from but it may have originated in a popular 1940s US cartoon strip featuring a madcap fireman, Smokey Stover, whose catch phrase was 'where there's foo, there's fire'. Alternatively 'foo' may come from the French word for fire as the phenomenon was often being described as resembling a fireball.

Whatever its origin, while 'foo-fighter' was a term familiar to aircrew serving with the United States Army Air Force (USAAF), it would have been unfamiliar to RAF pilots who observed similar lights during missions over Europe. Their reports were referred to by the Air Ministry as 'night phenomena' and 'balls of fire'. Research by my colleague Andy Roberts has revealed that individual RAF aircrew developed their own terminology for UFOs they saw during combat missions. Based on information gleaned from interviews with surviving aircrew and accounts from personal logbooks, he discovered 'The Light', or 'The Thing' was used by RAF crews from 1942.

A number of baffled aircrew, like Horton's, tried to rationalize their experiences as evidence of advanced Axis secret weapons or guided 'rockets', referring to them in those terms in flight logs and debriefings—but evidence soon emerged that the phenomenon was being observed by men on all sides. Dr R.V. Jones, director of intelligence for Britain's Air Staff during the war, later said the Air Ministry was unable to explain the reports it received, 'and when we asked German night-fighter crews they said they had seen them as well.'[9] Similar reports were also made by aircrew in the Far East theatre of war, and one classic photograph appears to show 'foo-fighters' accompanying a flight of Japanese Takikawa-Kawasaki 98 fighters over the Suzuka Mountains during 1945.

FIG. 6 A photograph said to show 'foo-fighters' following Japanese fighter aircraft over the Suzuka Mountains in 1945.

In the First World War, the British government was led to pour scarce resources into the investigation of phantom airships and mysterious 'floating lights' in case it offered evidence of enemy activity. In the Second World War, the allies investigated foo-fighters for exactly the same reason. Air Ministry and United States Army Air Force inquiries during the Second World War reached similar conclusions to the GHQ study in 1916.

Allied Air Intelligence had access to a wealth of information on all kinds of unexplained radar trackings and reports of 'mystery' aircraft and unusual rockets and flak. Each sighting was carefully analysed in the context of known weaponry, enemy tactics and the psychological problems of misperception. For his part, R.V. Jones recalled that 'we tended to interpret them as either aberrations under the stress of operation, or misinterpretations of some phenomena or other.'[10]

FIG. 7 Dr (later Professor) Reginald Victor Jones was director of intelligence for the Air Ministry during the Second World War. Later, as head of scientific intelligence at the Ministry of Defence, he became involved in the investigation of the UFO mystery.

Dr Jones's conclusions are echoed in the words of the late *Goon Show* star Michael Bentine who served as an intelligence officer in RAF Bomber Command during 1943–4. In a 1992 interview he described debriefing several crews who had seen unidentified lights in the sky during raids on the Baltic coast.

> 'They fired at the lights, which didn't shoot back. These lights didn't seem to do anything, just pulse and go round. We put it down to fatigue, but later, after I had sent the reports in, an American G2 Intelligence Officer told us that their bombers saw lights in the sky — "foo-fighters" he called them.'[11]

Bentine also described how he debriefed a Polish bomber unit based in England. They claimed that silver-blue balls appeared near their wing on six missions during the autumn of 1943. These tailed the planes as they raided the Nazi V-weapons base at Peenemunde. The crews told Bentine it must be a new weapon. 'But what did it do to you?' Bentine inquired. 'Nothing,' they replied. 'Well it was not a very effective weapon, was it?' he pointed out. Bentine's last statement accurately sums up the conclusions reached by the Air Ministry and USAAF during their study of these phenomena. Whatever the foo-fighters were, they did not appear to pose a threat to aircraft.

Radar Angels

A parallel mystery to UFOs encountered in the air is that of UFOs tracked on radar, something that is often a key element of modern accounts. Even before news of the first sightings of foo-fighters reached the Allies, operators had been perplexed by strange blips that appeared and disappeared on their screens as they controlled aircraft movements. Sometimes these appeared to move at incredible speeds, faster than any man-made aircraft of the day.

Radar was developed by British scientists during the 1930s as an early warning system against German bombers. Before the outbreak of war the Air Ministry secretly built a string of radar stations, known as Chain Home or CH, along the east coast of England that was to provide a crude first warning of German air raids. In 1940 during the Battle of Britain this 'secret weapon' gave the RAF a crucial tactical advantage over the superior strength of the Luftwaffe. Although at this time British radar was the most advanced in the world it was far from foolproof, as demonstrated by a series of strange incidents the following year.

Late on the night of 20 March 1941, with the threat of a German invasion still strong, RAF Fighter Command was placed on alert when the CH system reported an attack on Britain's south coast. Records at the National Archives show that up to five separate stations saw what seemed to be a massive formation of blips moving slowly across the channel precisely as would be expected if a large-scale night raid by German bombers was under way. As tension grew the blips approached from the direction of the Cherbourg peninsula until they reached a point 40 miles from the Dorset coast when they faded from the screen. The following night the blips returned and for a period of weeks CH stations continued to report both mass formations and individual echoes. Senior officers began to fear these could be part of a sophisticated German plot to jam British radar with false signals as aircraft or towed gliders prepared for a real invasion.[12]

A few years ago I had the opportunity to discuss these weird incidents with Sir Edward Fennessy CBE, who served on the RAF scientific staff responsible for the CH radars during the war. He said the radar sightings were taken seriously as the RAF was expecting a German invasion.

> 'Immediate orders were given to intercept, but when fighters were in position to intercept no targets could be found. Ground radar continued to plot the targets and we urgently contacted the Radar Research Station (TRE) then based in Swanage. They suggested various adjustments to the CH to eliminate false plots, but [they] remained tracking towards England until after some time they faded.'[13]

After the war Sir Edward had told this story at a dinner party where he entertained guests with his theory that the echoes were really guardian angels, 'the souls of British soldiers killed in France over the centuries returning to defend their country.' Although it was intended as a joke, this idea caught the imagination of serving airmen who were regularly seeing 'ghosts' on their radar screens that became known as 'radar angels'.

Up to five separate stations saw what seemed to be a massive formation of blips moving slowly across the channel precisely as would be expected if a large-scale night raid by German bombers was under way

More than imagination?

During the Second World War, Sir Edward recalled that no explanation was ever found for radar angels and pointed out that 'busy fighting a war we spent no time investigating this phenomena.' However, as in the First World War, the government sometimes did feel forced to act. By 1945 so many puzzling foo-fighter reports were reaching the Allies that scientific intelligence officers attached to Supreme Headquarters Allied Expeditionary Force (SHAEF), commanded by the US General Dwight D. Eisenhower, were asked to investigate. In February 1945 British officers attached to SHAEF told the Air Ministry

> 'it would seem that there must be something more than imagination behind the matter, and in view of the fact that pilots and crew are becoming slightly worried by them, it is considered that everything possible should be done to get to the root of the matter.'[14]

Responding on 13 March, Group Captain E.D.M. Hopkins of the Air Ministry said intelligence officers in London had carefully studied the sightings. They decided, 'a few of the alleged aircraft may have been Me 262 [Luftwaffe jet fighters] and for the rest, flak rockets are suggested as the most likely explanation.' He added: 'The whole affair is still something of a mystery and the evidence is very sketchy and varied so that no definite and satisfactory explanation can yet be given.'[15]

FIG. 8 Extract from an Air Ministry file on mysterious 'hovering echoes' tracked over the English Channel by RAF radars during 1941. Senior officers initially believed these were part of a German invasion force, but fighters sent to investigate found nothing. AVIA 7/1070

The one consistent feature that concerned the Allies was that foo-fighters paced and followed aircraft in a controlled, seemingly intelligent manner. At the time the Allies knew the Germans were experimenting with a host of unorthodox weapons, including jet aircraft such as the Me 262 and futuristic-looking bat-wing shaped 'flying wings'. When the allies overran Nazi Germany in 1945 they captured a number of designs for advanced aircraft, but they found the Axis forces did not have the capability to produce guided weapons that could twist and turn whilst following an airplane and certainly not for the lengths of time reported.

During this period a scientific intelligence officer serving with SHAEF called Bob Robertson carried out a study of the sightings reported by American aircrew. Robertson was a friend of Britain's R.V.

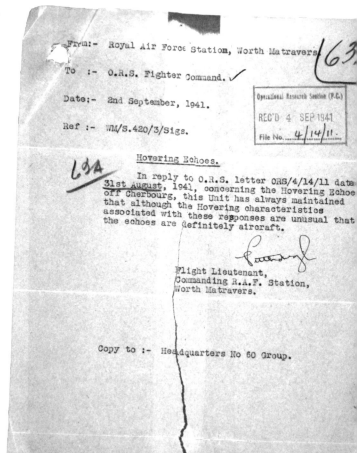

Jones and was an eminent physicist in his own right. After the war, in his role as a scientific advisor to the CIA, Robertson was asked to convene a secret panel to examine any potential threat posed by UFOs to national security. Although copies of his wartime foo-fighter study have sadly not survived, Robertson summarized his findings for a CIA panel on UFOs that he convened in 1953. In the panel's report he described foo-fighters as

> 'unexplained phenomena sighted by aircraft pilots during World War II in both European and Far East theatres of operation, wherein "balls of light" would fly near or with the aircraft and maneuver rapidly. They were believed to be electrostatic (similar to St Elmo's Fire) or electromagnetic phenomena or possibly light reflections from ice crystals in the air, but their exact cause or nature was never defined.'[16]

The Roberston panel concluded, as Michael Bentine had done in 1943, that foo-fighters were 'unexplained but not dangerous'. Once it had been ascertained that these UFOs did not explode, open fire on Allied aircraft or display aggressive characteristics, Air Intelligence was content to let the matter drop, maintaining a watching brief. There was a war on and they could not afford to waste time and money chasing phantoms of the skies.

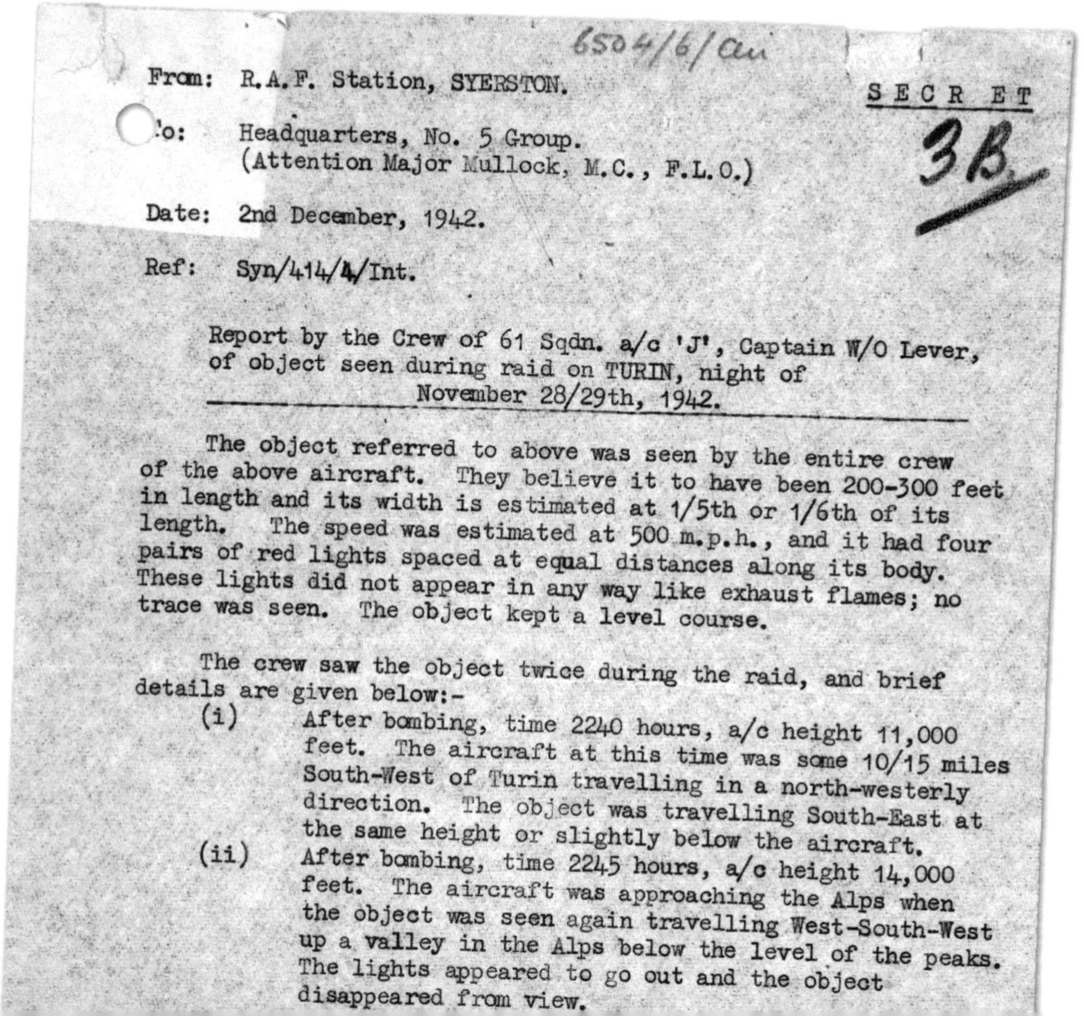

FIG. 9 During the Second World War the Air Ministry collected a number of reports of 'rocket phenomena'. This extraordinary example was made by a bomber crew during a raid on Turin on the night of 28/29 November. AIR 14/2076

6504/6/air

From: R.A.F. Station, SYERSTON.

To: Headquarters, No. 5 Group.
(Attention Major Mullock, M.C., F.L.O.)

S E C R E T

3B

Date: 2nd December, 1942.

Ref: Syn/414/4/Int.

Report by the Crew of 61 Sqdn. a/c 'J', Captain W/O Lever, of object seen during raid on TURIN, night of
November 28/29th, 1942.

The object referred to above was seen by the entire crew of the above aircraft. They believe it to have been 200-300 feet in length and its width is estimated at 1/5th or 1/6th of its length. The speed was estimated at 500 m.p.h., and it had four pairs of red lights spaced at equal distances along its body. These lights did not appear in any way like exhaust flames; no trace was seen. The object kept a level course.

The crew saw the object twice during the raid, and brief details are given below:-

(i)   After bombing, time 2240 hours, a/c height 11,000 feet. The aircraft at this time was some 10/15 miles South-West of Turin travelling in a north-westerly direction. The object was travelling South-East at the same height or slightly below the aircraft.

(ii) After bombing, time 2245 hours, a/c height 14,000 feet. The aircraft was approaching the Alps when the object was seen again travelling West-South-West up a valley in the Alps below the level of the peaks. The lights appeared to go out and the object disappeared from view.

Both Bob Robertson and Dr R.V. Jones remained interested in reports of unexplained phenomena and would eventually play significant roles in official investigations during the post-war UFO era. But Robertston clearly was not happy simply to dismiss the sightings just by giving them a name and he observed that 'if the term "flying saucers" had been popular in 1943–45, these objects [foo-fighters] would have been so labeled.'[17]

UFOs over the Alps?

Witness accounts and documentary evidence indicate the majority of foo-fighter sightings were of small spherical objects. Some seem similar to the accounts of ball lightning sent to the Meteorological Office in 1921, which has also, in more recent times, been recorded as pursuing and even entering aircraft during storms. However, among the testimonies of pilots in the Second World War, there are a few stories describing large, apparently structured objects.

One extraordinary example can be found in the Royal Air Force files at the National Archives. Stamped 'Secret', it was judged to be of such significance at the time that details were sent directly to the headquarters of RAF Bomber Command. A covering letter from the Air Vice-Marshal of No. 5 Group, RAF, was attached, which read:

> 'Herewith a copy of a report received from a crew of a Lancaster after a raid on Turin. The crew refuses to be shaken in their story in the face of the usual banter and ridicule.' (AIR 14/2076)

The report describes an aerial object seen by the entire crew of a Lancaster bomber during a bombing raid on Turin, northern Italy, during the night of 28/29 November 1942. Twice during the raid Captain Lever and the crew of the Lancaster from 61 Squadron, based at Syerston in Lincolnshire, saw an object 200–300 ft in length that travelled at a speed they estimated at 500 mph. They said it had four pairs of red lights spaced at equal distances along its body and flew on a level course. When first seen, after bombing at 10.40 pm, it appeared to be 10 or 15 miles southwest of the city travelling at the same height as the Lancaster. Five minutes later as the Lancaster approached the Alps at 14,000 ft the crew saw it again, travelling in a south-westerly direction up a valley but above the mountain peaks. It disappeared when the red lights it carried went out.

The report concluded by stating that

> '[Captain Lever] has seen a similar object about three months ago north of Amsterdam. In this instance it appeared to be on the ground and later travelling at high speed at a lower level than the heights given above along the coast for about two seconds; the lights then went out for the same period of time and came on again, and the object was still seen to be travelling in the same direction.' (AIR 14/2076)

It is difficult to know what to make of this sighting. RAF Bomber Command was impressed by the sincerity of Lever's report, and the fact that his crew was bold enough to repeat their fantastic story to their incredulous colleagues. Nonetheless, the object they saw resembles no known aircraft flying at that time and this case remains one of the most unusual UFO mysteries from the period.

Bombers' moon

One spectacular account from the penultimate year of the Second World War, however, seems to provide a classic description of a flying saucer from the pre-flying saucer age. In 1944 Ronald Claridge was a radio operator in a Lancaster from 7 Squadron, part of the Pathfinder Force that flew from RAF Oakington in Cambridgeshire. His Lancaster was returning from a night-time raid on oil refineries at Pelice in Southern France on 11 August when his close encounter began.

More than 50 years later Claridge recalled how he was hunched over the aircraft's radar, scanning for enemy night-fighters during the anxious flight home, when the screen suddenly went blank. As he reported the malfunction to his pilot, Squadron Leader (later Air Commodore) Brian Frow, he heard him yell: 'what the hell was that?' Claridge moved quickly into the astrodome of the bomber and immediately saw what appeared to be 'an enormous string of lights' on the starboard side of the plane. He recalls,

> 'the lights were circular, rather like portholes in a ship. The colour was a very bright yellow changing to intense white. My estimate was that they were about a thousand yards from our aeroplane. The ones nearest our Lancaster were the largest and brightest, they stretched fore and aft to what seemed infinity. After about thirty seconds I could see they were part of an enormous disc.'[18]

The watercolour painting Ronald Claridge produced illustrates just how large this UFO was, dwarfing the Lancaster in the night sky. All eight crew had been alerted by the intercom chatter and could now see the phenomenon and were left strangely transfixed by the experience. Claridge recalled: 'we had no feelings of fear but feelings of great calm … even our gunners who would normally open fire were helpless.' He timed the incident for his radar log at three minutes before the object 'suddenly shot ahead and was gone. We were travelling at 240 miles per hour but there was no turbulence. There was no noise of engines or vapour of any kind.'

The Lancaster crew were left stunned and spoke very little for the rest of the journey home. On return to Oakington they were debriefed by RAF intelligence who appeared more interested in their feelings of well-being than the details of their experience. Claridge recalls being warned not to discuss the incident or make any entry about it in his logbook. Nevertheless, he told me 'we all had sensed we were being watched by another force outside our knowledge'.

By the time Claridge made his sighting it was nearly 50 years since the airship scares that had so gripped Britain, and in that time military and commercial aircraft had become a common sight in our skies. Thousands of aircraft were now daily taking part in operations. The dramatic increase in air traffic naturally meant that if UFOs existed they would be seen and reported with corresponding frequency. But as the war came to an end there was still no widely recognized category into which airmen such as Ron Claridge could place their strange experiences until the age of the flying saucer finally arrived.

FIG. 10 A painting by Ronald Claridge depicting the huge disc-shaped UFO he and his crew saw during a raid on southern France in 1944.

TWO *'There may be flying saucers and there may not be. But this was something I have never seen before.'* Sunday Dispatch, 21 September 1952

THE FLYING SAUCER AGE

As the world emerged from the Second World War the idea that Earth could be under observation or visited by aliens from another world remained largely confined to the realms of science fiction and fantasy. As the Cold War began people in the West were initially preoccupied not with the idea of life on other worlds, but with the possibility of a future nuclear war with the Soviet Union. As a result the authorities and the media continued to seek terrestrial explanations for reports of strange flying objects in the sky.

The first appearance of flying saucers was preceded by reports of strange rocket-shaped flying objects from parts of Scandinavia during the summer of 1946. According to a British intelligence report in the Ministry of Defence's files at the National Archives, news of these sightings was seized on by the press who began using words such as 'ghost rockets' and 'spook bombs'. According to the report, the first sightings were made in Sweden:

> 'and for some months there was a considerable number of sightings, mostly in Sweden, but a few also in Norway, Finland and Germany. The descriptions given were usually of some sort of wingless missile travelling at a very high speed, cigar-shaped or circular, sometimes emitting bright lights, and occasionally sound.' (DEFE 44/119)

Scientist and wartime genius Dr R.V. Jones, who was then the Air Ministry's director of intelligence, recalled that colleagues at the Air Ministry believed these flying bombs could be modified v-2 rockets captured by the Russians at the end of the war. Western intelligence agencies, though, wanted to know for sure who had designed these 'ghost rockets' and what their purpose might be. Documents preserved at the National Archives show how both the War Office and the Air Ministry quickly became involved in secret negotiations with the Swedish government in an attempt to solve the mystery.[1] Secret agents were sent to Scandinavia and advanced radar equipment was offered to the Swedes to assist in tracing the flight path taken by the rockets.

Air intelligence produced two detailed papers summarizing their investigations. The contents of these reveal a simmering internal debate between those in the intelligence community who believed the rockets were Russian, and those who believed they were a case of post-war nerves.

The first of these reports, circulated widely within Western intelligence during September 1946, was written by R.V. Jones. He was sceptical about the Russian theory and compared the rocket scare with other pre-war social panics, such as rumours the Nazis had developed a death ray. In his memoirs Jones described the 1946 saga as 'a diversion … which no doubt arose from the general atmosphere of apprehension that existed in 1945 regarding the motives of the Russians, and which anticipated the flying saucer.'[2]

The coming of the saucers

The ghost rocket scare was followed, just nine months later, by the first sightings of 'flying saucers' over North America. During this intermediate period radar operators in England continued to be plagued by unexplained blips on their screens similar to those tracked during the Second World War (see p.25).

A fascinating example of one incident survives in the official Air Force records at the National Archives. According to these, RAF stations were placed on alert early in January 1947 after unidentified aircraft were tracked by Britain's wartime Chain Home radars. The most alarming incident occurred on the night of 16 January when a ground radar at Trimley Heath, near Felixstowe, tracked what was described as a 'strange plot' at 38,000 ft, 50 miles from the Dutch coast during a Bomber Command exercise over the North Sea. The unidentified blip appeared to be descending erratically and was calculated to be moving at a speed faster than sound. It is worth noting here that history records Chuck Yeager's flight in the experimental Bell XS-1 rocket plane some nine months later as being the first time the sound barrier was broken.

A concerned HQ Fighter Command immediately ordered a Mosquito to divert from the Bomber Command exercise to intercept the mystery aircraft. This was recorded in RAF Operation Books as a secret exercise code-named 'Operation Charlie'. A cat-and-mouse chase then ensued for up to 40 minutes as the Mosquito pursued the unidentified target towards the Norfolk coastline. The blip had descended to 17,000 ft when the Mosquito crew began their interception. However, although the aircraft's own radar appeared to detect the presence of *something* on at least two occasions, the pilot was unable to see it in the dark skies. Whatever was out there on that night appeared to take what was described as 'efficient controlled evasive action'. Soon afterwards the Mosquito crew lost their quarry and the interception was abandoned.[3]

This startling incident was just the first of a series that continued for a number of weeks. An investigation was launched, which led to some (though not all) of the blips detected on radar being identified to the Air Ministry's satisfaction as friendly aircraft and meteorological balloons. In April details were leaked to the *Daily Mail* which splashed the story across its front page under the headline: 'Ghost Plane over Coast: RAF spot it—can't catch it.'[4] Newspaper stories dubbed these unexplained radar blips as 'ghost planes' and speculation about their origin ranged from smugglers to Russian spy planes developed from captured Nazi technology.

> Whatever was out there on that night appeared to take what was described as 'efficient controlled evasive action'. Soon afterwards the Mosquito crew lost their quarry

Documents show that in August 1947 the United States Army Air Force were sent a secret summary of the events of 16 January by the Air Ministry. Their conclusion read: 'No explanation of this incident has been forthcoming.'[5] By this time, however, the United States Army Air Force had begun to be inundated with strange sightings of their own.

Kenneth Arnold's UFOs

The flying saucer age can be said to have truly begun shortly after 3.00 pm on 24 June 1947 as Kenneth Arnold, a private pilot, cruised above the Cascade Mountains of Washington State in his light aircraft. He was searching for the wreckage of a transport plane when his attention was suddenly attracted by 'a tremendous bright flash' towards Mount Rainier. As he scanned the sky he spotted a group of 'nine peculiar looking aircraft' directly in front of him, 25–30 miles away at around 10,000 ft. The aircraft were flying in echelon formation but were, he realized, of a most unusual shape, 'flat like a pie pan and somewhat bat-shaped', with the lead craft flying slightly higher than the rest. As he watched, this strange formation shone as it reflected the sun and appeared to be following the mountain ridges below in a peculiar undulating motion.

Initially Arnold had thought the objects were snow geese, but he quickly realized they were flying too high and at incredible speed. Timing them as they moved between distant mountain peaks, Arnold found that they were travelling at speeds unheard of at that date. Eventually they disappeared towards Mount Adams in the south.

On landing at Yakima Airfield, Arnold told his story and by the time he reached Pendleton in Utah the next day news had reached the press and he was asked to describe what he had seen. Arnold was later emphatic that he did not call them flying saucers, but that was to be the phrase that caught the world's imagination. Interviewed for the ITV programme *Arthur C. Clarke's Mysterious World* in 1980, four years before his death, Arnold said:

> 'When I was asked how the objects flew I said "they flew like a saucer would if you skipped it across water" … and then of course all of a sudden the terms flying disc, crescent-shaped and what-not was completely dropped and everyone started seeing flying saucers. And they've been seeing them ever since!'

FIG. 11 Kenneth Arnold's seminal sighting of 'flying saucers' in June 1947 featured in the first edition of the American magazine *Fate*.

This was a gift for headline writers and before June was out 'flying saucers' had become a household phrase around the globe. In Britain, for example, a trawl through the Mass Observation Project Archive records reveals the following charming diary entry by a woman who wrote on Sunday 6 July 1947:

> 'Husband much keyed up about the flying saucers over American skies. One of his pet subjects. Papers can't report enough about them to satisfy him. Just like a small boy about it.'[6]

As the historian Hilary Evans noted, 'looking back to that day ... when flying saucers arrived, we can see that they were unquestionably an idea whose time had come.'[7]

Newspapers were quickly inundated with stories of further sightings, some made months or even years before Arnold's report. Many of these described 'flying discs' but there were also wingless torpedo- and cigar-shaped objects that recalled the 'ghost rockets'; others were spherical or oval in shape, or simply luminous shapes seen in the night sky. At the time, Arnold has said he assumed the strange aircraft he saw were guided missiles or secret prototype aircraft—a possibility that was pounced on by the media but quickly denied by the US authorities.

This preoccupation with secret weapons was represented in the responses to the first opinion poll on the subject of flying saucers. Conducted by the Gallup organization and published less than two months after Arnold's sighting, the poll found an incredible nine out of ten Americans had already heard of flying saucers. Gallup found that 15 per cent of Americans believed that the saucers could be some new form of American military hardware, while, in a nod to Cold War tensions, another 1 per cent thought they could be Russian in origin.[8] But while a significant proportion of respondents believed that the saucers could be the result of misperception or an outright hoax, one possible explanation is at this stage conspicuous by its absence: the belief, later to become widespread, that flying saucers could be of extraterrestrial origin.

The Roswell incident

One final piece of the jigsaw had to fall into place before the genesis of the flying saucer legend could be complete. On 8 July 1947, whilst the news media was still buzzing with saucer stories, a press release arrived from Roswell Army Air Force base in New Mexico. This part of the US southwest was (and still is) home to some of America's most secretive defence establishments. It was here that the atomic bomb was developed and tested in great secrecy during the Second World War. After the war secret research continued on German v-2 rockets and aircraft captured from the Axis forces. Roswell itself was home to the US Army Air Force's 509th Bomber

Wing, at that time the only nuclear-equipped air force in the world.

The announcement from Roswell's press officer, Lieutenant Walter Haut, read as follows:

'The many rumours regarding the flying disc became a reality yesterday when the intelligence office of the 509th Bomb Group of the Eighth Air Force, Roswell Army Air Field, was fortunate enough to gain possession of a disc through the cooperation of one of the local ranchers and the sheriff's office of Chaves county.'

The statement said the flying object appeared to have landed, not crashed, on a ranch near Roswell a week earlier. It continued:

'Not having phone facilities, the rancher stored the disc until such time as he was able to contact the Sheriff's office, who in turn notified Major Jesse A. Marcel of the 509th Bomb Group Intelligence Office. Action was immediately taken and the disc was picked up at the rancher's home. It was inspected at the Roswell Army Air Field and subsequently loaned by Major Marcel to higher headquarters…'[9]

News that a 'flying saucer' had been captured by the US military spread like wildfire. Coming so soon after Kenneth Arnold's report it suggested the mystery could be solved very quickly. The initial excitement was though dampened almost immediately when the 8th Army headquarters at Fort Worth announced that the 'flying disc' had in fact been identified as a weather balloon and thus had nothing to do with flying saucers. According to the commanding officer, Brigadier Roger Ramey, when the remains were examined by meteorologists the 'disc' was found to be of 'flimsy construction, like a box-kite'.

This announcement killed the story and Roswell disappeared into obscurity for a further three decades. It did not make headlines again until 1980 when a book, *The Roswell Incident*, by Charles Berlitz and William Moore, resurrected the story. The authors interviewed Major Jesse Marcel,

FIG. 12 The 'Roswell incident' was widely reported by newspapers and radio bulletins across the world, including this example from the *Sheffield Telegraph*.

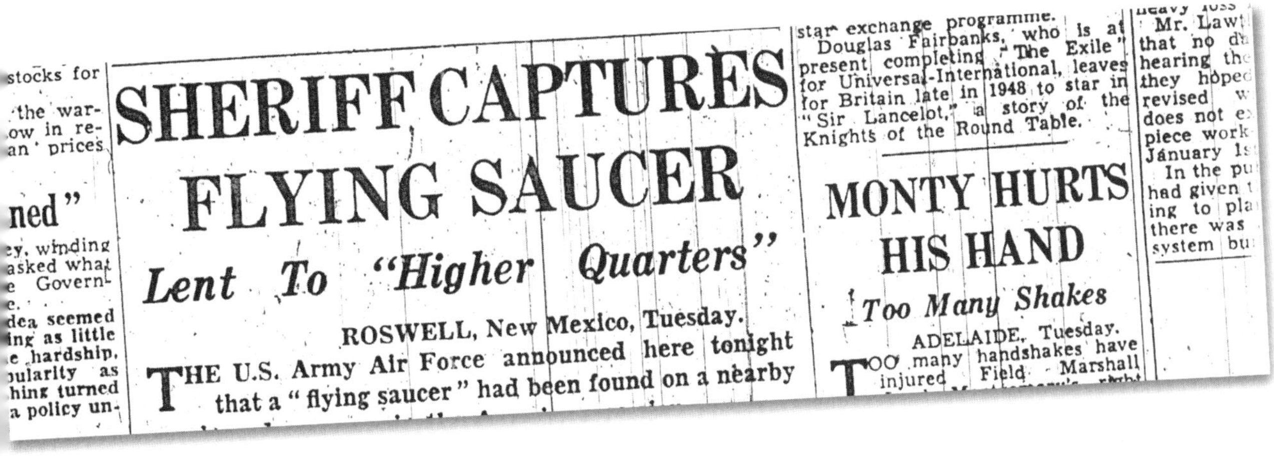

named in the original press release and now retired from the United States Air Force. Marcel had personally examined fragments of the wreckage found at the Roswell ranch in 1947.

Some 30 years afterwards, he said this consisted of small beams containing writing like hieroglyphics and metal like tinfoil that was extremely tough. He said: 'It was something I had never seen before, or since, for that matter ... I didn't know what it was but it certainly wasn't anything built by us and it most certainly wasn't any weather balloon.'[10]

The book also featured rumours that bodies of small creatures had been recovered from the wreckage of this and other saucer crashes in remote desert regions of the US southwest, all of which had been removed by the military under great secrecy. The authors claimed the truth—that the US Government had captured alien technology—had been concealed ever since. This account gave birth to one of the most enduring conspiracy theories of modern times, the UFO cover-up.

That something happened at Roswell is not in doubt. What is less certain is what that something might have been. The official explanation of what happened has changed several times since 1947 and this ambiguity has been seen by some as proof of Berlitz and Moore's claims. In 1993 a US congressman for New Mexico, Steven Schiff, asked the General Accounting Office (GAO), the investigative arm of the American Congress, to search the official files for evidence. His intervention led to the production of a report titled *The Roswell Files: Fact Versus Fiction in the New Mexico Desert*. Published in 1994/5, this concluded that there was after all a balloon connection. The 'disc' had been part of a classified Cold War project, code-named Mogul, which used elaborate balloon trains to carry scientific instruments to the upper atmosphere. However, rather than monitoring the weather, these balloons were used to monitor Soviet nuclear experiments. A balloon train from the Mogul project, launched from Alamogordo, New Mexico, on 4 June, was recorded as being lost in the Roswell area and the original descriptions of scattered debris and a 'box-kite structure' do appear to be consistent with the official explanation.

The Roswell report said the focus of military concern at the time 'was not on aliens, hostile or otherwise, but on the Soviet Union' and concluded:

'[results of our] research indicated absolutely no evidence of any kind that a spaceship crashed near Roswell or that any alien occupants were recovered therefrom, in some secret military operation.'[11]

Wherever the truth may lie, the Roswell incident demonstrated that flying saucers would remain inextricably bound up with military secrets. In the paranoid Cold War context of that time intense official interest in the subject was inevitable.

Project Sign

The United States Air Force (USAF) only became a separate branch of the military on 18 September 1947, but within 5 days of its formation Lieutenant General Nathan F. Twining of Air Materiel Command had sent a secret 'opinion on flying discs' to Brigadier General George Schulgen of the Army Air Force. His view was clear:

> 'The reported operating characteristics such as extreme rates of climb, manoeuvrability … and motion which must be considered evasive when sighted or contacted by friendly aircraft and radar, lend belief to the possibility that some of the objects are controlled either manually, automatically or remotely.'[12]

Significantly, there is no mention of the Roswell incident in Twining's summary, which was declassified in 1969. Indeed, he specifically refers to 'the lack of physical evidence in the shape of crash-recovered exhibits which would undeniably prove the existence of these objects'. If the wreckage of a spacecraft had been recovered at Roswell just two months earlier, Twining would surely have known about it. Nevertheless, he took the subject seriously, concluding: 'The phenomenon reported is something real and not visionary or fictitious' and recommended that a detailed study be undertaken.

As a direct result of the Air Force's concerns, on 30 December 1947 Project Sign was born, with a remit to collect and analyse reports of flying saucers. Within weeks the new project had to deal with the tragic case of a young Air National Guard pilot who died whilst pursuing a strange circular object over Kentucky. Captain Thomas Mantell was the leader of a flight of United States Air Force F-51s sent to investigate the UFO; he flew too high without oxygen, lost consciousness and crashed to his death. Flying saucers were now serious business and could no longer be dismissed as a joke. Following an investigation it was announced that Mantell—an experienced pilot—had actually pursued the planet Venus, which would have been dimly visible in the afternoon sky.

The unconvincing way in which this incident was dealt with provided ammunition to those who smelt a cover-up. The truth would emerge decades later, when it was revealed the object pursued by Mantell was a giant Skyhook balloon released by the United States Navy from a base in Minnesota earlier that day. The Skyhook project, like Mogul, was classified secret in

1948 when these events occurred, and the US authorities were prepared to go to great lengths to hide its existence and purpose.

As fears of communist expansion increased, it was logical for the military authorities to concentrate their attention upon the possibility that some of the unexplained saucer sightings could be of Soviet origin. It was known that the Russians had captured German scientists and blueprints of V-weapons and prototype aircraft, including versions of the Horten 'flying wing' at the close of the war. For a short time, one faction of the intelligence community believed it was plausible these had been developed to produce a disc-shaped aircraft that could reach the US mainland. When it became clear that no terrestrial aircraft could account for the incredible speeds and manoeuvres reported, other explanations had to be considered—and the 'secret weapon' hypothesis was replaced by the idea that saucers could be extraterrestrial in origin.

Captain Edward Ruppelt, who worked for Project Sign and has incidentally been credited as the man who coined the acronym UFO, claimed to have seen a top secret dossier prepared by Project Sign staff in 1948 that concluded flying saucers were probably interplanetary spacecraft. Among the unexplained sightings listed in the dossier, according to Ruppelt, were the Operation Charlie incidents, investigated by the RAF. The 'Estimate of the Situation', as it was named, was circulated as far as the Chief of the Air Force, General Hoyt Vandenberg, who was unconvinced and ordered all copies to be destroyed.[13]

This development marked a major change in the United States Air Force policy, perhaps a direct result of the CIA's growing interest and concern. On 16 December 1948 Project Sign was reborn as Project Grudge, a rebranding that reflected a U-turn from belief to disbelief. Captain Ruppelt summed up Grudge's philosophy as being based upon 'the premise that UFOs couldn't exist. No matter what you see or hear, don't believe it.'

The Flying Saucer Working Party

Flying saucers were regarded as largely an American phenomenon until 1950, when British newspapers began to take an interest in the growing mystery. During the spring and summer of that year a large number of sightings of mysterious fast-moving lights and objects in the sky were made by ordinary members of the public. Most of these observations were made after dark, but a few occurred during daylight. In April a woman from Chester reported seeing 'a round object, like a child's balloon magnified a hundred times, and very bright silver' flying against the wind; later in the year, disc- and globe-shaped objects were seen by many people in the West Country. In December a rugby match in Rhyl was halted as hundreds of spectators watched a 'flying tadpole' zoom across the sky trailing sparks.[14]

Public fascination continued to grow and in the autumn of 1950 two Sunday newspapers serialized the first books on the subject of 'flying saucers'. The most influential of these was the bluntly titled *The Flying Saucers are Real*, by a retired US Marine Corps Major, Donald Keyhoe, who appeared to have highly-placed sources in the American government. Keyhoe claimed the United States Air Force had privately concluded UFOs were of interplanetary origin but feared if this was admitted a mass panic, similar to that which followed the Orson Welles radio broadcast of *The War of the Worlds* in 1938, would result.

Although Keyhoe's claims were never officially confirmed, his writings were popular and had a wide impact on the media and public opinion. His books and those of others who followed led a number of senior figures in the British military establishment to treat the subject seriously for the first time. At the forefront of these was Churchill's son-in-law and future Minister of Defence, Duncan Sandys. He took a fairly pragmatic view, believing the evidence for flying saucers to be no different to the first reports of the German V-2 rockets during 1943, which the government's scientific advisors 'declared to be technically impossible'.

Alongside Sandys there were others such as Lord Mountbatten, who began collecting accounts of sightings in 1950 and encouraged his friend Charles Eade, editor of the *Sunday Dispatch*, to publish them without naming him as the source. In a letter to Eade of 26 March 1950 Mountbatten rejected the idea that flying saucers were secret weapons, stating:

> 'The available evidence will show that they are not of human agency, that is to say they do not come from our Earth. If that is so then presumably they must come from some heavenly body, probably a planet... Maybe it is the Shackletons or Scotts of Venus or Mars who are making their first exploration of our Earth.'[15]

Another influential establishment figure who took reports of UFOs seriously was the scientist Sir Henry Tizard. Best known for his work on the development of radar before the Second World War, his interest in flying saucers remained a secret until recently. Post-war Tizard became Chief Scientific Advisor to the Ministry of Defence and, following a number of sightings in the summer of 1950, argued that 'reports of flying saucers should not be dismissed without some investigation'. It was as a direct result of his influence that the British government was persuaded to set up a small working party to investigate the mystery, reporting to the Directorate of Scientific Intelligence/Joint Technical Intelligence Committee (DSI/JTIC), part of the Ministry of Defence.

The working party was created in August 1950. Chaired by G.L. Turney, head of scientific intelligence at the Admiralty, it included five intelligence officers, two of whom were scientists, the other three representing the intelligence branches of the Army, Navy and RAF. In June 1951, after 11 months of investigations, the working party produced its final report, *DSI/JTIC Report No 7 Unidentified Flying Objects.* The contents followed the lead taken by Project Grudge to debunk UFO sightings and concluded that flying saucers did not exist. Classified as 'Secret/Discreet', the team's brief six-page report poured cold water on the subject, maintaining that all UFO sightings could be explained as misidentifications of ordinary objects or phenomena, optical illusions, psychological delusions and hoaxes.

The team's brief six-page report [maintained] that all UFO sightings could be explained as misidentifications of ordinary objects or phenomena, optical illusions, psychological delusions and hoaxes…

Of the possibilities reviewed by the Flying Saucer Working Party, the idea that UFOs were spacecraft piloted by interplanetary visitors was given short shrift:

'When the only material available is a mass of purely subjective evidence it is impossible to give anything like scientific proof that the phenomena observed are, or are not, caused by something entirely novel, such as aircraft of extraterrestrial origin, developed by beings unknown to us on lines more advanced than anything we have thought of.' (DEFE 44/119)

In conclusion the report stated: 'We accordingly recommend very strongly that no further investigation of reported mysterious aerial phenomena be undertaken, unless and until some material evidence becomes available.'

A senior official from the CIA's Office of Scientific Intelligence, Dr Harris Marshall Chadwell, was present at the meeting in June 1951 when the report was delivered. The CIA had closely monitored the United States Air Force investigations since 1948 and was concerned by the growing public fascination in the subject. As a result there was a level of official paranoia concerning news of intelligence interest in UFOs leaking to the media. Circulation of the British report was therefore restricted within the MoD and CIA.

Its existence remained a closely guarded secret for 50 years, until reference to it surfaced in the minutes of a meeting that were tucked away among the documents released by the National Archives in 1998. One now declassified surviving copy was then discovered in the MoD archives in 2001 and released by the National Archives in the following year. Attached was a covering letter from Directorate of Scientific Intelligence head Bertie Blount to Sir Henry Tizard that read: 'This is the report on "Flying Saucers" for which you asked. I hope that it will serve its purpose.'[16]

Flying saucers over Farnborough

This cryptic remark, and the CIA's influence upon the report's recommendations, could be taken to imply that a hidden agenda lurked behind the Flying Saucer Working Party's conclusions — and this is the opinion of one of the UFO witnesses whose incredible story features in the report. In 1950 Stan Hubbard was an experienced test pilot based at the Royal Aircraft Establishment at Farnborough, site of one of the aeronautical industry's most important annual events, the September air show. On the morning of 15 August 1950, a dry, clear summer's day, Flight Lieutenant Hubbard was walking along the airfield runway towards his quarters. He later recalled his attention was attracted by what he described as 'a strange distant humming sound'. I had the chance to interview him in 2002 and he remembered then how, turning to investigate, he saw in the direction of Basingstoke an object that looked

> 'for all the world like the edge-on view of a discus, the sort of discus we used to throw at sports day in school … and it was rocking from side to side very slightly … but maintaining a very straight approach. That was something that has stuck in my mind very clearly, vividly, to this day.' [17]

As it approached the airfield the sound emanating from the object increased in intensity to become 'a heavy, dominant humming with an associated subdued crackling-hissing … which reminded me strongly of the noise inside a large active electrical power station.' He continued:

> 'It was light grey in colour, a bit like mother of pearl, but blurred. It was obviously reflecting light because as it rocked it looked like a pan lid as you rotate it, with segments of light rotating around. And I could see that around the edge as it went overhead, it was a different colour, it had a definite edge to it. And the whole of the edge was a mass of tiny crackling, sparkling lights. And associated with that, there was a real impact of a very strong ozone smell.

FIG. 14 RAF test pilot Stan Hubbard, whose 1950 sighting triggered a secret investigation by the MoD.

> 'There were no windows or portholes or any other characteristics at all. It was featureless, and the remarkable thing about it was there was no sound of air movement … as the object was coming closer and then went overhead I tried to estimate its size, altitude and speed, but with the absence of any readily identifiable feature it was difficult to gauge these factors with any confidence… I guessed that its height above ground

when first seen was probably between 700 and 1000 [ft] and since it certainly seemed to maintain altitude throughout the period of my observation, I guessed that it would have to be about 100 ft in diameter. It must have been travelling very fast, perhaps as high as 500 to 900 mph.'

Hubbard immediately reported this sighting to his commanding officer and soon afterwards was quizzed by members of the Flying Saucer Working Party. He recalled the questions included:

'"How high was it?" "How big was it?" "How fast was it?" "What was it?" ... and one question which I think reflects the tenor of the interview was: "What do you suppose the object was, and where would it have come from?" I replied simply that in my opinion it was not something that had been designed and built on this Earth. Clearly, from the effect it had on the team, it was the wrong answer.'

The working party's visit to Farnborough would not be the last. On the afternoon of 5 September 1950, just two weeks after Hubbard's first observation, he saw what he believes was the same object again. On this occasion he was standing with five other serving RAF airmen on the watch-tower waiting for a display by the Hawker P.1081 when he spotted the object in the sky to the south of the airfield, towards Guildford. 'I grabbed hold of the chap next to me,' he recalled, 'and said: "Hey, what do you think that is?" Pointing ... and he shouted "My God! Go get a camera quick! Go get some binoculars!"'

Hubbard and his colleagues then watched an incredible performance of aerobatics by what the official report describes as 'a flat disc, light pearl in colour [and] about the size of a shirt button.' Hubbard described it as

'fluttering, as though bordering on instability, in a hovering mode, the object would swoop off in a slight dive at incredibly high speed and in quite stable flight, then stop abruptly and go into another fluttering hover mode. This performance was repeated many times ... and it appeared that all this was taking place some eight to ten miles south of us over the Farnham area.'

The UFO was under observation for some 10 minutes during which the little crowd had swelled to more than a dozen RAF personnel. 'They were awestruck,' Hubbard recalls, 'but not one of them had a camera! I remember one of them saying "Sorry Stan, I didn't believe those first stories." It made my day.' Within 24 hours they were all questioned by the Flying Saucer Working Party. 'We were not given their names and we were strictly warned not to ask questions of them, nor make enquiries elsewhere in the Ministry', Hubbard said. 'We were also warned not to discuss the subject later, even amongst ourselves in private.'

Despite his misgivings Hubbard believed the assurance given by the Air Ministry member of the team that he 'had never had a more reliable and

authentic sighting than ours.' He was unaware of the outcome of this investigation until he got to see a copy of the working party's final report after its
release in 2001. In its summary of Hubbard's initial sighting the report said
there was no doubt the experienced test pilot had honestly described what
he had seen,

> 'but we find it impossible to believe that a most unconventional aircraft,
> of exceptional speed, could have travelled at no great altitude, in the
> middle of a fine summer morning, over a populous and air-minded dis-
> trict like Farnborough, without attracting the attention of more than one
> observer.' (DEFE 44/119)

Accordingly, they concluded he was 'the victim of an
optical illusion, or that he observed some quite normal
type of aircraft and deceived himself about its shape
and speed.' The report then turned its attention to the
second incident, which they described as 'an interesting
example of one report influencing another.' Although
Hubbard believed the objects he saw on both occasions
were identical, the authors felt this opinion was of little
value. While they had no doubt a flying object of some
sort had been seen,

The UFO was under observation
for some 10 minutes
during which the little crowd
had swelled to more than
a dozen RAF personnel.
'They were awestruck,'
Hubbard recalls

> 'we again find it impossible to believe that an uncon-
> ventional aircraft, manoeuvring for some time over a populous area,
> could have failed to attract the attention of other observers. We conclude
> that the officers in fact saw some quite normal aircraft, manoeuvring at
> extreme visual range, and were led by the previous report to believe it to
> be something abnormal.' (DEFE 44/119)

The working party were satisfied this solution was correct because of
another example of misperception reported to them by the Air Ministry
member of their team, Wing Commander Myles Formby. Whilst on a rifle
range near Portsmouth he spotted what he at first thought was a 'flying
saucer' in the distance.

> 'Visibility was good, there being a cloudless sky and bright sunshine. The
> object was located and held by a telescope and gave the appearance of
> being a circular shining disc moving on a regular flight path. It was only
> after observation had been kept for several minutes, and the altitude of the
> object changed so that it did not reflect the sunlight to the observer's eye,
> that it was identified as being a perfectly normal aircraft.' (DEFE 44/119)

Sceptics and believers

The conclusions of the Flying Saucer Working Party set the pattern for all
future British government policy on UFOs. After the report was delivered
the team was dissolved and official investigations ended. However, during

the summer of 1952 there was a new wave of sightings across the world. In America more than 500 sightings were reported to the United States Air Force in July alone, leading future CIA director Major General Charles P. Cabell to launch a new UFO project, Blue Book, under the control of the Air Technical Intelligence Center with Captain Ruppelt as its director.

For the Americans, the most alarming of these sightings occurred in the US capital, Washington DC. On 19 and 20 July 1952, strange moving blips appeared on radars at Washington's National Airport and at Andrews Air Force Base. The phenomena reappeared the following weekend, sometimes moving slowly, then reversing and moving off at incredible speed. Aircraft were scrambled, but the crews saw nothing, despite being vectored towards targets that were visible on ground radar. At the same time, civilian aircrew and ground controllers reported seeing strange lights whilst the phenomena were visible on radar. These events alarmed the Truman administration and led the *New York Times* to demand why 'a jet fighter of Air Defence Command, capable of a speed of 600 miles an hour, failed to catch one of the "objects"'.[18]

A huge press conference was called at the Pentagon as officials moved to calm public fears. High-ranking figures, including the director of United States Air Force intelligence, Major General John Samford, reassured the assembled media the radar blips were probably the result of temperature inversions created by the hot summer weather. These types of unusual conditions, he said, could produce false echoes on radar screens.

Samford's public reassurances followed those given to authority figures in private: President Harry Truman himself had been sufficiently concerned to phone Captain Ruppelt asking for an explanation. And Truman was not the only national leader who read the newspaper headlines. On 28 July, the day before the Washington press conference, the British Prime Minister Winston Churchill had sent a memo to his Secretary of State for Air and copied it to Lord Cherwell, one of his most trusted scientific advisors. This demanded:

> 'What does all this stuff about flying saucers amount to? What can it mean? What is the truth? Let me have a report at your convenience.'
> (PREM 11 / 855)

The Prime Minister received a reassuring response from the Air Ministry on 9 August 1952. Preserved alongside Churchill's memo at the National Archives, it said UFOs were the subject of 'a full intelligence study in 1951' that had concluded all incidents reported could be explained by natural phenomena, misperceptions of aircraft, balloons and birds, optical illusions, psychological delusions and deliberate hoaxes. Churchill was told that an earlier investigation, carried out by Project Grudge in 1948–9 had reached a similar conclusion and that 'nothing has happened since 1951 to make the

Air Staff change their opinion, and, to judge from recent Press statements, the same is true in America.'

The government's Chief Scientist, Lord Cherwell (Frederick Lindemann) said he 'agreed entirely' with the Air Ministry and, in a minute circulated to Cabinet members, dismissed the American saucer scare as 'a product of mass psychology'. But not everyone was so convinced. A 2009 release by the Churchill Archives included a letter from Duncan Sandys, then Minister of Supply, to Cherwell that stated: 'There may, as you say, be no real evidence of the existence of flying saucer *aircraft*, but there is in my view ample evidence of some unfamiliar and unexplained phenomenon.'[19]

The division in the establishment between those who 'believed' that reports of flying saucers should be taken seriously, such as Duncan Sandys and Lord Mountbatten, and those who dismissed the whole subject as 'mass hysteria' was growing. The sceptics tended to be scientists, who applied cold logic to the UFO question and demanded solid evidence, and their opinion was ultimately the most influential.

The Topcliffe incident

With the debate ongoing, events were to take another unexpected turn when a fresh series of sightings occurred during a major NATO exercise in Europe, Operation Mainbrace. The most dramatic was reported by a group of Shackleton aircrew who saw a circular silver object above the airfield at RAF Topcliffe, North Yorkshire, on the afternoon of 19 September 1952. A report made to Topcliffe's commanding officer by one of the men, Flight

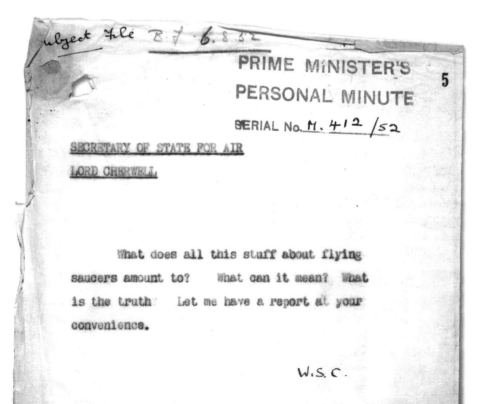

FIG. 15 Following a 'flap' of UFO sightings over Washington DC, British Prime Minister Winston Churchill asked the Secretary of State for Air: 'What does all this stuff about flying saucers amount to?'
PREM 11/855

Lieutenant John Kilburn of 269 Squadron, can be found among the Fighter Command papers preserved at the National Archives. In this Kilburn said he was standing on the airfield with four other Shackleton aircrew watching a Meteor fighter descending:

'The Meteor was at approximately 5,000 feet and approaching from the east. Flt Lt Paris suddenly noticed a white object in the sky at a height between ten and twenty thousand feet some five miles astern of the Meteor. The object was silver in colour and circular in shape, it appeared to be travelling at a much slower speed than the Meteor but was on a similar course. It maintained the slow forward speed for a few seconds before commencing to descend, swinging in a pendular motion during descent similar to a falling sycamore leaf. This was at first thought to be a parachute or engine cowling. The Meteor, meanwhile, turned towards Dishforth and the object, while continuing its descent, appeared to follow suit. After a further few seconds, the object stopped its pendulous motion and its descent, and began to rotate on its own axis. Suddenly it accelerated at an incredible speed towards the west turning onto a south easterly heading before disappearing. All this occurred in a matter of fifteen to twenty seconds. The acceleration was in excess of that of a shooting star. I have never seen such a phenomenon before. The movements of the object were not identifiable with anything I have seen in the air and the rate of acceleration was unbelievable.' (AIR 16/1199)

As in America, the year 1952 was to be a busy one for UFOs and the Topcliffe incident was just the first in a series of reports made by military personnel that reached the Air Ministry. There were also a growing number of incidents involving the tracking of fast-moving unidentified objects on RAF radars. For example, on 21 October 1952 a flying instructor and his Royal Navy student were in a Meteor jet on exercise from the RAF's central flying school at Little Rissington, Gloucestershire, when they saw three saucer-shaped UFOs. Flight Lieutenant Michael Swiney, who later served in air intelligence and retired at the rank of Air Commodore, vividly remembers this encounter. The circular, plate-like objects were also clearly observed by his student, Lieutenant David Crofts. They became visible when the Meteor punched through a layer of cloud at around 12,000 ft. Initially Swiney thought they were three parachutes descending towards them. Crofts described them as elliptical in shape and iridescent, like circular pieces of glass reflecting the sun.

Shaken, Swiney abandoned the training flight and reported the sighting to ground control. The objects, stationary at first, appeared to change position and then vanished. Subsequently he learned that aircraft were scrambled by Fighter Command to intercept these UFOs. When I interviewed

Michael Swiney in 2004 he recalled his reaction:

'I was frightened, I make no bones about it. It was something supernatural, perhaps, and when I landed someone told me I looked as if I had seen a ghost. I immediately thought of saucers, because that was actually what they looked like… I even put an entry in my logbook, which reads: "saucers! … 3 'flying saucers' sighted at height, confirmed by GCI [radar]."'[20]

On landing at Little Rissington the two men were ordered to remain in their quarters until the following day, when an Air Ministry team arrived to

FIG. 16 A sighting of a 'flying saucer' by RAF Shackleton aircrew in Yorkshire during a NATO exercise made news headlines in September 1952.

FIG. 17 Details of the Topcliffe incident were circulated to Air Ministry intelligence in this message dated 20 September 1952.
AIR 20/7390

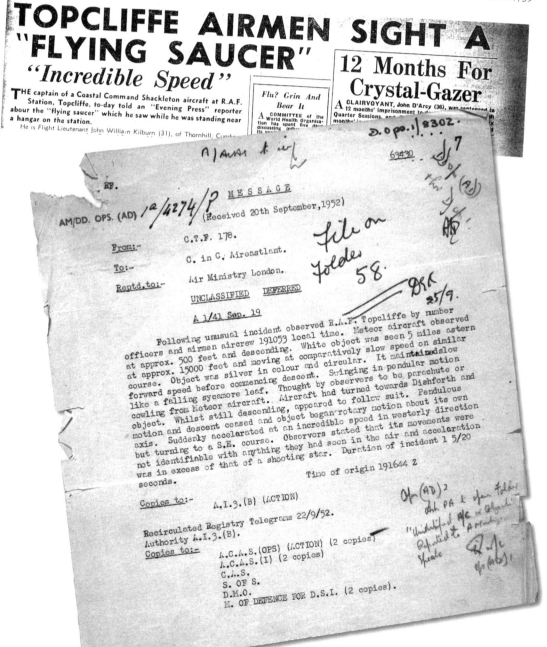

interview them. The team took statements and asked the men to draw what they had seen. Swiney's student, David Crofts, recalled he was told 'they [Air Intelligence] had been in communication with every country in the world that was likely to have that sort of aircraft in the vicinity and drew a blank.' When I interviewed him in 2004 he remembered: 'They also said they [the UFOs] had been picked up on radar; fighters had been scrambled and the target had a ground speed of 600 knots, heading east but the fighters saw nothing, didn't make a contact and returned to base.'[21]

Despite this clear testimony it appears the men's statements describing this dramatic incident were subsequently destroyed. On his retirement, Air Commodore Swiney made inquiries with the MoD hoping to locate a copy of his original report on the incident. He was amazed to learn that most records of UFOs before 1962 had been routinely shredded. Today all that remains in the files at the National Archives is a single surviving reference in the flying school's operations record book which simply records how the two men 'sighted three mysterious "saucer-shaped objects" travelling at high speed at about 35,000 feet whilst on a high level navigation exercise.' The document adds that air traffic control later reported radar plots that appeared to confirm their report 'but Air Ministry discounted any possibility of "extra terrestrial objects."'[22]

FIG. 18 An extract from the Operations Record Book of RAF Little Rissington that includes a sighting of 'three mysterious saucer-shaped objects' by the crew of a RAF Meteor jet on 21 October 1952. AIR 29/2310

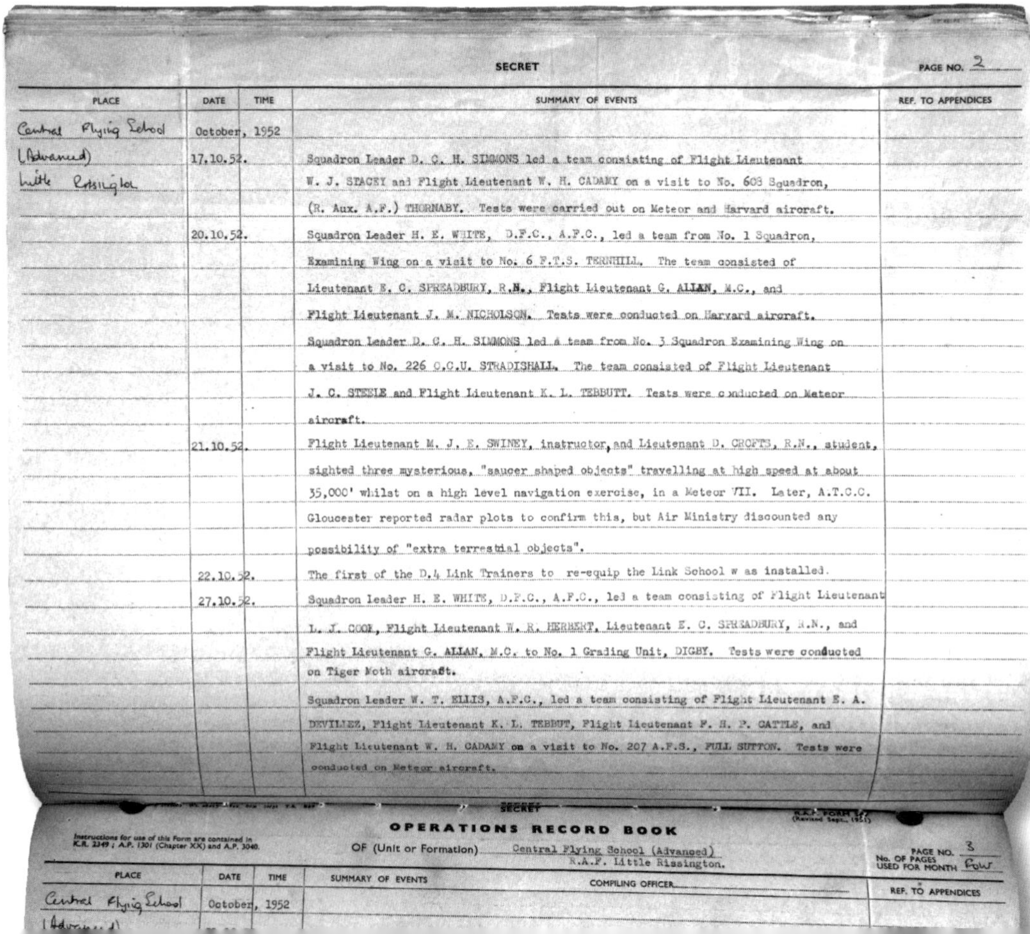

Writing in 1988 Ralph Noyes, who was private secretary to the Vice Chief of the Air Staff, Air Chief Marshal Sir Ralph Cochrane, at the time recalled their 'own embarrassed unease, widely shared by the [RAF] operations staff, that "our own people" had begun to fall for "that saucer nonsense".' Indeed, as a direct result of these incidents a decision was taken in 1953 that the Air Ministry should investigate UFO reports on a permanent basis and responsibility was delegated by the Chief of the Air Staff to a section of the air technical intelligence branch, DDI (Tech). The memoirs of Captain Edward Ruppelt refer to an exchange visit to Project Blue Book's base at Wright-Patterson airfield, Ohio, by two RAF officers shortly afterwards. In his *Report on Unidentified Flying Objects*, published in 1956, Ruppelt revealed the officers were in the USA 'on a classified mission' during which one admitted the sightings during Operation Mainbrace had 'caused the RAF to officially recognise the UFO.'

From angels to aliens

One of the features of the UFO phenomenon that most concerned the Air Ministry was visual sightings that appeared to be corroborated by radar operators, as featured in the report by Michael Swiney and David Crofts. Unexplained phenomena had been tracked on RAF radars early in the Second World War (see p.25) and again during the 'ghost plane' flap of 1947 (see p.33), but until 1952 none of these had involved visual sightings.

In his history of UK air defence radar systems, *Watching the Skies*, Jack Gough says that 'angel' and 'ghost' echoes continued to plague RAF radars during the early 1950s. They sometimes appeared from the ground 'as a cloud of responses very similar to the echoes obtained by small aircraft'. When tracked as individual echoes they could easily be mistaken for military aircraft as they followed a steady course and were plotted at heights from 2,000 ft to 10,000 ft.[23]

The Air Ministry turned to their scientists to provide a solution to this problem. Initially there were two competing theories to explain 'angels'. The first was they were caused by unusual conditions in the atmosphere that created pockets of air that bent and reflected radar beams to produce false targets on radars. This appeared likely, but could not explain how some 'angels' moved against the prevailing winds or faster than measured wind speeds.

The second more improbable-seeming theory was that angels were really formations of birds flying to and from their breeding grounds as part of their annual migrations. At the time the few ornithologists who were using radar to study bird movements had problems persuading the RAF to take this theory seriously. However, during the war staff at coastal radar stations had linked 'angels' on their screens with flights of seabirds spotted with the naked eye. On rare occasions large individual birds had been known to cause chaos. Barry Huddart, who served with Fighter Command HQ in 1957, recalled one incident 'when fighters were scrambled to intercept an echo on a radar screen which turned out to be a Golden Eagle at 25,000 ft in a jet stream, very unusual but nonetheless true.'[24]

By 1957 Fighter Command HQ was so concerned by the 'angel' problem that it ordered a secret investigation by its Research Branch. The two-year study was to combine the skills of its radar technicians with the expertise of British ornithologists. Selected RAF radar stations around the east coast were asked to send film from their radar cameras for analysis. Meanwhile, morbid experiments were carried out to measure the echoing area of various types of birds. Dead animals were obtained from bird sanctuaries and their bodies were wrapped in cellophane and then whirled around whilst radar was bounced off them to measure their 'echoing area'.

Staff at coastal radar stations had linked 'angels' on their screens with flights of seabirds spotted with the naked eye.

On rare occasions large individual birds had been known to cause chaos

The investigation was concentrated around one key radar station where 'angels' had been frequently reported. RAF Trimingham on the north Norfolk coast was one of the first to be equipped with a new powerful radar, the Type 80. Ornithologist David Lack used this to track 'angel' echoes for a year. His study revealed the heaviest 'angel' activity occurred during the spring and autumn months, usually at night in calm weather when birds were migrating over the sea. Lack and his colleagues were able to demonstrate that what the radar operators were actually seeing were flocks of small birds migrating to and from East Anglia and Continental Europe. These observations led the RAF inquiry to conclude in 1958 that most 'angel' echoes on radar were caused by birds after all.[25]

Nevertheless, a big problem remained. How could 'angels' be eliminated from radar without playing havoc with the tracking and control of military aircraft? The answer was a gadget that simply tuned out the 'noise' created by the presence of smaller birds and other clutter from radar screens whilst at the same time increasing the strength and visibility of echoes created by aircraft. This system was simplified further when all 'friendly' aircraft were fitted with transponders that transmit a coded identification signal to ground stations.

Advances in radar technology may help explain why the majority of accounts describing UFOs on radar were made during the 1940s and 1950s, before technological innovations removed the noise that plagued older systems. The older post-war radars appear to have been more effective detectors of a range of natural and unusual phenomena including 'angels'. Once computers were used to remove anything that did not behave like an air-craft from screens, reports of UFOs on radar became fewer. This was brought home to me during a visit to a busy RAF radar control centre in 2005. When I asked one of the operators if they ever detected radar UFOs she replied, with a smile: 'Sometimes, but when we spot one we just send for the technicians who come along and tune them out.'

UFOs at RAF West Freugh

Nonetheless, the main purpose of air defence radars is to detect unidenti-fied aircraft that might pose a threat to the security of the UK. On rare occasions some radar UFOs defied all attempts to explain them as 'angels' or other naturally occurring phenomena. One of the best examples took place on 4 April 1957 when a formation of UFOs was tracked over the Irish Sea. Unlike other similar incidents that were kept secret, the radar operators in this case were civilians and the story appeared in the national media. Newspapers discovered the objects had been seen on radar at a record-breaking 70,000 ft, far beyond the capability of most aircraft of the day. This led to speculation these UFOs could have been long-range Russian or American spy planes. This incident caused a major panic within the Air Ministry and led to questions in Parliament and at the Joint Intelligence Committee.

Wing Commander Peter Whitworth, who was commanding officer of RAF West Freugh in 1957, sent the following detailed account of this inci-dent to the MoD in 1971 after he was approached by a UFO researcher. He asked the MoD for permission to release details, which were protected by the Official Secrets Act, writing:

'The radars used at West Freugh were extremely accurate and reliable. They were used for "blind-bombing" if weather conditions were too bad for the bomb-aimer to see the target in Luce Bay. The plotting of the UFO was thus a true and accurate plot, confirmed by two radar oper-ators, 14 miles apart. At the time of the sighting, there was unbroken cloud at approximately 1,000 ft over the whole area. The UFO was not seen or heard … [it] was first seen when the radar at Balscalloch, near Corsewall Point, north of Stranraer, "locked-on" to the object. This showed the UFO to be over the sea, about 20–25 miles N-West of Stran-raer; it was at approx: 51,000 ft and absolutely stationary in space. This so surprised the radar operator, he called up the other operator at Ard-well (14 miles away) and asked if he had anything on his screen. The Ardwell operator switched on his set and at once the radar picked up the UFO. Both operators then tracked the UFO until it disappeared from their screens, approx four minutes later.

'After remaining stationary for a short time, the UFO began to rise

vertically, with no forward movement, rising rapidly to approx 60,000 ft in much less than a minute. The UFO then began to move in an Easterly direction, slowly at first but later accelerating very fast and travelling towards Newton Stewart, losing height on the way. Near Newton Stewart the UFO made a very sharp turn to the South-West, still at very high speed and losing height approx 15,000 ft, it continued on the S-West course towards the Isle of Man, when radar contact was lost … the sharp turn made near Newton Stewart would be impossible for any aircraft travelling at similar speed, according to one of the radar operators.'
(AIR 2/18564)

This letter survives at the National Archives alongside a detailed report covering the investigation of the incident. This confirms most of the details in Whitworth's account written 15 years after the event. It says that five objects were detected by three radars at least one of which rose to an altitude of 70,000 ft where it remained, while at other times the formation moved at speeds of around 240 mph. Shortly before the objects disappeared the operators saw up to four smaller objects moving in line astern about 4,000 yds from each other.

> After remaining stationary for a short time, the UFO began to rise vertically, with no forward movement, rising rapidly to approx 60,000 ft in much less than a minute

The report notes how 'the radar operators [said] the sizes of the echoes were considerably larger than would be expected from normal aircraft. In fact they considered that the size was nearer that of a ship's echo.' It adds that nothing could be said of physical construction of these UFOs 'except they were very effective reflectors of radar signals, and that they must have been either of considerable size or else constructed to be especially good reflectors.' Inquiries ruled out aircraft, meteorological balloons and thunderclouds as explanations and the report concluded with a startling statement that is the closest the Air Ministry ever came to an admission that UFOs did exist:

> 'It is concluded that the incident was due to the presence of five reflecting objects of unidentified type and origin.' (AIR 20/9320)

After the story appeared in the press the Air Ministry was questioned about UFOs at a meeting of the Joint Intelligence Committee at the Cabinet Office. In response to their concerns, Air Vice-Marshal Bill McDonald reassured the committee that 'all of these phenomena have … been satisfactorily explained through mistakes in radar interpretation, maladjustment of sets, as balloons or even as aircraft'[26]. Plainly this was not the case as the West Freugh incident was one of a number listed as 'unexplained' in air intelligence files.

The Cold War was now at its height and UFOs remained a persistent and troubling problem for the air forces of the world. In a 1989 interview,

Ralph Noyes, who rose to the rank of Assistant Under Secretary of State for Defence in the course of his career, admitted to me that West Freugh and other incidents left the Air Staff in 'little doubt something had taken place for which we had no explanation.' He added:

'Not once, however, was there the faintest suggestion that extraterrestrials might be in question. We suspected the Russians. We suspected faulty radar. We wondered whether RAF personnel might be succumbing to hallucinogens. But we found no evidence of any such things and in the end, and fairly swiftly, we simply forgot these uncomfortable "intrusions".'

FIG. 19 No two UFOs are identical. In the years that followed the first flying saucer sightings reports of many different sized and shaped UFOs would be received, as demonstrated by this 1971 spread from the *UFO Register*, a magazine produced by Contact UK.

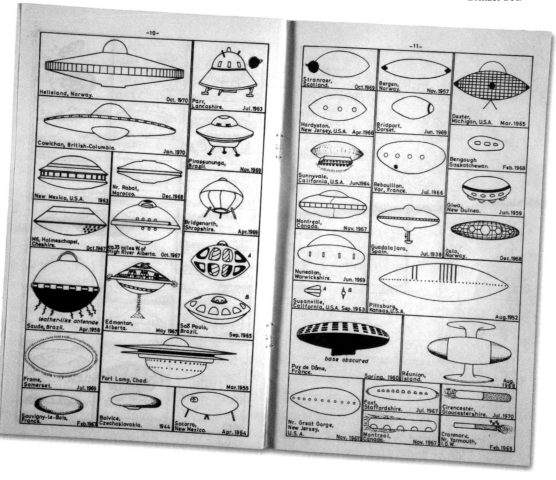

THREE *'…in an age when the wartime Spitfire is now just an old-fashioned flying machine, a Flying Saucer could so easily be just the newest prototype out on its test flight.'* Daily Express, 29 July 1954

COLD WAR UFOS

PRIOR TO 1950 flying saucers had been widely seen as an American phenomenon, but within just four years people across Britain were seeing them—and believing in them. At this early stage British sightings lacked a little drama in comparison with those that were being reported in America. Even so there were some fascinating accounts from eyewitnesses, such as this incident reported by Flight Lieutenant James Salandin, who was a pilot flying with the RAF's auxiliary air force:

'On 10 October 1954 I took off from North Weald on a normal routine flight in a Meteor 8 aircraft. Whilst climbing I noticed a number of trails in the Chatham/Gillingham area at 12 o'clock… When at 15,000 feet I saw what I presumed at the time to be two aeroplanes flying on a reciprocal course to myself but out to my port side…I could not identify these two objects and I could not follow them due to the fantastic speed they were travelling. The first one appeared to be a goldy colour and the second silvery, flying in what appeared to be a loose battle formation. Upon looking ahead again, I saw coming straight towards me at the same height a silvery spherical object with a bun on top and below. When at what I should imagine was only a few hundreds yards distance it went over to my port side… also travelling at some terrific rate of knots. I was completely shaken by the incident and it took me five or ten minutes to pull myself together. Had I not been so shaken I could probably have taken a head-on cine film of the third object…'[1]

Pilots were not the only people to see flying saucers. On 15 February the same year 13-year-old Stephen Darbishire took a photograph of a UFO he saw swooping over the Coniston mountains of Cumbria. Early that morning he was walking on the lower fells with his 8-year-old cousin, Adrian Meyer, 'when Adrian suddenly shouted "Look! What on Earth's that?" and pointed to the sky over Dow Crag.' The two boys then saw an object 'glistening like aluminium in the sunlight' coming towards them. Stephen said:

'You could tell the outline of it very plainly indeed and see port-holes along the upper part, and a thing which looked like a hatch on top ... I took the first picture when it was moving very slowly about three or four hundred yards away and then it disappeared from my view... When it came into sight again I took another picture but then it suddenly went up into the sky in a great swish.' [2]

In the wake of the UFO panic in Washington DC in 1952, the CIA had taken a close interest in Project Blue Book's investigations and were told by the United States Air Force that around 90 per cent of the sightings reported to them could be explained. However, the CIA's Dr Harris Marshall Chadwell remained concerned that a small residue of sightings, those he described as 'incredible reports from credible observers', could not be ignored. The agency feared that a UFO panic engineered by the Russians could overload the US air defence system with so many spurious reports that it would not be able to distinguish real aircraft from what he called 'phantoms'.

CIA Director Walter Bedell Smith felt that even if 'there was only one chance in 10,000 that the phenomenon posed a threat to the security of the country ... even that chance could not be taken.' [3] Accordingly, in January 1953 the CIA convened a panel of non-military scientists in Washington, chaired by the physicist Dr Bob Robertson, to study the most impressive cases reported to date. Dr Robertson, of the California Institute of Technology, was an interesting choice as chair. Eight years earlier he had taken part in an inquiry into the foo-fighter mystery whilst serving as a scientific intelligence officer in Europe during the Second World War (see p.27).

Other members of the panel included Nobel Prize winner and radar specialist Dr Luis Alvarez, nuclear physicist Dr Samuel Goldsmit and Dr Lloyd Berkner of Brookhaven National Laboratories. During a period of four days, this team scrutinized two movie films showing UFOs and reviewed a number of case histories presented by Project Blue Book personnel.

They emerged unconvinced that any of the incidents discussed could not be explained through the application of existing scientific knowledge. The panel could find no evidence that any sightings were observations of extraterrestrial spaceships, or posed any threat to national defence. Their findings underlined the CIA's desire to control the release of information on unexplained incidents. They also recognized the danger posed by UFO 'false alarms' clogging military communication channels at tense periods that might lead the authorities

'to ignore real indications of hostile action ... and the cultivation of a morbid national psychology in which skilful hostile propaganda could induce hysterical behaviour and harmful distrust of duly constituted authority.'[4]

This paranoid language was typical of the McCarthy era and this was reflected in the panel's recommendation that federal agencies 'take immediate steps to strip the Unidentified Flying Objects of the special status they have been given and the aura of mystery they have unfortunately acquired.'

The panel toyed with ideas of elaborate public education campaigns to debunk UFOs, even to the extent of enlisting the resources of the Walt Disney corporation to put out an anti-UFO message to the public. None of these suggestions appears to have been implemented, but attempts were made both in America and in Britain to restrict the release of information about sightings reported by military personnel unless they could be adequately explained.

UFOs in Parliament—'All balloony?'

Later that year attempts by the British Air Ministry to control the spread of information about UFO sightings reported by RAF personnel were dealt a major blow. On the morning of 3 November 1953 a Vampire night-fighter from RAF West Malling in Kent was on a routine exercise at 20,000 ft over the Thames Estuary when the crew spotted a very bright object straight ahead at a much higher altitude. The UFO was stationary when first seen and shaped like a doughnut with 'a bright light around the periphery'. As they watched it disappeared in a south-easterly direction. Their story leaked to the *Daily Express* who discovered that later that same day a Territorial Army unit tracked 'a very large echo' on their radar moving at 60,000 ft over London. Through a telescope, a sergeant then reported seeing 'a circular or spherical object' high in the sky.

This story caused a sensation when it appeared on the front page of the *Daily Express* under the headline 'Mystery at 60,000 feet'. Questions were tabled in the Commons and on 24 November the Secretary of State for Air, Nigel Birch, moved to reassure MPs there was 'nothing peculiar about either of the occurrences'. The object seen on radar over London, Birch explained, had been traced to balloons released by the Meteorological Office station at Crawley. They were fitted with 'a special device to produce as large an echo on a radar screen as an aircraft'. Laughter erupted when an MP asked if the Minister agreed that 'this story of flying saucers is all balloony'.

Files at the archives show that orders were sent to all RAF stations in the wake of the unwelcome publicity that followed the West Malling incident, warning that in future all UFO reports 'are to be classified "Restricted" and personnel are warned not to communicate to anyone other than official persons any information about phenomena they have observed, unless officially

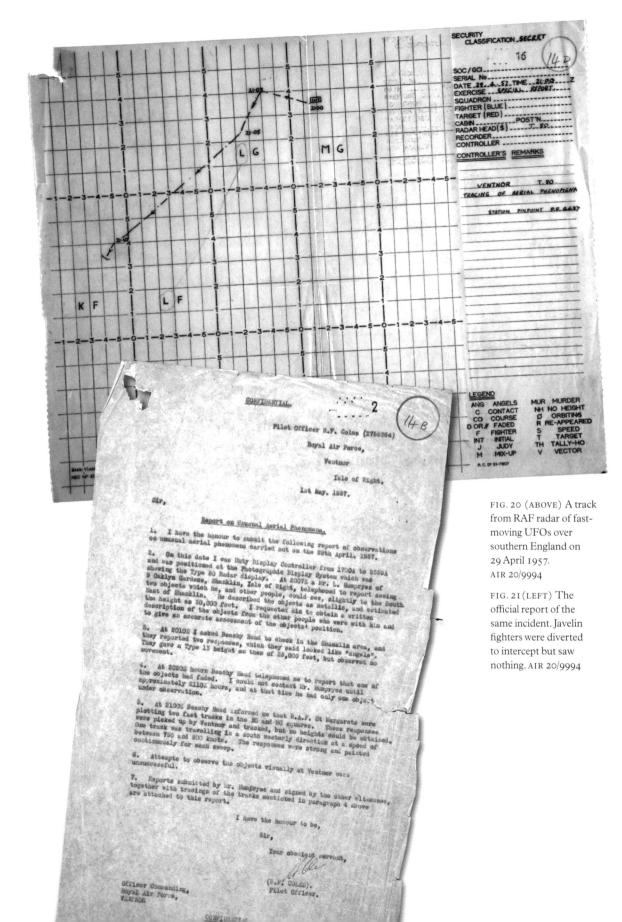

CONFIDENTIAL.

2   14 B

Pilot Officer R.F. Coles (2755364)

Royal Air Force,

Ventnor

Isle of Wight.

1st May. 1957.

Sir,

Report on Unusual Aerial Phenomena.

1. I have the honour to submit the following report of observations on unusual aerial phenomena carried out on the 29th April. 1957.

2. On this date I was Duty Display Controller from 1700A to 2359A and was positioned at the Photographic Display System which was showing the Type 80 Radar display. At 2007Z a Mr. L. Humphreys of 9 Oaklyn Gardens, Shanklin, Isle of Wight, telephoned to report seeing two objects which he, and other people, could see, slightly to the South East of Shanklin. He described the objects as metallic, and estimated the height as 50,000 feet. I requested him to obtain a written description of the objects from the other people who were with him and to give an accurate assessment of the objects' position.

3. At 2010Z I asked Beachy Head to check in the Shanklin area, and they reported two responses, which they said looked like "angels". They gave a Type 13 height on them of 25,000 feet, but observed no movement.

4. At 2020Z hours Beachy Head telephoned me to report that one of the objects had faded. I could not contact Mr. Humphryes until approximately 2110Z hours, and at that time he had only one object under observation.

5. At 2100Z Beachy Head informed me that R.A.F. St Margarets were plotting two fast tracks in the MG and MG squares. These responses were picked up by Ventnor and tracked, but no heights could be obtained. One track was travelling in a south westerly direction at a speed of between 750 and 800 knots. The responses were strong and painted continuously for each sweep.

6. Attempts to observe the objects visually at Ventnor were unsuccessful.

7. Reports submitted by Mr. Humphryes and signed by the other witnesses, together with tracings of the tracks mentioned in paragraph 4 above are attached to this report.

I have the honour to be,

Sir,

Your obedient servant,

(R.F. COLES).
Pilot Officer.

Officer Commanding,
Royal Air Force,
VENTNOR

CONFIDENTIAL

FIG. 20 (ABOVE) A track from RAF radar of fast-moving UFOs over southern England on 29 April 1957. AIR 20/9994

FIG. 21 (LEFT) The official report of the same incident. Javelin fighters were diverted to intercept but saw nothing. AIR 20/9994 authorised to do so.' The RAF order dated 16 December 1953 said reports should be sent to the intelligence branch DDI (Tech) who were now responsible for the investigation of all UFO reports. It said because

'the public attach more credence to reports by RAF personnel than to those from members of the public ... it is essential that the information should be examined at Air Ministry and that its release should be controlled officially.' (AIR 20/9994)

This decision marked the first coordinated attempt to define and codify sighting reports reported to the Air Ministry. In January 1953, shortly after the Robertson panel met, RAF Fighter Command had issued the first reporting guidelines for 'unusual targets' detected by radar stations. These required that special reports should be made about any targets

'moving at a ground speed exceeding 700 knots at any height and at any speed above 60,000 feet...When an unusual response is seen, the supervisor ... should be informed and he should then check that the echo is not spurious, and arrange for the necessary records to be made.' [5]

Later the same year the first Air Ministry UFO report form was drawn up, based upon a template of questions used by Project Blue Book staff. The form listed key facts in 10 categories that included date/time and location, name and address of the witness, the height, speed, shape, size and colour of the phenomena observed and classification of sighting as explained or unexplained. Modified versions of this form, with categories of information listed under alphabetical numerals, were still in use by the MoD until quite recently.

From 1954 the new Air Ministry UFO project produced a yearly report 'summarising all UFO sightings by types'. An analysis of 80 reports received to the end of 1954 formed the basis of an article in a classified publication known as the Air Ministry Secret Intelligence Summary (AMSIS) during March 1955. This summary, based upon a longer air intelligence report now lost, was classified 'Secret—UK Eyes Only'. Its existence was revealed in May 1955 when the Conservative MP Major Patrick Wall asked the Secretary of State for Air, in a Parliamentary Question, if he would publish the 'report on flying saucers recently completed by the Air Ministry.' Wall had learned about the report from an informant within the Ministry who told him, via a third party, 'there are in fact two reports; the first is a full length report going into some 10,000 words. It does include a number of things which the authorities would certainly consider as secret.' [6]

In his Commons reply the Air Minister George Ward avoided answering Wall's question directly. Instead he gave a formal statement that said:

'reports of "flying saucers" as well as any other abnormal objects in the sky, are investigated as they come in, but there has been no formal inquiry. About 90 per cent of the reports have been found to relate to meteors, balloons, flares and many other objects. The fact that the other 10 per cent are unexplained need be attributed to nothing more sinister than lack of data.' (AIR 2/16918)

The figures were similar to those issued during 1955 by the United States Air Force's Project Blue Book.

Although Major Wall was unaware of it at the time, Ward's statement was evidence of a major change of mind on the part of the British Government. The Flying Saucer Working Party report of 1951 had concluded, in secret, that all UFO reports could be explained (see p.42). After four years of further investigations, the Air Ministry was now admitting publicly that 10 per cent of UFO reports could not after all be accounted for, even after investigation. The reason given for the continued interest in UFOs was 'there is always the chance of observing foreign aircraft of revolutionary design.'[7]

The saucers that came in from the cold

As chilly East–West relations cooled even further during the 1950s, both sides poured money into military technology. The British and Canadian governments flirted with a number of designs for unorthodox aircraft that were inspired by the flying saucer craze. The most famous of these was a saucer-shaped aircraft, code-named Project Y, that was designed by British engineer John Frost for A.V. Roe in Canada.

Extravagant claims were made by the company to attract government investment in the project, such as vertical takeoff and a high supersonic speed. Photographs taken in a hangar near Toronto in 1953 show a sleek delta-shaped aircraft that sat on its tail like a rocket. A prototype was built but the British government were unimpressed and the project was taken over by the United States Air Force the following year. The American version reverted to the classic saucer-shape but the two prototype 'Avro-cars' produced performed poorly in tests and the project was cancelled in 1961.

At the same time, both the United States and the Soviet Union became increasingly concerned about what the other was up to, developing hi-tech aircraft capable of making covert, long-range missions to spy on enemy territory. One result of this was the top-secret Skyhook programme. Skyhooks were balloons constructed from special plastics with diameters of more than 200 ft and a gas capacity double that of the Hindenburg airship. From the late 1940s thousands were

FIG. 22 A photograph showing a futuristic 'flying saucer' prototype – Project Y – designed by British engineer John Frost and developed by Avro-Canada in 1953. AVIA 65/33

launched from Holloman Air Force Base, near the White Sands missile range in New Mexico. This was the base whose Mogul balloon trains have been linked to the crash of a 'flying saucer' near Roswell in 1947 (see p.38).

As with Mogul, these were no weather balloons. Their actual purpose was to ride the jet stream to the Soviet Union where sophisticated payloads of cameras suspended in a gondola below the balloons took photographs of sensitive military facilities on the ground. After over-flying Soviet territory their payload dropped into the ocean where radio beacons guided US planes to collect them.

One of the most dramatic American UFO incidents, when United States Air Force pilot Captain Thomas Mantell crashed to his death whilst chasing a 'flying saucer', was later revealed to be linked to a Skyhook launched by the US Navy in 1948 (see p.39). Skyhooks may also lie behind a number of British sightings, including the RAF West Malling incident of 1953. A declassified history of balloon operations produced by the USAF Missile Development Center in 1958 reveals that balloon number 175, launched from Holloman, New Mexico, on 27 October 1953, failed to drop into the Atlantic at the end of a scheduled 12-hour flight. Six days later it was this, cruising at high altitude over Kent, that was spotted by the RAF crew and which prompted 'flying saucer' questions in parliament.

A former member of the Skyhook project staff, Duke Gildenberg, revealed in 2004 that British intelligence concluded this UFO was the Skyhook balloon but could not reveal the truth because the project was classified top secret at the time. When the Secretary of State for Air, Nigel Birch, was quizzed in Parliament his explanation simply reflected the official weather balloon line that did not reveal any military secrets.[8]

The fact that Skyhook flights occasionally triggered UFO panics as they cruised the stratosphere was an unexpected, though not unwelcome, by-product. At sunset and dawn the huge balloons reflected sunlight to appear as classic silvery 'flying saucers' to observers below. Gildenberg said Skyhook staff often monitored long-distance Skyhook flights by following 'flying saucer' reports published in newspapers across the world.

From 1951 new bases were opened in Scotland, from where the United States Air Force planned to release up to 3,500 of the giant balloons. The project was eventually scrapped in 1956 after achieving only limited success. In total 461 balloons were launched, just half of which penetrated Russian airspace, and of these just 42 gondolas were recovered intact.[9]

'An unidentified high-flying aircraft'

When the Skyhook balloon programme failed to produce satisfactory results, the CIA began testing their high-altitude U-2 spy plane, developed from 1955 at Lockheed's 'Skunk Works' in Burbank, California. The plane

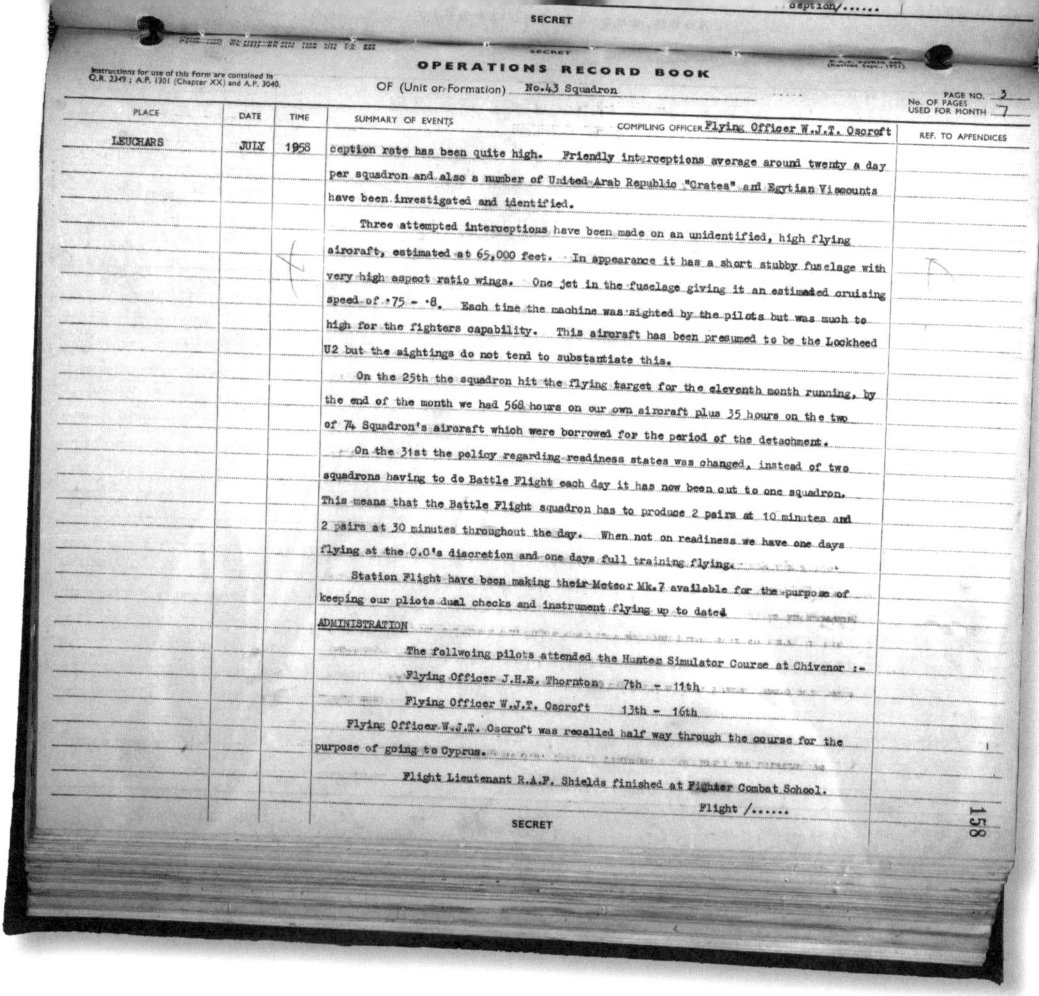

OPERATIONS RECORD BOOK

OF (Unit or Formation) No. 43 Squadron

Instructions for use of this form are contained in
Q.R. 2349 ; A.P. 1301 (Chapter XX) and A.P. 3040.

PAGE NO. 3
No. OF PAGES USED FOR MONTH 7

PLACE	DATE	TIME	SUMMARY OF EVENTS COMPILING OFFICER Flying Officer W.J.T. Oscroft	REF. TO APPENDICES
LEUCHARS	JULY 1958		...ception rate has been quite high. Friendly interceptions average around twenty a day per squadron and also a number of United Arab Republic "Crates" and Egyptian Viscounts have been investigated and identified.	

    Three attempted interceptions have been made on an unidentified, high flying aircraft, estimated at 65,000 feet. In appearance it has a short stubby fuselage with very high aspect ratio wings. One jet in the fuselage giving it an estimated cruising speed of .75 - .8. Each time the machine was sighted by the pilots but was much too high for the fighters capability. This aircraft has been presumed to be the Lockheed U2 but the sightings do not tend to substantiate this.

    On the 25th the squadron hit the flying target for the eleventh month running, by the end of the month we had 568 hours on our own aircraft plus 35 hours on the two of 74 Squadron's aircraft which were borrowed for the period of the detachment.

    On the 31st the policy regarding readiness states was changed, instead of two squadrons having to do Battle Flight each day it has now been cut to one squadron. This means that the Battle Flight squadron has to produce 2 pairs at 10 minutes and 2 pairs at 30 minutes throughout the day. When not on readiness we have one days flying at the C.O's discretion and one days full training flying.

    Station Flight have been making their Meteor Mk.7 available for the purpose of keeping our pilots dual checks and instrument flying up to date.

ADMINISTRATION

    The follwoing pilots attended the Hunter Simulator Course at Chivenor :-
        Flying Officer J.H.E. Thornton   7th - 11th
        Flying Officer W.J.T. Oscroft   13th - 16th
    Flying Officer W.J.T. Oscroft was recalled half way through the course for the purpose of going to Cyprus.

    Flight Lieutenant R.A.F. Shields finished at Fighter Combat School.
                                        Flight /......

SECRET

158

---

could fly at an altitude of 60,000 ft to avoid Soviet radars, way beyond the capabilities of most civil aircraft of the time. The early U-2s were silver, tended to reflect sunlight and often appeared as 'fiery objects' to the crews of airliners and military aircraft sent to intercept them. According to the CIA, their staff were able to attribute more than half of all UFO reports made to Project Blue Book from the late 1950s through the 1960s to flights by advanced reconnaissance aircraft such as the U-2 and the SR-71 Blackbird over the US mainland.

As the United States Air Force received thousands of UFO reports during this period, many of which had other explanations, this estimate seems excessive. However, the operations record book of 43 Squadron based at RAF Nicosia records three occasions in July 1958 when fighter crews tried to intercept 'an unidentified, high-flying aircraft, [at an estimated height] of 65,000 feet' over the Mediterranean and above the RAF's own capability. Crews assumed this aircraft, which had 'a short stubby fuselage with very high aspect ratio wings' was the U-2, but the RAF could not confirm this identification as the project was highly classified at the time.[10]

Spy plane missions were made in radio silence without notification even

FIG. 23 An extract from the Operations Record Book of No 43 Squadron, RAF, describing attempted interceptions of 'an unidentified high-flying aircraft' over the Mediterranean in 1958. The aircraft was most likely to have been the CIA's U-2 spyplane.
AIR 27/2775

to friendly countries on their flight path or indeed the United States Air Force's own air defences. As a result U-2 and SR-71 flights often triggered early-warning systems in the UK and along the Soviet border in Germany. Some researchers believe a number of unexplained UFO reports, such as that from RAF West Freugh in 1957, where objects were plotted on radar at 70,000 ft, may have been triggered by secret U-2 missions (see p.53).

On the other side of the Iron Curtain the Soviet Union officially denounced UFOs via a 1961 article published in *Pravda* as 'fantastic fairy-tales' spread by the Americans. Here too, however, they occasionally provided a useful cover for military activities the Soviet military wished to conceal from the West. For example, in September 1977 residents of the city of Petrozavodsk were terrified by the appearance of a glowing object like a 'giant jellyfish' that lit up the skies as far west as Leningrad and Helsinki. This UFO was quickly identified by astronomers as the burning tail of a rocket used to launch a spy satellite into orbit from the space centre at Plesetsk. But the Soviet press continued to publish statements from official spokesmen who claimed the spectacular sighting remained unexplained.[11]

The Lakenheath–Bentwaters Incident

Although a number of Cold War UFO reports could be put down to spy planes, balloons and rocket tests, there were many others made by military pilots from both sides of the Iron Curtain that intelligence agencies have struggled to explain. One of the best known unexplained incidents occurred at the nuclear-armed United States Air Force airfield at RAF Lakenheath in Suffolk, where the U-2 had been based in April 1956 shortly before the Suez crisis.

On the evening of 13 August 1956 airfield radars at RAF Bentwaters in Suffolk detected a number of unexplained blips, including one travelling at hypersonic speed. Airmen on the ground, and travelling in a C-47 transport above the base, reported seeing bright lights, but aircraft sent to investigate could find nothing unusual. Later that night more UFOs were seen on radar by United States Air Force personnel at RAF Lakenheath, 40 miles (65 km) to the northeast; these moved erratically at speeds of between 400 and 600 mph. Lakenheath then alerted RAF Neatishead, a radar station on the Norfolk Broads that defended England's east coast.

The RAF chief controller at Neatishead, Flight Lieutenant Freddie Wimbledon, came forward in 1978 to describe publicly what happened next. He admitted to being initially sceptical, but on checking his radars he was amazed to see an unidentified target at a height of between 10,000 ft and 20,000 ft. The target moved at tremendous speeds and then stopped suddenly, behaviour that was totally unlike any aircraft he had seen on radar before.

Immediately he gave orders to scramble RAF Venom interceptors. When I spoke to him in 2001 he remembered what happened next:

'After being vectored onto the tail of the object by the interception controller the pilot called 'contact' then a short time later 'Judy' which meant the navigator had it fairly and squarely on his own radar screen and needed no further help from my controller. After a few seconds, in the space of one sweep of our screens, the object appeared behind our own fighter and our pilot called out: "Lost contact, more help." '12

The second aircraft sent to intercept this UFO appears to have been flown by Squadron Leader Tony Davis, a veteran of the Second World War, who was Commanding Officer of 23 Squadron in 1956. In a brief account of his experience written 20 years later, Davis says he was vectored by RAF ground control towards a suspected UFO, but his radar operator could not make contact with it and he found himself 'chasing a star'.

For his part, Wimbledon remembered the blip on his radar vanishing before the second aircraft approached, almost as if it had given up the chase.

I remember saying to the pilot:
  'CONTACT… there it is
out 45 starboard now at one mile
…and he kept saying to me:
'Where is it? Where is it?
  I can't see it!'
  as we rushed past.

He maintained the target was strong and clear, of similar size to a fighter aircraft, but capable of 'terrific acceleration' from a standing start.

More UFOs were spotted on Lakenheath radars in the early hours of 14 August, and again Venoms were scrambled to intercept them. The crews of two Venoms came forward with their accounts in 1995 for a BBC programme on Cold War UFOs. The radar operator on the first aircraft, Squadron Leader John Brady, kept a note in his flying logbook that shows his Venom was scrambled at 2.00 am to investigate something seen by United States Air Force radars at low altitude near RAF Lakenheath. He later recalled:

'The USAF were directing us towards this thing at around 7,000 feet. The first run we had at it I saw nothing. The next time we turned onto a reciprocal heading and I then obtained a contact which I held 10–15 degrees off dead ahead and noticed that it raced down the tube at high speed. We were flying at around 350–400 mph. I remember saying [to the pilot]: "CONTACT … there it's out 45 starboard now at one mile" … and he kept saying to me: "Where is it? Where is it? I can't see it!" as we rushed past. And it would go down the right hand side or the left hand side [of the Venom]. Two further runs were made with the same result and it was fairly obvious that whatever it was, it was stationary. [The pilot] looked out on each run but could see nothing. My radar contact was firm but messy, but there was something there!'13

A second Venom sent to assist had no more success and both aircraft returned to base, low on fuel, without identifying their target. Shortly afterwards the UFO disappeared from the United States Air Force's radar and did not return.

Ralph Noyes, who was working at the Air Ministry at the time, later recalled the panic this incident created. Interviewed in 1989 he said:

'Here we had a number of objects seen coming in across the North Sea on coastal radar. It looked like a Russian mistake. Jet aircraft were scrambled. The objects were travelling at quite impossible speeds and simply made rings round our fastest aircraft. Inevitably this led to the sort of inquiry that you would put in hand if you had any military responsibilities, but we did not particularly want to make public statements about that. Not for something that we had no explanation for.' [14]

FIG. 24 The Air Ministry report on UFOs, published as part of their 'Secret Intelligence Summary' in 1955, concluded that 90 per cent of sightings could be explained. AIR 40/2769

Although details of the Lakenheath incident were recorded by Project Blue Book, the file was kept secret until 1969 when scientists at the University of Colorado were allowed access to it. In 1956 Blue Book investigators had concluded the blips seen on radar were probably spurious echoes caused by 'unusual weather conditions' as the events happened on a humid August evening. When university staff reviewed the case their radar expert Gordon Thayer said the Lakenheath event was 'the most puzzling and unusual case in the radar-visual files', adding:

'The apparently rational, intelligent behaviour of the UFO suggests a mechanical device of unknown origin as the most likely explanation for this sighting.' [15]

Unfortunately, by that time the British Air Ministry had decided to destroy its own records of this remarkable incident. The single surviving reference to it occurs in an intelligence briefing to the Under Secretary of State for Air, George Ward MP, in May 1957. Under the category of 'unexplained radar incidents' the note plays down its significance, referring to:

'a report of an unusual object on Lakenheath Radar which at first moved at a speed of between two and four thousand knots [2300–4600 mph] and then remained stationary at a high altitude. No visual contact was made with this object by the Venom sent to intercept it and other radars failed to pick it up.' (AIR 20/9320)

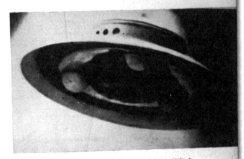

Flying Saucers

"An Object was reported ..."

The origin of the term " flying saucer," as applied to strange objects sighted in the sky, remains obscure, although authorship is claimed by a British journalist. According to him, whilst sitting in a Bronx café talking with three New York reporters, one of whom was doodling on a piece of paper, he observed that the drawing looked like a " flying saucer." One of the Americans decided that they " had something " there and, within the hour the term was in use. Within two, it is claimed that ninety people had reported having seen one.

(Restricted)

Man has always instinctively looked to the sky for signs and portents, nor has he, even to-day, quite lost his inclination to discern and report celestial manifestations. It is not the object of this article to decry or deprecate such reportings—as Shakespeare wrote " There are more things in heaven and earth Horatio, than are dreamt of in your philosophy "—but it is the intention to encourage a rational approach both to the objects themselves and to the method of their reporting.

Generally, reports are of commonplace objects which would normally pass unobserved but which attract attention in the light of more sensational stories, and lend support to them. Thus a meteor or a radio sonde balloon, or even a conventional aircraft, assumes in the perception of some observers speeds, shapes and movements which are entirely uncharacteristic. A well-known astronomer has declared that his experience of the reports of ordinary observers prompts him to reject 95 per cent of what they say, particularly when he knows that they have been startled by a sudden phenomenon which they could have

observed for no more than a few seconds. With such reports we are not seriously concerned. There are a number of other reports on flying saucers which are emphatic statements of visitations from neighbouring planets, and suchlike ; these derive both from the imaginings of zealots, admittedly quite serious and sincere in their beliefs, and from charlatans.

VISUAL SIGHTINGS

Reports of sightings themselves reveal certain stereotyped patterns. They usually describe objects as being projectile-shaped, round, oval, or ellipsoidal ; they are dazzling-bright, light, shiny, blue-green and generally speaking, iridescent. They move at fantastic speeds in lateral and longitudinal directions ; they also hover. Such are the basic lines of description, with inevitable variations.

Practically all of these objects can be roughly identified as follows :—

(a) conventional aircraft viewed by observers from unaccustomed angles

(b) present-day jet aircraft, flying at great speeds and great heights, mistaken by untrained and, on occasion, by experienced observers

(c) sunlight reflections from aircraft and balloons which themselves are too distant to be observed

(d) car headlights reflected on low cloud

(e) meteorological, radio sonde and cosmic research balloons of all types

(f) bright meteors and fireballs

(g) planets observed at certain times of the year

(h) birds

(j) cloud formations

(k) meteorological phenomena, such as mock moons and mock suns.

There are other reports of visual sightings which are admittedly very strange and difficult to classify. They tell of objects which appear to change shape quickly, which move erratically and at fantastic speeds across the sky. Under no consideration could these reports be classified in terms of the objects listed above. It is firmly believed that these reports are made in all sincerity and are in fact

Page 3

Intercept UFO!

Even the dramatic Lakenheath incident pales in significance compared to the story told by a retired United States Air Force pilot who claims he was ordered to shoot down a UFO over East Anglia. Lieutenant Milton Torres first spoke publicly about his experience at a squadron reunion in 1988 and a written account was sent to the Ministry of Defence shortly afterwards. When the file containing the letter was opened by the National Archives in 2008 it threw new light upon one of the many dramatic UFO incidents reported by front-line fighter pilots at the height of the Cold War. This story has been pieced together from a number of different sources, including my own correspondence with Milton Torres.

> Torres recalls being vectored to a point 32,000 feet over East Anglia…
>
> Ground control were tracking an unidentified target that had been… displaying 'very unusual flight patterns'

In 1956 Lieutenant Torres flew F-86D Sabre Dogs with the 406th Fighter Bomber Wing based at RAF Manston in Kent. It was from the runway at Manston that Torres, then a 25-year-old pilot, was scrambled near midnight one 'typical English night' late that year. Whereas other fighter aircraft of the period carried a pilot and navigator, with the F-86D the pilot had to both fly the aircraft and operate the airborne radar. This was used to 'lock onto' the target once it was within a range of 15 miles.

On this particular night Torres received his orders from a RAF controller who was tracking a UFO from an underground radar station at Kelvedon Hatch in Essex. Torres recalls being vectored to a point at 32,000 ft over East Anglia before the action began. Ground control briefed him that the RAF were tracking an unidentified target that had been orbiting the area for some time, displaying 'very unusual flight patterns', for example remaining motionless for long periods.

Then orders came to fire afterburners and Torres, with his wingman following slightly behind him and below, turned towards the target. Over the radio the controller asked both pilots to report any visual contact but they could not see anything. Torres then received a startling order to fire a full salvo of rockets at the UFO. The order was so unusual that it remains vivid in his memory today; so unusual that he stalled, demanding authentication before he opened fire. The F-86D had a formidable armoury of 24 unguided rockets—dubbed 'Mighty Mouse'—carried in a missile tray beneath the fuselage. Each weighed 18 lbs and had the explosive power of a 75-mm artillery shell.

As seconds passed authentication was confirmed and in the darkness of his cramped cockpit Torres struggled to select his weapons. His account sent to the MoD in 1988 says:

'I used my flashlight, still trying to fly and watch my radar…The final turn was given, and the instructions were given to look 30 degrees to port for my bogey … there it was exactly where I was told it would be … burning a hole in the radar with its incredible intensity.' (DEFE 24/1931/1)

In this account Torres describes the size of the blip visible on his radar scope as similar to that produced by a giant B-52 bomber. He remains convinced that it was the best target he could remember having locked onto during his entire flying career. Torres told me what happened next when I interviewed him in 2003: 'After we were on our final vector I called "Judy" at 15 miles…The F-86D was flat out and at about .92 Mach and we were closing very fast.'

In the files released during 2008 the MoD admit that all Air Ministry UFO records from this period have been destroyed and there is no mention of the incident in Project Blue Book

With just 10 seconds to go Torres saw the target begin to move away from him and was asked again if he could see anything. On his radar screen the blip had broken lock and was now leaving his 30-mile range. He reported the UFO had gone, only to be told the blip had also left the ground scope, in two sweeps of the radar, which he later realized indicated 'a speed in excess of 1,000 knots (more like double or triple Mach numbers)'.

With the UFO gone the two pilots returned to Manston with orders to contact the RAF by landline. They were told little other than the mission was considered classified, but the following day Torres was debriefed by a civilian who arrived from London. In his statement sent to the MoD and released by the National Archives in 2008 he wrote:

'The civilian looked like a well-dressed IBM salesman, with a dark blue trenchcoat ... he immediately jumped into asking questions about the previous day's mission. I got the impression that he operated out of the States, but I don't know for sure. After my debriefing of the events he advised me that this would be considered highly classified and that I should not discuss it with anybody, not even my commander. He threatened me with a national security breach if I breathed a word about it to anyone.' (DEFE 24/1931/1)

Some 30 years passed and it was only after retirement that Torres felt confident to talk publicly about his experience. Compounding the mystery is the almost complete lack of contemporary records relating to the incident. In the files released during 2008 the MoD admit that all Air Ministry UFO records from this period have been destroyed and there is no mention of the incident in Project Blue Book. Only intelligence briefings prepared by the Air Ministry for the Secretary of State George Ward in 1957 have survived at the National Archives. Ward was told there had been three 'unexplained radar incidents' during 1956, one of these being the report from

RAF Lakenheath. Another, which described an object seen on radar by a United States Air Force base in Essex, and 'momentary contact' by one of the two aircraft sent to intercept, certainly could tally with Torres' account.[16]

The documents briefly mention four other radar incidents from 1957 that remained 'unexplained' and are also possible candidates, including one when 'unusual responses which did not resemble aircraft' were detected by RAF radars on the east coast. Again, there is mention of a fighter aircraft being scrambled but on this occasion no contact was apparently made.

Others too have pursued missing records. Ralph Noyes said he was shown gun-camera film taken by RAF aircrew during this period at a secret briefing attended by MoD officials held at Whitehall in 1970. In 1989 he told me: 'I saw short clips showing fuzzy objects, self luminous, rather dark against a light sky. Never anything like a structured craft. Always globular, capable of moving very fast. Nothing more sensational than that, but puzzling nonetheless.' National Archives files reveal that following his retirement Noyes wrote to the MoD asking if these films had survived. He was told no trace of them could be found.

UFOs in the swinging sixties

As public fascination with UFOs increased during the late 1950s the Air Ministry decided to offload responsibility for dealing with the public and the press onto a more suitable department. This was S6 (Air), an Air Staff secretariat that routinely dealt with questions relating to RAF activities such as low flying complaints. Civil servants, rather than military officers, were seen as the best choice for those occasions when questions about UFOs required a careful response. A civil servant with S6, David West, set the tone for future UFO policy by noting in 1958 that when dealing with the public he would consult intelligence branches only when it was necessary, 'but for the most part we expect to be politely unhelpful.'[17]

From that point onwards, S6 and its successors became known publicly as 'the UFO desk', the central—and only officially acknowledged—focus for public correspondence on the subject. Although the name of the department dealing with UFOs changed periodically, from S6 to S4 in 1964 and then to DS8 and Sec(AS) during the 1980s, the civil servants responsible for answering letters and Parliamentary questions maintained, in public at least, the same level of official disinterest displayed by David West.

During the course of the next 50 years, even at the busiest times, responding to letters and UFO reports and drafting responses to MPs occupied only a tiny fraction of a desk officer's duties. As a small part of the department's wider responsibilities, UFOs were largely looked upon as at best an interesting distraction and at worst a nuisance. As David West explained in 2006:

'Our policy was largely reactive. When questions were asked by MPs or stories were published in the newspapers we responded. But we were not really focused on UFOs. At that time we were far more concerned with the Suez crisis.'[18]

Despite its nickname, it was never the responsibility of those who manned 'the UFO desk' to investigate those reports that could not be easily explained. Following the abolition of the Air Ministry and the creation of the unified Ministry of Defence in 1964, this duty was passed to branches of the Defence Intelligence Staff. Publicly, the MoD said their 'UFO desk' dealt with *all* UFO matters and staff only took advice from other branches when it was necessary. Files at the National Archives make it clear that in the few cases 'where no immediate satisfactory explanation can be determined—i.e. they are truly UFOs', these were passed to the Defence Intelligence Staff for further investigation.

The Men in Black

A number of Defence Intelligence Staff branches were secretly involved in UFO investigations, but from 1967 all unexplained incidents were reported to DI55. Their primary role was to collect intelligence on Soviet guided missiles and satellite launches that were occasionally reported as UFOs. Despite the risk involved in making inquiries into UFO sightings on occasions intelligence officers felt they had no option but to follow up incidents that received national publicity.

In 1962 the *News of the World* published a black and white photograph apparently showing a fleet of flying saucers over Sheffield, taken by a 14-year-old schoolboy, Alex Birch, with his Box Brownie camera. When Alex's father wrote to the Air Ministry offering the print for analysis officials were placed in a dilemma. If they were seen to reject his offer they could be accused of neglecting their defence responsibilities. Alternatively, if they displayed any interest at all this would be interpreted as evidence of 'secret Government investigations'. In the end, there was no other choice but to invite Alex and his father to visit the Air Ministry in London where officials examined the camera and photo. S6's explanation, in a letter sent to Mr Birch senior, was that the saucer-shaped objects on the photo were most likely produced by sunlight reflecting from 'ice crystals' in the smoky atmosphere. This kind of conclusion satisfied no one and as the United States Air Force had already discovered, simply encouraged members of the growing UFO movement to believe officials were involved in a cover-up.

When the Ministry received UFO reports from credible witnesses such as airline pilots and police officers it would sometimes, in exceptional circumstances, send intelligence officers to interview them. It is possible some of these visits were responsible for stories about the sinister 'Men In Black', that would be made famous by the movies staring Will Smith and Tommy

FIG.25 A black and white photograph showing a UFO fleet over Sheffield in 1962, taken by 14-year-old Alex Birch on his Box Brownie camera.

Lee Jones. The MIB are mysterious figures who, it has been claimed, pay visits to UFO witnesses to collect evidence and attempt to persuade them not to talk about their experiences. Their immaculate black suits and cars have led some UFOlogists to believe the MIB are employed by some secret government agency.

One example of such a visit followed a sighting in January 1966 made by a Cheshire police constable, Colin Perks. The constable, then 28, reported seeing a glowing green object hovering behind a row of houses in Wilmslow whilst on early morning patrol. A copy of his report was sent to the Ministry of Defence. In his police statement Perks reported how:

'about 4 a.m. on [7 January 1966] I was checking property at the rear of a large block of shops which are situated off the main A34 Road (Alderley Road) Wilmslow. At 4.10 am I was … facing the back of the shops when I heard a high-pitched whine … for a moment I couldn't place the noise as it was most unfamiliar to the normal surroundings. I turned around and saw a greenish/grey glow in the sky about 100 yards from me and about 35 feet up in the air … I stopped in my tracks and was unable to believe what I could see. However, I gathered myself together after a couple of seconds and made the following observations.

'The object was about the length of a bus (30 feet) and estimated at being 20 feet wide. It was [elliptical] in shape and emanated a green grey glow which I can only describe as an eerie greeny colour. It appeared to be motionless in itself, that is there is no impression of rotation. The object was about 15 feet in height [with] a flat bottom.

'At this time it was very bright and there was an east wind although it was cold there was no frost… The object remained stationary for about five seconds then without any change in the whine it started moving at a very fast rate in an East-South-East direction. It disappeared from view very quickly. When it started moving it did not appear to rotate but move off sideways with the 30 foot length to the front and rear.'

PC Perks ended his report:

'There is no doubt that the object I saw was of a sharp distinctive, definite shape and of a solid substance. However I did not notice any vents, port-holes or other place of access. The glow was coming from the exterior of the object and this was the only light which was visible. I checked with Jodrell Bank and Manchester airport control shortly after the incident but they could not help or in any way account for what I had seen.'
(AIR 2/17983)

Afterwards Perks drew a sketch that shows an elliptical object similar to an upturned jelly-mould. The police constable's account was deemed to be so reliable and detailed that the MoD sent a defence intelligence officer, Flight Lieutenant M.J.P. Mercer, to interview Perks. Details of this visit were kept secret until 1997 when the MoD file containing his report was opened at the National Archives. In Mercer's report to headquarters he said that PC Perks

'had not read any books on the subject [of UFOs] nor had he seen any-thing similar before. There is no reason to doubt the fact that this con-stable saw something completely foreign to his previous experience.'
(AIR 2/17983)

Mercer visited the scene of the encounter and checked radar records but found nothing unusual had been detected. He concluded his report with the following:

'On the evidence available … it is not possible to arrive at any concrete conclusion. This is always likely to be the case with such "one man" sightings… On the information available it would be unwise if [we]

FIG. 26 (BELOW) A map drawn by PC Perks showing the position of the UFO he encountered in January 1966 in a car park behind a row of shops in Wilmslow, Cheshire in 1966.
AIR 2/17983

FIG. 27 (BELOW RIGHT) A drawing of the same UFO. PC Perks esti-mated it to have been 30 ft in length.
AIR 2/17983

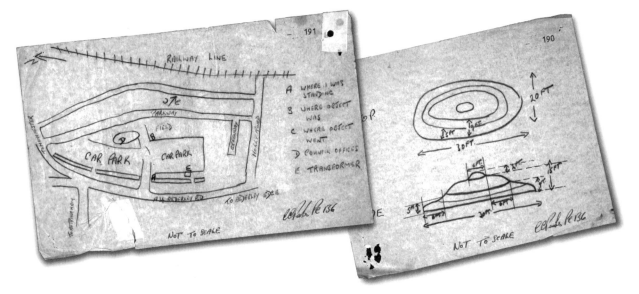

speculated on possible explanations … [but] it is perhaps pertinent to quote from an article by Dr Allen Hynek, an American astronomer who advises the USAF on the subject of UFOs: "…so far I have come across no convincing evidence that any of these mysterious objects come from outer space or from other worlds." We would agree with this conclusion.' (AIR 2/17983)

The flying cross

During the summer and autumn of 1967 Britain experienced one of its most intense UFO flaps, as such panics became known. The MoD received almost 400 sighting reports from a variety of sources including large numbers from police officers. The greatest number of sightings occurred during October 1967 when a spectacular report by police officers triggered off a surge of new sightings. In the early hours of 24 October PCs Roger Willey and Clifford Waycott were on patrol in their police car near Holsworthy in North Devon when they saw a strange light in the sky that appeared to be at treetop height. PC Willey described the UFO as 'a star-spangled cross radiating points of light from all angles.' The pair drove immediately towards the light, which appeared to move away from them. Giving chase, at one stage their patrol car reached speeds of up to 90 mph as it pursued the UFO along narrow and twisting country lanes on the edge of Dartmoor. PC Roger Willey, speaking at a televised news conference afterwards, said:

> 'At first it appeared to the left of us, then went in an arc, and dipped down and we thought it had landed. It seemed to be watching us and wouldn't let us catch up… It had terrific acceleration and seemed to know we were chasing it.' [19]

Eventually they gave up the chase and pulled up behind a parked Land Rover to wake the sleeping occupant, 29-year-old Richard Garner. He said one of the policeman pointed to the horizon, where a bright light was hovering in the sky. 'I thought I was having a nightmare when they woke me up… They said they wanted confirmation of what they had seen. I don't know what it was, but this object was much too bright for a star.' [20]

The policeman's story was featured on TV news and the press dubbed the UFO 'the flying cross'. For a full week UFOs dominated the headlines and dozens of new reports of the 'flying cross' were reported in the early hours across Hampshire, Sussex and Derbyshire. The MoD file on the events of 1967 at the National Archives contains 79 reports from the month of October alone. One came from retired RAF Wing Commander Eric Cox who spotted a UFO shortly after watching a television news report on the Devon police officer's experience. Cox was driving with his wife near Fordingbridge in the New Forest the following night when they saw 'seven lights in the sky at low altitude, very bright but not dazzling.' He said:

'They appeared to be in a "V" formation and stayed absolutely still for about three minutes after which time the three on the right-hand side appeared to recede or fade. The remaining four lights then formed into a perfect formation of a cross or plus sign. These remained for about three minutes when they too faded or receded rapidly.'

Cox ended his account:

'I do not believe in "little green men" nor in flying saucers but I am certain they cannot be dismissed as easily as authority would deem. I have never before seen anything like them and incidentally I am a tee-totaller.' (AIR 20/11889)

The UFO panic led to a series of questions in Parliament and demands for an official study similar to that underway in America, where the University of Colorado had received its contract to produce a scientific report based upon the sightings recorded in Project Blue Book's files. The MoD resisted pressure for a similar inquiry in Britain but considered calling upon Professor R.V. Jones, now in retirement, to act as a consultant if the sightings continued. Towards the end of the year, a briefing prepared for the Labour Secretary of State for the RAF, Merlyn Rees MP, revealed the vast majority of sightings (150) had been identified as aircraft. Satellites and space debris accounted for 57 reports, balloons 42 and bright stars and planets a further 26.

The UFO panic led to a series of questions in Parliament and demands for an official study similar to that underway in America…

A residue of 46 reports remained 'unexplained' but as UFO desk head Jim Carruthers told Mr Rees, these simply lacked 'information vital to their explanation'. He said there was 'nothing in any of them to suggest that the incidents to which they relate are any different in nature to those mentioned in the reports that have been explained.' Most were generated not by an increase in UFO activity, he continued, but as a result of an increase in public awareness of the subject. People were looking at the sky,

'impelled either by the good weather or by Press-aroused curiosity … [and] the increased number of reports show that it is becoming fashionable to see UFOs.' (DEFE 31/119)

Meanwhile DI55 sent a scientific officer, Dr John Dickison, to interview the two Devon police constables. His brief report concluded the most likely explanation was they had seen and pursued a bright star or planet, possibly Venus:

'when questioned … one of the police constables indicated that … he had decided that the light [they saw] came from a spaceship. They did not see a spaceship but only a light and his conclusion appears to have no factual basis.' (DEFE 31/119)

Many of the 'flying cross' incidents reported during October 1967 described bright lights seen in the early hours on the eastern horizon, where Venus remained a bright, conspicuous celestial object. In fact, Venus is so often mistaken for a UFO that she has been called 'the Queen of UFOs'. It's a mistake even future presidents of the United States have made. Two years later Jimmy Carter was with a group of 10 people who watched a brilliant light low on the horizon that appeared to move towards them and then away whilst changing in brightness, size and colour. They estimated the distance as between 300 ft and 100 ft and said the UFO was at times as big and bright as a full moon. Carter reported the sighting to Project Blue Book in 1973 and when details were checked by an astronomer it was found he was looking directly at the brilliant planet Venus.

Daydream or reality?

The 1967 UFO flap made the MoD look again at how they dealt with UFOs. Forced into action by pressure from MPs and the media, they assembled a small team of experts drawn from the RAF and the Defence Intelligence Staff, who were placed on stand-by to make field investigations of credible reports. The team included Dr Dickison, Leslie Ackhurst from the 'UFO desk' and a RAF psychologist, Alex Cassie. One report scrutinized by this three-man team is among the strangest ever to reach the MoD.

A file at the National Archives contains details of the sighting by Angus Brooks, a retired BOAC Comet Flight administration officer. Brooks claimed he had a 'close encounter' on the Dorset coast in daylight on 26 October 1967, at the height of the 'flying cross' flap. Brooks said he had taken his two dogs for a walk on the Moigne Downs during a fierce gale and found shelter by lying flat on his back in a hollow. In his report to the MoD he said the UFO suddenly appeared 'descending at lightning speed' towards him. It then 'decelerated with what appeared to be immensely powerful reverse thrust to level out at approximately a quarter of a mile to the south of my position at 2–300 foot height.'

Brooks described this object as 150 ft long with a central circular chamber from the front of which extended a long 'fuselage'. Three more long fuselages extended from the rear and these moved to positions equidistant around the centre of the craft, so that it took the shape of a giant cross. Brooks said he remained frozen to the spot for the 20 minutes the UFO remained visible fearing that he might be 'captured' if he moved. He noticed that the silent object was constructed from some translucent material as '[it] took on the colour of the sky above it and changed with clouds passing over it.' Then the two central fuselages folded back to their original position and the UFO disappeared in the direction of the Winfrith Atomic Research Station. Brooks' pet Alsatian returned to his side at this point and appeared distraught. He believed that she might have been distressed by a VHF sound emitted by the UFO although he heard nothing during the experience.

Suspecting the object may have been interested in the power station or a nearby US naval base, Brooks reported his sighting to the police and MoD. When the MoD team, whom Brooks referred to as 'the James Bond department', arrived at his home they were taken to the spot where the UFO hovered and Brooks relived his experience in detail. In a letter Brooks wrote to the MoD he said:

> 'we had a long chat, first at home and then I "rusticated" them to the location … they all seemed rather surprised that such lonely country existed in the south of England. I do hope the fresh air and violent exercise did them no real harm. Actually I think they rather enjoyed it all. They certainly asked some very interesting questions and made the whole thing seem to me to be a very matter-of-fact happening, which is really just what it was.' (AIR 20/11890)

In their own report 'the James Bond department' described how they were immediately suspicious that such a large object could have hovered for the length of time claimed without anyone else having spotted it. They decided it was more likely Brooks had seen something ordinary, such as a kite or a hawk, and this had become transformed into a UFO 'whilst he was in a dream or a near sleep state'. The psychologist member of the MoD team, Alex Cassie, believed that Brooks may have experienced 'a vivid daydream' when he lay down to shelter from the wind. He suggested the dream could have been influenced by the news reports of the 'flying cross' or triggered off by a piece of dead skin, moving in the fluid of his eyeball.

Cassie discovered that Brooks had lost the sight in his right eye in an accident, but this had been restored by a corneal graft. He speculated this operation might have made Brooks more prone to seeing elaborate 'floaters'. But he admitted these would not have remained visible for 20 minutes and he could only account for the whole experience by turning to the 'day dream' theory. In his opinion:

FIG. 28 A report and drawing by Angus Brooks describing the transparent 'flying cross' he saw hovering above the Moigne Downs, Dorset, on 26 October 1967. AIR 20/11890

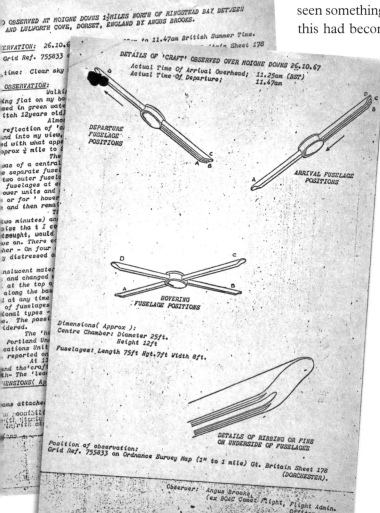

'[Brooks'] instant knowledge and certainty of the size and distance of the UFO and its intent, are all suggestive of the immediate and inexplicable awareness which are characteristic of many dreams.' (AIR 20/11890) Although he could not prove his theory was correct Cassie concluded 'it just seems possible, even likely.' But he could not resist adding a caveat, albeit tongue-in-cheek, to his report: 'if his experience can't be explained in some such way, then maybe he saw an Extra Terrestrial Object!' DI55 agreed, but added that '[we] think that the probability of there being an E.T.O. is of a very low order.'

Brooks circulated his report to UFO magazines and newspapers before the MoD team produced their conclusion. The Ministry were acutely aware from past experience that any statements they made in writing would receive maximum publicity. In the letter sent to Brooks, Ackhurst carefully explained their theory and said the team did not doubt that he had an experience 'for which no proven explanation can be given' but added: 'we have concluded that you did not see a 'craft' either man-made or from outer space.'[21]

As *Daily Express* science writer Robert Chapman noted at the time, the MoD's attempts to explain away Angus Brook's experience were doomed to failure because 'the explanations themselves are as far-fetched as, if not more so than, the actual sightings.' Privately MoD officials felt that all rational explanations should be explored first before turning to fantastic explanations such as extraterrestrial visitors. As Flight Lieutenant Mercer had noted in his report on the Cheshire police officer's sighting, 'if it were possible for a scientific investigation team to be present at the instant of [a] sighting these "unknown" phenomena would probably be quite easily explained.'[22]

'Amazing pictures of a flying saucer'

For these reasons doubt would always continue to surround those UFO experiences where the only evidence was the testimony of a single witness. In a few rare cases, however, an explanation came to light that left no shadow of doubt. One of these happened in March 1966 when Joan Oldfield and her husband Tom, from Helmshore, Lancashire, were passengers on an airliner flying from Manchester to London. The couple were on their way to say goodbye to relatives who were emigrating to Australia and carried a cine camera with them.

As the aircraft cruised at 9,000 ft over Staffordshire at 8.00 am on a bright sunny morning Mrs Oldfield, glancing out of a window, spotted what she first thought was a small plane tracking them. She immediately picked up her cine camera and filmed the object, which was totally unlike any other aircraft she had ever seen. As the film rolled the flat cigar-shaped

UFO appeared to pull away and retract four fin-like objects into its body before disappearing. When the couple replayed their cine film they discovered they had captured 160 colour frames featuring the UFO, running to seven seconds of viewing time.

The story was flashed around the world and stills from the film were proclaimed by the *News of the World* as proof that 'craft from outer space' had visited Britain. The film was sent to the MoD for study, but it was the BBC who solved the mystery. On 21 April the popular BBC1 evening science programme *Tomorrow's World* sent a reporter, Francis Greene, to reconstruct the Oldfield's exact flight, using the same plane and taking pictures from the same seat the couple used. His film conclusively proved the 'craft from outer space' was actually a distorted reflection of the airliner's tailplane, visible only from one specific spot inside the cabin. As a MoD official noted, the tailplane had been 'distorted by the optical effects of the curvature of the "porthole glass" [and] the images all appear towards the rear of the porthole, where the glass is curved in towards its mounting.'[23]

FIG. 29 The UFO that wasn't. An optical illusion produced by the curvature of the glass in an aeroplane's window seemed to show a shape-changing UFO over Staffordshire.
AIR 2/17983

This example illustrates the difficulties faced by official investigations of UFOs where time and resources are always in short supply. The author of the Air Ministry's Secret Intelligence Summary appreciated this problem when he wrote:

'the investigation of [UFOs] presents very apparent difficulties, the major one of which is that, ninety-nine times out of a hundred, the scent is completely cold. It is only fair to point out that in every other case, i.e. when reports are telephoned and promptly checked on the spot, the sighted object has been identified as a balloon or a conventional aircraft.' (AIR 40/2769)

CLOSE ENCOUNTERS

N JUNE 1969 Norfolk police sent the Ministry of Defence details of two strange experiences that had occurred within 24 hours of each other. The first of these came from an electrical engineer, Robin Peck, who they described as 'a very level headed person who has been genuinely frightened by [his] experience.' Peck made this statement concerning his sighting at 12.25 am on 19 June 1969:

> 'I was passing through Bircham when the lights on my vehicle started to dim. Within a few moments they had dimmed to such an extent that I was unable to see, and pulled up on my nearside. As I did this the engine also cut out and I could get no ignition light. Suspecting a fault with the battery, I got out and went to the bonnet. It was then that I experienced a feeling that the air was full of static, and my hair felt to be standing on end. I then saw an object in the sky about 100 feet from the ground. This object appeared to be like an inverted mushroom, approximately the size of a row of several cottages. It was of a very pale blue colour surrounded by a golden glow. The object emitted no sound whatsoever and remained in this position for at least a minute. It then moved off towards King's Lynn, still without a sound. When it moved off the blue colour appeared to leave a haze trail following the object. I went back and sat in my vehicle for some minutes rather shaken, then by reflex rather than anything else I tried to start the engine and found that everything worked perfectly again.' (AIR 20/12061)

Police linked Peck's experience with a report from 17-year-old Arthur Hendry, a trainee carpenter, who lived nearby. Before midnight on the next day, 20 June, he was getting ready to cycle home when he heard a strange whistling noise above him, but could see nothing. In a statement to police

he said the noise then became louder and intensified to a powerful throb-
bing. 'I suddenly felt as if every muscle in my body locked, and I was unable
to release my grip on my cycle,' he said in a police statement. 'After a few
seconds the noise disappeared and I felt almost normal again ... it had felt
as if I was receiving a severe electric shock and electricity was passing
through my body from my head to my feet.' (AIR 20/12061)

MoD scientists suspected the two men may have experienced a type of
rare atmospheric phenomena similar to ball lightning (see p.19). Checks
by the Meteorological Office, however, found the skies over East Anglia
were clear with no thunderstorms at the relevant time. Unable to explain
the strange electromagnetic effects reported, a desk officer concluded
'[this] sounds like a genuine UFO' and closed the file.

The Condon report

The last three years of the 1960s were a remarkable time for UFOlogists, as
those who studied UFOs had become known. Hardly a day seemed to pass
without a newspaper story about a new sighting somewhere in the country.
Even that bastion of Britishness, the BBC, got in on the act with the documentary *Flying Saucers and the People Who See Them*, which was inspired by
the 1967 UFO 'flap'. Then in 1969, with UFOs already firmly embedded in
popular culture, NASA's Apollo programme reached its apogee with the
moon landings. Many people who had previously scoffed at the idea of visitors from space began to reconsider. If we could visit the moon and possibly other planets why couldn't intelligent extraterrestrials, if they existed,
visit us?

Heightened public awareness of UFOs was continuing to pose a problem for the MoD, who were still struggling to talk down calls for a govern-
ment-sponsored scientific study. In November 1967 UFO desk head, James
Carruthers, summarized their policy in a briefing for ministers. He said the
MoD had kept a statistical analysis of reports received since 1959 but 'has
found no evidence to suggest [UFOs] have other than mundane explanations.' He added that the MoD 'does not consider that a separate study
by [UK] Government departments or by a university or other independent
organisation would produce results to justify the expenditure, time and
money involved.'[1]

Meanwhile in America the study conducted by scientists at the University of Colorado, led by the physisist Dr Edward Condon, had reached a
series of conclusions and recommendations. In summary these stated that:

About 90 per cent of all UFO reports prove to be plausibly related to
ordinary phenomena, both natural and man-made.

No UFO report had ever given any indication of a threat to national
security.

There was no evidence that sightings categorized as 'unexplained' were extraterrestrial spaceships.

Little, if anything, had come from the study of UFOs in the past 21 years that had added to scientific knowledge and further extensive study of UFO sightings was not justified.

These findings were later endorsed by a panel of the American National Academy of Sciences and following publication of the university's final report, *The Scientific Study of Unidentified Flying Objects*, in 1969, the United States Air Force took the opportunity to close Project Blue Book and draw a line under their official interest in UFOs.

Britain followed the USA's lead and few further reports, apart from those from members of the armed forces, were subject to the type of detailed field investigations undertaken by the MoD in 1967–8. However, the UFO desk did continue to copy all the reports it received to the Defence Intelligence Staff and the RAF—'just in case'.

By early 1974 cuts in defence expenditure led the MoD to discontinue annual statistical analysis of UFO reports. Since the 1950s they had been allocating sightings, often in a haphazard fashion, to various explained categories, providing those who had contacted them with a brief summary of the MoD's assessment. With the subject now a low priority, members of

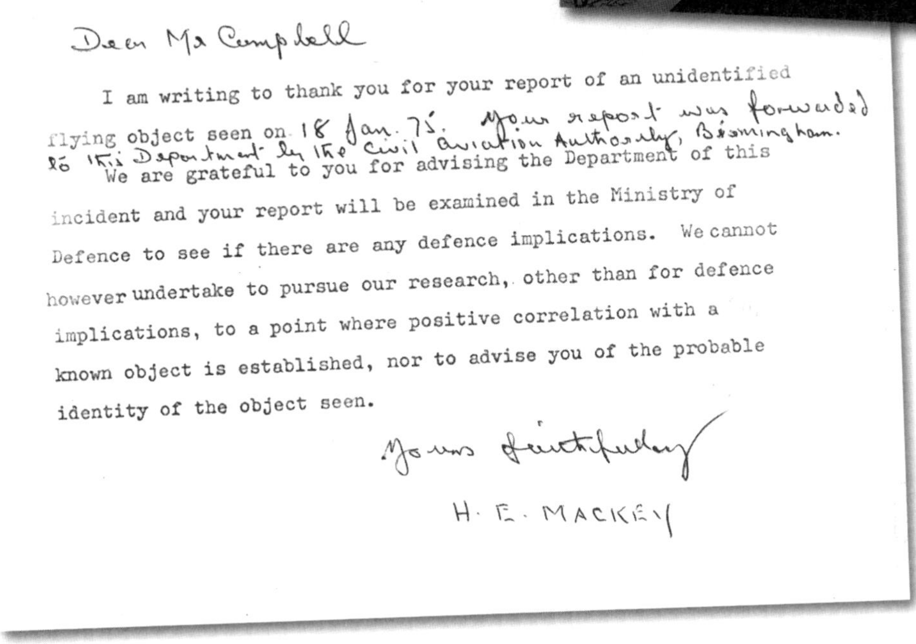

FIG. 30 (ABOVE) 'A delightful hand-coloured painting' of a UFO sighted over Harborne, Birmingham, in January 1975, which prompted an exchange of letters with UFO desk personnel. AIR 2/18961

FIG. 31 (LEFT) By the mid 1970s most reports sent to the MoD received a standard letter in reply. AIR 2/18961

Dear Mr Campbell

I am writing to thank you for your report of an unidentified flying object seen on 18 Jan. 75. *Your report was forwarded to this Department by the Civil Aviation Authority, Birmingham.* We are grateful to you for advising the Department of this incident and your report will be examined in the Ministry of Defence to see if there are any defence implications. We cannot however undertake to pursue our research, other than for defence implications, to a point where positive correlation with a known object is established, nor to advise you of the probable identity of the object seen.

Yours faithfully,

H. E. MACKEY

the public who reported sightings to the MoD would from now on receive a polite acknowledgement in the form of a standard letter outlining probable causes. These included aircraft, satellites and meteors, balloons, bright stars and planets, aside from the 10 per cent that would continue to be listed as 'unexplained' in the official files.

'Like a flattened avocado pear'

Despite the reduction in official interest, ordinary members of the public continued to report puzzling and sometimes frightening close encounters with UFOs to the authorities. In a letter sent to the MoD, Mrs Anne Taylor from Romford, Essex, described a strange experience that happened around 9.00 pm on 17 September 1973. She was returning to her farm after walk-ing her three dogs when:

> 'I noticed a green light very near the cowshed. My first reaction was that this was one of the many light aircraft from nearby Stapleford Aero-drome, and that he was a bit low. I continued walking and watching this light, which started to move very slowly towards me. I then thought it was possibly a helicopter but suddenly realised there was no noise. By this time I had reached a line of trees with a thin wire fence dividing one field from another. The two terriers, who don't normally wander very far, were against my legs, whining and cringing.'

Mrs Taylor stopped, standing by one of the trees, and watched as the light kept coming slowly towards her until it was only a few feet from her, sus-pended some 12 ft from the ground. At this point

> 'I could then make out a ball-shaped outline, but no noise whatsoever. I whistled [for the Doberman] who came up to me, looked at the green light and started to howl. I looked at my watch and found it had stopped. Suddenly my spine started to tingle. I can't say that I was terrified; I think it was slight apprehension and certainly a great deal of curiosity. Next there was the sound of a jet plane in the distance; the green light went out and there was a sound which I can only describe as an electric whirring, and the ball went straight up until I could see it no more. As soon as the light went out, the dogs returned to normal. I walked home, looked at my watch and it was going again.' (AIR 20/12552)

Mrs Taylor guessed her sighting had taken place in the space of three min-utes, adding: 'Let me assure you that I had not been drinking anything stronger than coffee and that I am not a reader of science fiction which this sounds rather like!' On receiving her letter, a scientist at the Meteorological Office reached the same conclusions as one of his colleagues had in the cases of Peck and Hendry four years earlier; a belt of heavy thundery rain had passed over eastern England shortly before the sighting and there was, he believed, 'a possibility that Mrs Taylor witnessed an example of ball lightning ... a rare and transient phenomenon which is not properly under-stood'. Several features of the experience were not, however, consistent with the theory: 'For example, ball lightning is usually described as white, red, yellow and uncommonly blue. Green has seldom been noted and the dur-ation of the phenomenon is usually a matter of seconds rather than minutes.'

In other cases MoD scientists could be more confident about expla-nations for UFO reports sent in by members of the public. One example was reported to RAF St Mawgan by Mrs Good who saw three mysterious objects in the sky over Porthcothan Bay, Cornwall on the evening of 7 July 1973. She was closing the curtains of her house at 10.00 pm. It was still light outside and she was amazed to see two dark semi-cigar shaped objects hov-ering in the sky over the bay. These were positioned on either side of a glow-ing, symmetrical ring. After a few seconds the ring appeared to enter the left object and the two 'shot off at terrific speed' upward and into the dis-tance. Shortly afterwards the remaining object also disappeared, following the same path.

On checking date and time, RAF St Mawgan found their duty meteoro-logical officer had seen a rare meteorological phenomenon known as 'sun dogs' or parhelia shortly before the sighting. The base commander con-cluded this offered 'a very credible explanation to the [UFO] sighting, although [it] was made one to two hours later than that of the Met Officer.' Mrs Good was far from convinced by this and remained sure of what she had seen. She wrote back, finishing her reply by saying 'I do realise it is one thing to be told of such things and another to see for yourself. I wonder if you were to see for yourself would anyone believe you?'[2]

As this was a detailed report from a distinguished diplomat, the MoD had no option but to investigate further...

In 1977 the British Ambassador to Switzerland, A.K. Rothnie, sent a detailed account of his UFO experience near Rolvenden in Kent on 15 October. He was driving at 6.45 pm when

'through my car windscreen I sighted to the north of me, somewhere near the spire of the church, an object in the sky at an inclination of some 18 or 20 percent above the horizon, travelling fast from south to north and shaped somewhat like a flattened avocado pear. The blunt and lead-ing end seemed to be rimmed horizontally by some sort of phosphor or bronze metal which shone quite distinctly. The general body of the object was emitting a pronounced bluish light and from the tapering or trailing end there was a stream of golden sparks. The whole sighting took only a matter of one or one and a half seconds but my impression of what I had seen was so vivid that when a few minutes later I entered the "Ewe and Lamb" public house for a well-deserved pint of bitter (after a hard day's work in the garden) I immediately announced to the landlord that I had just seen my first UFO.' (DEFE 24/1205)

Mr Rothnie decided to report his sighting to the MoD after his local newspaper carried a story describing how groups of other people had seen 'a glowing mango-shaped UFO' at the same time. As this was a detailed report from a distinguished diplomat, the MoD had no option but to investigate further and DI55 scientists used a computer to check a range of possible explanations. In a letter Rothnie was told the MoD did not usually advise observers of the possible identity of the UFOs, but 'the incident at Rolvenden has been examined rather more fully than usual and it has been established that debris from a Soviet space satellite entered the earth's atmosphere on 15th October. We cannot say definitely, but this is possibly the explanation.' (DEFE 24/1205)

Dancing lights and an aerial circus

By the late 1970s it was unusual for UFO witnesses to receive such a detailed response from the MoD. The majority of those who wrote in and whose letters can today be perused in the National Archives reading rooms would only have received a standard letter. Their reports, however sincere, were rarely investigated further. One example was a report submitted by civil servant Alan Lott, who worked at the Atomic Weapons Research Establishment at Aldermaston. In his account he describes how he felt compelled to make an official report of 'an extraordinary sighting' made by himself and his wife, Clarice, on the night of 31 January 1975. Mr Lott had left his home in Caversham, near Reading, to walk their dog just before 10.30 pm when he spied a group of bright lights in the sky to the east over a neighbour's bungalow. He immediately called his wife and they both examined the lights through a pair of binoculars. Mr Lott's account continued:

'I discovered that they were moving slowly in a straight line almost exactly east to west and were now directly above my house. It was clear to the naked eye that there were three extremely bright lights of an orange/yellow colour arranged as a large equilateral triangle. There were two other very small lights, one red and one white ... all steady with no flashing [and] there were no beams of light as with searchlights, just the steady brilliant glare.' (AIR 2/18961)

The couple were puzzled at the lack of sound and could see no evidence of any outline of a fuselage that would be expected if the object was a low-flying aircraft. 'The separation of the light suggested a very large body flying very low but the UFO was travelling so slowly that it could not have been any conventional aircraft,' Mr Lott added. The formation of lights disappeared after five minutes, vanishing silently behind houses and trees further down the road. He ended his account by saying:

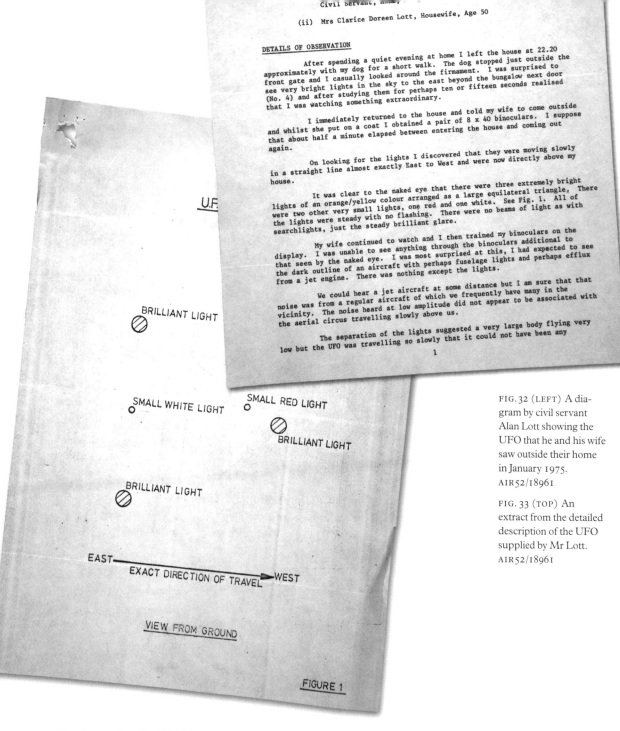

Civil servant, ...,

(ii) Mrs Clarice Doreen Lott, Housewife, Age 50

DETAILS OF OBSERVATION

After spending a quiet evening at home I left the house at 22.20 approximately with my dog for a short walk. The dog stopped just outside the front gate and I casually looked around the firmament. I was surprised to see very bright lights in the sky to the east beyond the bungalow next door (No. 4) and after studying them for perhaps ten or fifteen seconds realised that I was watching something extraordinary.

I immediately returned to the house and told my wife to come outside and whilst she put on a coat I obtained a pair of 8 x 40 binoculars. I suppose that about half a minute elapsed between entering the house and coming out again.

On looking for the lights I discovered that they were moving slowly in a straight line almost exactly East to West and were now directly above my house.

It was clear to the naked eye that there were three extremely bright lights of an orange/yellow colour arranged as a large equilateral triangle. There were two other very small lights, one red and one white. See Fig. 1. All of the lights were steady with no flashing. There were no beams of light as with searchlights, just the steady brilliant glare.

My wife continued to watch and I then trained my binoculars on the display. I was unable to see anything through the binoculars additional to that seen by the naked eye. I was most surprised at this, I had expected to see the dark outline of an aircraft with perhaps fuselage lights and perhaps efflux from a jet engine. There was nothing except the lights.

We could hear a jet aircraft at some distance but I am sure that that noise was from a regular aircraft of which we frequently have many in the vicinity. The noise heard at low amplitude did not appear to be associated with the aerial circus travelling slowly above us.

The separation of the lights suggested a very large body flying very low but the UFO was travelling so slowly that it could not have been any

1

U.F.

BRILLIANT LIGHT

SMALL WHITE LIGHT   SMALL RED LIGHT

BRILLIANT LIGHT

BRILLIANT LIGHT

EAST
EXACT DIRECTION OF TRAVEL ➤ WEST

VIEW FROM GROUND

FIGURE 1

FIG. 32 (LEFT) A diagram by civil servant Alan Lott showing the UFO that he and his wife saw outside their home in January 1975.
AIR52/18961

FIG. 33 (TOP) An extract from the detailed description of the UFO supplied by Mr Lott.
AIR52/18961

'In observing the UFO(s) one's first subjective impression was of an immense delta aircraft of the size of say a 747 flying at about 1,000 ft altitude and a speed of, say, 50 knots. However the three brilliant lights and the two small lights are not compatible with any type of aircraft known to me … I am quite unable to account in any way for this "aerial circus". It was quite unlike anything I have seen.' (AIR 2/18961)

Possibly the most bizarre story among the MoD's UFO files for the 1970s came from a young couple. They decided at the last moment to remove their names from the letter they sent to the MoD because they did not wish to be identified. The man described how he and his partially-sighted fiancée were returning home from a holiday in Cornwall late on 25 June 1977 to avoid holiday traffic. As they were driving along the deserted A303, near Warminster in Wiltshire, they noticed a triangle of three white lights ahead of them. 'My first conclusion was that they probably marked an obscured railway crossing or perhaps a low bridge,' he wrote.

'As they drew nearer it became apparent that there was something singularly unusual in the glow that emitted from whatever object it was that I was gazing upon. I muttered to my fiancé, "look at these", and immediately became aware that she had seen the mysterious objects, which by this time were almost upon us. At this juncture, to my amazement the three objects broke away from their self-disciplined triangle and became three independent bodies. One then drifted away to the side of the road, to finally disappear into the bushes. The remaining two then ranged themselves alongside the car, very much to my fiancé's disquiet and consternation. Then the most amazing thing of all occurred. The objects, which danced with elf-like impishness alongside us, gently and with a "bubble-blowing-like action" changed both their colour and shape. From the centre of the white light an orange/golden-like globe emerged ... these two globes ... dwelt for a short space of time alongside the car and then moved to the rear, where I picked them up in my rear-view mirror as they continued to dance along behind us, before they soon disappeared.' (DEFE 24/1207)

The letter-writer added:

'My reactions were only of surprise—certainly not fear—[and] at no stage was there an atmosphere of anything in the least bit unwelcome or sinister—so that I was able to view that which took place with a large degree of detachment and with considerable fascination.' (DEFE 24/ 1207).

The Welsh Roswell

One of the best-known UFO mysteries of the 1970s has become known as 'the Berwyn Mountains incident'. On the evening of 23 January 1974 many people across Britain and Wales sighted brilliant coloured lights streaking across the sky. Astronomers at Leicester University recorded up to four separate sightings of fireball meteors between 7.00 pm and 10.00 pm. Fireballs are bright meteors that fly close to the earth's atmosphere, forming vivid bursts of colour as they burn up in the atmosphere, leaving a trail of sparks in their wake.

One of these fireballs was seen over North Wales just minutes before a huge explosion shook villages at the foot of Cader Bronwen mountain near Bala. For many who saw lights in the sky and experienced the earth tremor, not knowing their source, it *appeared* that something, perhaps a plane, had crashed. Police switchboards were jammed with calls and, as the Berwyns had been the scene of several earlier military jet crashes, police and a mountain rescue team were sent out in case a real disaster had taken place. The team, from RAF Valley, was sent to Llandrillo at the foot of the range and joined local police to search the mountains the following day. They found no trace of a crash and the operation was called off when they learned the British Geological Survey had identified the source of the 'explosion' as an earthquake, measured at between 4 and 5 on the Richter scale, with its epicentre in the Bala area.[3]

> For many who saw lights in the sky and experienced the earth tremor…
>
> it appeared that something, perhaps a plane, had crashed

The Berwyn event received a great deal of media coverage but was not directly linked with UFOs at the time. When it became clear the meteor shower and the earth tremor were unrelated, other than by coincidence, the story was quickly forgotten. However, by the 1990s the popularity of the Roswell incident in books and TV documentaries led some UFO enthusiasts to resurrect the Berwyn event as a possible example of a UFO crash covered up by the authorities—a 'Welsh Roswell'. In common with the original Roswell (see p.36), in these later accounts witnesses, often anonymous, were quoted decades after the actual events. Some claimed roads leading to the Welsh hillsides had been closed off by the army whilst teams searched for the crash site, while others alleged that alien bodies had been retrieved and taken for examination at the secret Porton Down biological weapons plant in Wiltshire.

Despite numerous claims and counter-claims there is no evidence of any official involvement in the Berwyn incident apart from the initial search by the RAF mountain rescue team. No other military personnel visited the scene and stories of officials interviewing residents have been traced back to a subsequent field survey by scientists from the British Geological Survey. The MoD's records contain accounts of seven UFOs sighted on the evening of 23 January 1974, but none of these were reported from Wales. The sightings were made in the Home Counties, Lincolnshire and Sussex. Most described a bright greenish light high in the northwest that appeared to fall towards the horizon. One observer in Lincoln said the object appeared to break up, followed by a brilliant flash of green light. According to the files, observers recorded the time as just before 10.00 pm, which coincides with the last and most dramatic of the fireballs recorded by astronomers.[4]

In May 1974 Welsh MP Dafyd Ellis Thomas asked Defence Minister

Brynmoor John if any official investigation was made into the Berywn inci-
dent. Files released at the National Archives in 2005 show the MoD con-
sulted the Meteorological Office and DI55 who said the meteor display was
the most likely explanation for what had been seen in North Wales. The MP
was told that 'no official enquiry' was made by the MoD other than the initial search by the RAF Valley Mountain Rescue team, which found nothing.[5]

UFOs over the North Sea

Of all UFO sightings, those reported by police officers or military witnesses
and corroborated by radar contacts tend to provide the most impressive
evidence for the existence of UFOs. One of the most puzzling reports in the
MoD files for this period was made by personnel at RAF Boulmer, which is
an important air defence radar station on the northeast coast near Alnwick,
Northumberland. In the early hours of 30 July 1977 airmen on the night
shift were alerted by a call from a civilian who could see two bright objects
hovering over the North Sea. When the duty controller Flight Lieutenant
A.M. Wood and a group of airmen emerged from the control room they
realized that they too could see the mysterious objects. In a signal sent to
the MoD, Wood described them as being close to the shore and hovering at
a height estimated at 4,000–5,000 ft. They appeared to slowly move apart
and then back together as they climbed into the clear sky. His report said:
'No imagination was required to distinguish the shape ... westerly object
[was] conical with apex at top ... [it] seemed to rotate and change shape to
become arrowhead in shape. The easterly object was indistinct.' Wood said
the UFO closest to the base was 'round, luminous, [and] 4 to 5 times larger
than a Whirlwind helicopter.'[6]

Flight Lieutenant Wood's story was supported by two airmen on duty at
a picket post on the base perimeter, who were described as 'reliable and
sober'. Incredibly, they said the westerly UFO moved 'and changed shape
to become body-shaped with projections like arms and legs.' In his report
Wood says that shortly after they disappeared from sight, two unidentified
targets were detected on RAF Boulmer's radars at a range of between 20
and 30 miles out to sea. These slowly moved northeast as they climbed, 'then
parted, one climbing to 9,000 feet [estimated] and moving east, the other
holding 5–6,000 ft.' Wood contacted the controller at RAF Patrington, a
second radar station some miles to the south near Flamborough in Yorkshire.
Personnel there said they could also see two targets on the radar screens.

A senior intelligence officer commented on this incident when I interviewed him in 2005. He said he was left 'infuriated' at the lack of an immediate response to Boulmer's report by the RAF despite the wealth of
evidence. The UFOs were visible for 1 hour 40 minutes and this fact led
him to suspect the UFOs might have been drifting balloons or even bright

stars, but he felt an opportunity had been missed to resolve the mystery. He added: 'I sent a rocket to the [Commanding Officer] demanding to know why they hadn't scrambled an aircraft to see what it was.'

Vulcan crew encounter UFO

The RAF Boulmer incident was one of the more intriguing sightings in the 1970s by military personnel to be revealed when the MoD released its files to the National Archives. Perhaps the most amazing of all, however, is that made by the entire crew of a Vulcan bomber based at RAF Waddington in Lincolnshire. According to a restricted signal dated 26 May 1977, the captain and his four crewmen were on a training flight 43,000 ft over the North Atlantic when they saw a strange lighted object some 40 nautical miles distant. The UFO appeared to track them for around 15 minutes whilst turning onto the same course slightly above them. At first the UFO resembled an aircraft's landing lights, 'with a long pencil beam of light ahead', but as it turned towards them the lights appeared to go out leaving a diffuse orange glow with a bright fluorescent green spot in the bottom right-hand corner. Then suddenly, both the captain and co-pilot saw an object 'leaving from the middle of the glow on a westerly track … climbing at very high speed at an angle of 45 degrees.'[7]

As they continued to scan the sky the bomber crew detected interference on their radar screen, originating from the same direction in which the UFO was seen. This continued for 45 minutes as the Vulcan turned back towards the British Isles. On its return to RAF Waddington the camera film from the aircraft's radar was examined by experts. This confirmed the Vulcan's radar had recorded a 'strong response' from the direction of the sighting. It appeared to consist of three separate radar returns at varying distances, the

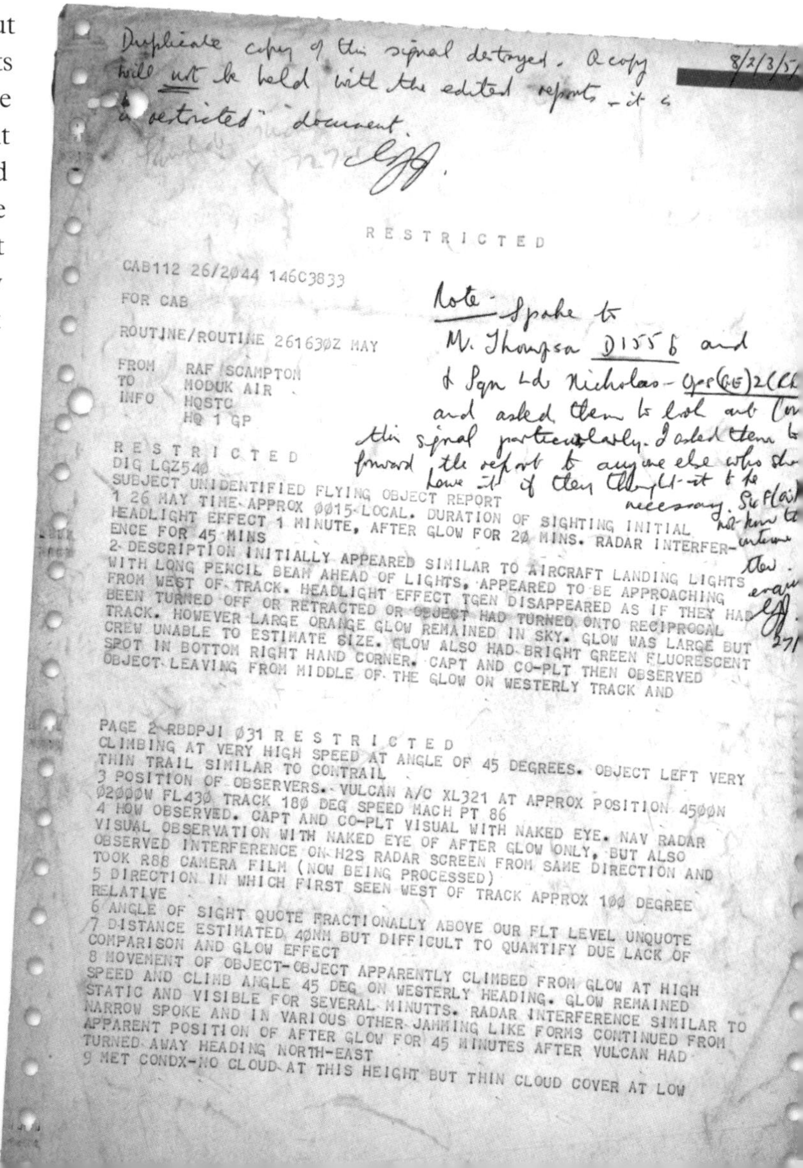

FIG. 34 A signal from RAF Scampton reporting a Vulcan bomber's extraordinary UFO sighting over the North Atlantic in May 1977. DEFE 71/34

third made up of three targets all 200 yds wide. On the film the UFO appeared as 'an elongated shadow', indicating an object of 'large size' at a similar height to the Vulcan.

An intelligence summary sent to the MoD later the same day said the crew 'were unable to offer a logical explanation for the sighting' but noted that foreign shipping was present in the area and the interference evident on the radar suggested an attempt had been made to jam the Vulcan's instruments. The signal, marked 'restricted', said the description resembled 'surface or sub-surface launched missile firing' perhaps by American or Soviet forces. When the UFO desk passed the report on to DI55 for further investigation they were informed that it would 'not know the outcome of their inquiries' due to the report's sensitive content.

The Welsh triangle

By now, as the UFO mystery evolved in complexity, the idea was beginning to arise that some places were more prone to visits from UFOs and their occupants than others. In the 1960s, for example, Warminster, a small town on the edge of the Army training grounds at Salisbury Plain in Wiltshire, become Britain's first UFO hotspot or 'window'. The strange sighting of 'impish' moving lights described earlier (see p.86) was reported in this area of Wiltshire, which would later become a focus for the crop circle mystery (see p.110).

The Warminster phenomenon actually began when residents reported a rash of strange aerial noises and mysterious lights in the sky during the Christmas holidays of 1965. Within two years the town was overwhelmed at weekends and bank holidays by crowds of UFOlogists who took up positions on surrounding hills to watch for 'The Thing' as it was described by the town's residents. Hundreds of sightings were logged by a local journalist, Arthur Shuttlewood, who claimed to have himself observed numerous flying objects in and around the town. Enthusiasm for skywatching at Warminster had, however, ebbed away by the late 1970s when media attention moved to a new UFO hotspot on the rugged coastline of West Wales.

The West Wales flap began at lunchtime on 4 February 1977 when 15 children at Broad Haven Primary School announced they had watched a silver cigar-shaped UFO in fields behind the building. Some of the group, aged 9 to 11 years, claimed they saw a silver man with pointed ears emerge from the craft. These stories were initially put down to a combination of over-active imaginations and too much television, but the children were so adamant they had seen something unusual that they were allowed to hand in a petition at the police station. Their school's head later asked them to draw the UFO and was amazed at how similar their pictures were.

Here Welsh UFO enthusiast and veterinary surgeon Randall Jones Pugh was, like Arthur Shuttlewood, instrumental in bringing a local story to the attention of the national media. Journalists and TV crews flocked to the Welsh coast from across the country and flying saucers were soon the main topic of conversation in the principality. By May straightforward lights in the sky had been replaced by stories of giant humanoid figures in spacesuits, similar to those used by Apollo astronauts, who had been seen prowling around remote parts of the Welsh countryside late at night.

Details of these strange happenings were chronicled in three books, one of which, *The Welsh Triangle* by Peter Paget, had been partly inspired by a headline in the *Sun* newspaper, 'Spaceman Mystery of the Terror Triangle'. The idea of UFO sightings and other strange phenomena being linked up to form a 'triangle' when plotted on a map was a direct outcome of popular fascination with the 'Bermuda Triangle', made famous by a book of that name published in 1974. Author Charles Berlitz invented the term as shorthand for an area of the western Atlantic between Bermuda and Florida where he claimed 'over 1,000 people and 100 aeroplanes have vanished without trace'. The disappearance of aircraft and people had become a popular theme in UFO literature since the death of United States Air Force Captain Mantell in 1948 (see p.39), and the idea of a 'zone of terror' appealed to the tabloid media. What exactly constituted the Welsh version of the Bermuda Triangle was not entirely clear, but according to various books and tabloid articles it included most of the southeast corner of St Bride's Bay along with the towns of Milford Haven and Haverfordwest.

> By May, straightforward lights in the sky had been replaced by stories of giant humanoid figures in spacesuits… prowling around remote parts of the Welsh countryside late at night

Opinion was divided on what was responsible for the Welsh UFO flap. Could it be as journalist Hugh Turnbull, who worked for the local weekly newspaper, the *Western Telegraph*, came to suspect, 'something military'? A more extreme version, favoured by Paget, was that aliens had established an underground base beneath the Stack Rocks in St Bride's Bay, where UFOs had been seen to hover and disappear. In fact within a 20-mile radius of Broad Haven, where many of the sightings occurred, there actually were a number of sensitive military bases. To the north was the rocket testing station at Aberporth, while RAF Brawdy, near St David's, trained pilots and housed both a Tactical Weapons Unit and a US Navy research station.

The silver spacemen

As press coverage continued demands grew for an official inquiry into the West Wales UFO mystery. One lady resident wrote to her MP, Nicholas Edwards, to ask the Ministry of Defence to investigate a UFO experience that left her 'greatly agitated and disturbed'. According to her letter, in the early hours of 19 April 1977 she was disturbed by a strange humming noise and, on looking out of her window, saw an oval-shaped object 'like the moon falling down' land behind her home in St Bride's Bay. As she watched in amazement two very tall human-like figures appeared in front of the UFO that was about the size of a mini-bus. The figures had blank faces and pointed heads and wore white outfits like boiler suits. They appeared to 'take measurements or gather things' and climbed a grassy bank in the field. When she returned to the window after calling members of her family both the object and the 'humanoid' figures had vanished.

As she watched in amazement two very tall human-like figures appeared in front of the UFO … The figures had blank faces and pointed heads and wore white outfits like boiler suits.

Within days of the MP's intervention the MoD asked Squadron Leader J.A. Cowan, who was the Community Relations Officer at RAF Brawdy, to visit the town. According to a report dated 3 June 1977 he examined the area indicated by the woman 'which is in a field adjacent to a Royal Observer Corps underground monitoring post but could find no evidence of a landing.' He added: 'I can offer no explanation of [this] sighting but can confirm that it is not connected with the operations of RAF Brawdy.' Squadron Leader Cowan also discounted the idea that secret military activities were responsible for what the press called 'the Broad Haven Triangle'. He thought it was more likely some of the sightings were caused by 'the high level of flying activity that is generated by the military and civil airfields and to a lesser extent the Royal Aircraft Establishments; the area is also overflown by transatlantic aircraft'.[8] RAF Brawdy had also received several calls describing 'men in silver suits' and an official noted that 'it is perhaps not irrelevant that a local factory manufactures protective clothing of this type for the oil installation at Milford Haven. One of these "silver suits" is also on display in a shop at Brawdy village.'

Suspecting a prankster was at work, the then head of the UFO desk, J.A. Peduzie, took the unusual step of asking the Provost & Security Service (P&SS) to begin a 'discreet enquiry' into events in Wales. The Provost & Security Service are the RAF's police force and are also responsible for the investigation of complaints about low-flying aircraft. In his letter to them Peduzie wrote: 'We have not invoked the assistance of P&SS before on UFOs … and the last thing I want to do is involve you in extraneous problems which would divert you from your more immediate work.' He asked them to assess

'the volume of local interest and/or alarm and whether there is a readily discernable rational explanation, or whether there is prima facie evidence for a more serious specialist enquiry.' (DEFE 24/1206)

Peduzie went to some length to emphasize his request must be treated in confidence, adding: 'I have not even told the Minister I am consulting you.'

Due to the discreet nature of this inquiry, no final report on the Welsh UFO mystery has survived, but in December 1977, in a briefing on UFO policy submitted to the MoD's Defence Intelligence Staff, Mr Peduzie wrote: 'There is always a steady public interest in UFOs and from time to time it tends to increase unaccountably... [In the summer] there was some concern in Wales, although the RAF Police thought this could have been the work of a practical joker.'[9] In 1996 this suspicion was confirmed when one of the men involved confessed in an interview with the *Western Mail* newspaper. He said the spaceman outfit 'had a solid in-built helmet so I would have looked about 7ft tall. Alien sightings were all the rage so I took a stroll around for a bit of fun.'[10]

Nevertheless, the sighting by the Broad Haven schoolchildren that triggered the Welsh UFO flap has never been adequately explained and the witnesses, now adults, continued to stick by their stories when interviewed for a TV documentary in 2008. And the MoD's files reveal they were not the only schoolchildren to see UFOs during that year. At 2.45 pm on 4 October 1977 a group of 10 children, aged from 7 to 11 years, spotted something strange hovering between two trees whilst they were in the playground of Upton Primary Junior School in Macclesfield, Cheshire. Their teacher immediately separated them and asked them to draw what they had seen. She, like her counterparts at Broad Haven, was so astonished at the remarkable consistency of the drawings that she passed them to the police. They took the report seriously and checks were made with Manchester airport who found

FIG. 35 One of a number of crayon drawings showing a UFO sighted by children from the playground of Upton Primary Junior School at Macclesfield in Cheshire in 1977. Their teacher sent the drawings to the MoD. DEFE 24/1206

nothing unusual had been detected by their radar. A letter sent to the children's teacher by the MoD thanked her for sending the drawings and then reassured her with the standard words that

'simple explanations are found for the great majority of UFO reports, the most common single source of sightings being aircraft or the lights of aircraft seen under unusual conditions. Investigations over a number of years have so far produced no evidence that UFOs represent a threat to the air defences of this country.' (DEFE 24/1206)

We are not alone — Spielberg's UFOs arrive

Opinion polls show that 1978 marked the high water mark for public belief in UFOs as extraterrestrial spacecraft. A Gallup survey that year found around half of all Americans believed in some form of extraterrestrial life and 57 per cent thought UFOs were 'real', with 9 per cent reporting a personal sighting. These figures reflect high public awareness of the subject created by the release of Steven Spielberg's science fiction film *Close Encounters of the Third Kind*. The film, with a $19 million budget, opened in UK cinemas during February 1978. The plot involved benevolent aliens who slowly make their presence known to world governments and selected individuals via escalating UFO flaps. This build-up culminates in a final spectacular landing and contact hidden from the public by an ingenious cover-up by the US government. The plot, though fictional, seemed to reflect what many thousands believed was *really* going on and the overlap between fact and fiction was underlined by the presence of former Project Blue Book consultant astronomer Dr J. Allen Hynek as Spielberg's consultant. Hynek had coined the phrase 'close encounters' to describe categories of UFO experience, with the 'third kind' involving sightings of alien creatures such as those reported in Wales during 1977.

The effect of the film on UFO reports in Britain was dramatic. Files at the National Archives show the number of sightings reported to the MoD during 1978 reached a record-breaking 750, almost double the figure for 1977 and the highest total on record. When the *Daily Express* set up a UFO reporting bureau to coincide with the film's release, hundreds more came forward to describe experiences they had never spoken about publicly before. Others simply 'saw' the fantastic craft from the film for themselves. In July, a man from Ealing Common in London rang the MoD to report 'a gigantic saucer' lit up with coloured lights, 'just like a scene from *Close Encounters of the Third Kind*'. It seemed, he said, echoing the compulsive feelings experienced by characters in Spielberg's film, 'as if I was meant to see this object.'[11]

Memories of 1978–9 are dominated by the economic crisis and industrial chaos that eventually swept the Labour Government from power. During what became known as the 'winter of discontent' there was one moment when the gloomy headlines were replaced by exciting news of dramatic UFO sightings across the world. The night of 31 December 1978 was cold and clear, and across the British Isles people were out of doors bringing in the New Year. A few minutes after 7.00 pm many hundreds were amazed to see a bright light with a long trail behind it streaking across the heavens on a northwest to southeast path. In the space of just a couple of hours the MoD received a total of 120 separate sighting reports and civilian UFO groups received hundreds more. The source of this spectacular flap was quickly identified by the RAF's early warning base at Fylingdales in North Yorkshire as the re-entry into Earth's atmosphere of a booster rocket that had launched a Russian satellite, *Cosmos 1068*, into orbit on Boxing Day. The rocket burned up over northern Europe, with pieces falling to the ground in Germany.

Although most observers gave an accurate description of the New Year's Eve UFO a few provided wildly inaccurate details, particularly of its size and altitude. Exact estimation of the height of an object in the dark sky is extremely difficult, if not impossible. For example, some observers believed the object was as low as 1,000 ft, when in reality it was many miles above the Earth. Others gave a time for their sighting that was one hour or more in error. Several described what they had seen in imaginative terms, for example 'cigar-shaped, very bright, with lighted windows' (Manchester), 'similar to a German v-2 rocket' (Bradford) and 'train-shaped, 120 ft long tapering at the front with 40 plus bright lights all along the side' (Newmarket). A few refused to believe the UFO was a Russian rocket at all. One, who served five years in the RAF, said he was familiar 'with meteors and re-entry

FIG. 36 A letter sent to MoD in 1971 by 7-year-old Colin Davis from Leicester describing his sighting of 'a UFO and a monster'. DEFE 24/1206

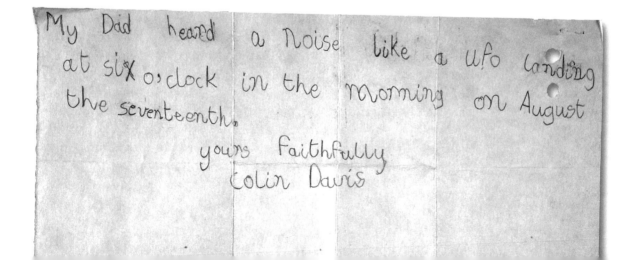

of space debris [and] found it difficult to accept the [MoD's] explanation for this occurrence.'[12]

No sooner had this story died away when news broke of a remarkable film that showed UFOs following a freighter aircraft above the east coast of New Zealand. The film was shot by a camera crew from an Australian TV station who joined the flight after hearing news of an earlier sighting by the crew of an Argosy freight plane flying between south and north islands a week earlier. Dramatic images from the New Year's Eve footage were shown on TV news across the world the following day and quickly became a media sensation. The pilot of the aircraft involved in the second incident, Bill Startup, had more than 20 years flying experience. He said the mysterious lights appeared just before midnight as the Argosy hugged the coast of South Island near Kaikoura, on a flight from Wellington to Christchurch. Startup described the lights as behaving in an intelligent, playful manner similar to the accounts of 'foo-fighters' described by wartime pilots in Europe and the Pacific. He was quoted as saying:

> '[The UFO] appeared to stay still until we got within ten miles then it turned with us as I changed course … it then went above us and circled and came down beneath us. It was making definite movements in relation to [the plane].'[13]

Further evidence in support of the crew's story was provided by air traffic controllers at Wellington airport, who reported unusual targets tracking the aircraft on both nights, some of which tallied with the visual sightings.

UFOs in the House of Lords

These developments were welcomed by a prominent UFOlogist, Lord Clancarty (Brinsley le Poer Trench) who was busy writing a speech for what was to become a historic debate in the ornate setting of the British House of Lords. Questions about UFO sightings and government investigations had been tabled in the Commons as early as 1953, but the motion Clancarty intended to present in the Upper Chamber was unique in being the first full debate on UFOs held in the British Parliament. Clancarty had become fascinated by UFOs early in the 1950s and helped to found the magazine *Flying Saucer Review*, which he edited from 1956–9. With his stock in UFOlogy rising he went on to found his own organization, Contact International, in 1966 and wrote seven books on UFOs and 'ancient astronauts', whom he believed had visited Earth millions of years ago. In a BBC TV interview during 1977 he expanded on this belief by claiming aliens had established bases inside the Earth and their flying saucers entered the atmosphere by flying out from holes in the poles. The ever-so-British eccentricity displayed by Clancarty in his TV appearances is equally evident in the transcript of the UFO debate preserved in Hansard.

Lord Clancarty had succeeded his half brother as 8th Earl in 1976 and immediately used his seat in the Lords to pressurize the government on the issue. His elevation to the Lords added to the problems faced by the Ministry of Defence who anticipated he would use the opportunity to ask the government to make a public statement about UFOs. In December 1977, with assistance from the Foreign Office, the MoD used its influence to talk down a call by another highly placed UFO enthusiast. This was Sir Eric Gairy, president of the small Caribbean island republic of Grenada, a member of the British Commonwealth.

Gairy wanted the United Nations to set up an international agency or department to conduct UFO research, but Britain's diplomats at the UN refused to sanction such a move. Records show one official described this as 'a ridiculous proposal that will only bring the United Nations into disrepute'.[14] Gairy withdrew his original proposal but continued his campaign for a full debate, calling on the UN General Assembly to make 1978 'the year of the UFO'. Gairy was at the UN in New York pressing for further UN action on UFOs early in the following year when he was deposed by a military coup in Grenada.

> Gairy withdrew his original proposal but continued his campaign for a full debate, calling on the UN General Assembly to make 1978 'the year of the UFO'

Meanwhile the dramatic events unfolding in the southern hemisphere led the Royal New Zealand Air Force to launch its own UFO inquiry. To quell public concern they sent out a squadron of Orion aircraft for a seven-hour UFO hunt three days after the New Year sightings. They investigated 14 separate unidentified radar targets seen by air traffic control radar, but nothing was seen. A copy of the air force's draft report was sent by the British High Commission in Wellington to DI55 officials in London, who were preparing the MoD's response to Lord Clancarty in the Lords. This said radars at Wellington airport had been plagued by 'spurious returns' for some time and during the New Year period 'atmospheric conditions [were] conducive to freak propagation of radio and light waves.'

The UFOs seen by the aircrew were, it decided, probably caused by the lights of squid boats distorted by unusual atmospheric conditions or the planet Venus which 'was rising in the eastern sky at this time of the year and is unusually bright in appearance' (in fact Venus did not rise above the horizon until 3.15 am, over one hour *after* the sightings). The report concluded, in lieu of a more detailed scientific study that: 'almost all the sightings can be explained by natural but unusual phenomena.'[15]

Lord Clancarty had originally intended his UFO debate to be held in June 1978 but his motion was withdrawn at the last minute because he feared poor attendance before the summer recess. When it was re-tabled later that year Patrick Stevens, head of the UFO desk, warned colleagues at Whitehall: 'We do not take this lightly because Lord Clancarty is an acknowledged

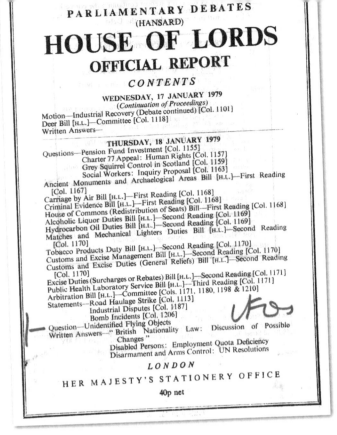

PARLIAMENTARY DEBATES
(HANSARD)

HOUSE OF LORDS
OFFICIAL REPORT

CONTENTS

WEDNESDAY, 17 JANUARY 1979
(Continuation of Proceedings)
Motion—Industrial Recovery (Debate continued) [Col. 1101]
Deer Bill [H.L.]—Committee [Col. 1118]
Written Answers—

THURSDAY, 18 JANUARY 1979
Questions—Pension Fund Investment [Col. 1155]
Charter 77 Appeal: Human Rights [Col. 1157]
Grey Squirrel Control in Scotland [Col. 1159]
Social Workers: Inquiry Proposal [Col. 1163]
Ancient Monuments and Archaelogical Areas Bill [H.L.]—First Reading [Col. 1167]
Carriage by Air Bill [H.L.]—First Reading [Col. 1168]
Criminal Evidence Bill [H.L.]—First Reading [Col. 1168]
House of Commons (Redistribution of Seats) Bill—First Reading [Col. 1168]
Alcoholic Liquor Duties Bill [H.L.]—Second Reading [Col. 1169]
Hydrocarbon Oil Duties Bill [H.L.]—Second Reading [Col. 1169]
Matches and Mechanical Lighters Duties Bill [H.L.]—Second Reading [Col. 1170]
Tobacco Products Duty Bill [H.L.]—Second Reading [Col. 1170]
Customs and Excise Management Bill [H.L.]—Second Reading [Col. 1170]
Customs and Excise Duties (General Reliefs) Bill [H.L.]—Second Reading [Col. 1170]
Excise Duties (Surcharges or Rebates) Bill [H.L.]—Second Reading [Col. 1171]
Public Health Laboratory Service Bill [H.L.]—Third Reading [Col. 1171]
Arbitration Bill [H.L.]—Committee [Cols. 1171, 1180, 1198 & 1210]
Statements—Road Haulage Strike [Col. 1113]
Industrial Disputes [Col. 1187]
Bomb Incidents [Col. 1206]
Question—Unidentified Flying Objects
Written Answers—" British Nationality Law: Discussion of Possible Changes "
Disabled Persons: Employment Quota Deficiency
Disarmament and Arms Control: UN Resolutions

LONDON
HER MAJESTY'S STATIONERY OFFICE
40p net

FIG. 37 (ABOVE) A copy of the Hansard publication covering the historic House of Lords UFO debate, tabled by Lord Clancarty and held in January 1979 at the height of the Winter of Discontent.

FIG. 38 (FACING) An extract from the House of Lords debate, in which Lord Gainford described his sighting of lights in the sky over Loch Fyne on New Year's Eve 1978.

expert on UFOs, whilst MoD has no experts on UFOs' adding the sarcastic caveat, 'for much the same reasons as we have no experts on levitation or black magic.' With public interest in the subject higher than ever he warned colleagues there was now a real risk the government would be persuaded to conduct the dreaded study of UFOs, 'or at least to examine the mass of evidence that Lord Clancarty and his fellow UFOlogists have assembled in the last 30 years.' And he added: 'Should the Government's defences break, I need hardly warn you that responsibility for the study could very likely fall on [our] department!'[16]

Steven's research revealed there had never been any British 'scientific study of UFOs' and he had to rely upon the combined expertise of military and scientific advisors during his preparation for the debate. One of the most revealing briefings came from Group Captain Neil Colvin, a senior officer overseeing the RAF's air defences. He told Stevens: 'Of the [UFO] reports reviewed to date we can find no evidence of extraterrestrial visitation to either earth, its atmosphere or near space,' but he was reluctant to dismiss the entire phenomenon as nonsense. 'The almost total lack of primary radar observations of unnatural phenomena leads us to be sceptical of Lord Clancarty's claims,' Colvin wrote, 'although we would not wish to state categorically that "UFOs" do not exist.'

The task of speaking for the government in the Lords debate fell upon Lord Strabolgi (David Kenworthy), who was Labour's chief whip in the Upper Chamber. After six months of preparation Stevens recommended the government adopted 'an unequivocal and uncompromising line' on UFOs but after much internal debate the MoD agreed to remain open-minded, taking the line 'that there really are strange phenomena in the sky, but there is no need to introduce the highly questionable hypothesis of alien space craft.'

The debate arrived on 18 January 1979 in the middle of a national strike, but the industrial crisis did nothing to dampen interest in UFOs. It was one of the best attended ever held in the Lords, with 60 peers and hundreds of onlookers, including several famous UFOlogists, present in the public gallery. Lord Clancarty opened the three-hour session at 7.00 pm 'to call

[Lord Gainford.]

receive every possible encouragement to take part in many debates in the future. My main contribution to this debate is to assure the noble Earl, Lord Clancarty, of any support that I can give. If we are going to have a study group in your Lordships' House I shall be glad to be a volunteer to take part whenever I have the opportunity. I also thank him and others for initiating this debate, and for the pleasure of having such a refreshing subject to discuss in the midst of the present period of crices and strikes.

I am the 10th person to speak in this debate. I have noticed that so far none of your Lordships have actually reported a sighting, so here goes! I am going to stick my neck out, open my big mouth and trust I am not going to put my foot in it! I saw a UFO a little while ago. It was on 31st December about 8 p.m. All right, my Lords, have a good laugh, it was Hogmanay! Up in Argyll it was a New Year's Eve party and somebody said there was something funny flying across the sky. Fifteen of us came out to have a look, including some children. They had been drinking soft drinks anyway! The object was like a bright white ball with a touch of red followed by a white cone. In fact the whole object had the appearance of a small comet. It was heading eastwards and seemed rather low in the sky, passing over the hills between Loch Sweyne and Loch Fyne. The position from which we viewed it was outside the village of Tayvallich in Argyllshire on the West coast of Scotland about the same latitude as Glasgow.

As the ball disappeared into the distance it seemed to divide into two parts. It may have been a comet or a meteorite, but I should like to know what it really was. It would have been very beneficial if there had been some sort of centre to which I could write or telephone to report such an incident. No doubt setting up such an organisation would be an invitation to pranks, but for starting such a centre I suggest that volunteers could readily be found from the ranks of the former Civil Defence Service and/or the Royal Observer Corps. The Royal Observer Corps still exists but it has literally, if not metaphorically, gone underground where it is preparing to report and advise on nuclear fallout in the case of war. But there are many who used to serve it

and who have not yet disappeared from the scene who could make valuable use of their past experience in establishing centres in various districts throughout the country—and I do not suggest that we start opening up the old observer posts in the countryside—to receive and analyse any reported sightings from the public. Such people with a sense of responsibility could, with a little experience, sift the genuine reports from the false.

Suggesting that such an organisation be set up, particularly at times like these, can naturally give rise to a protest about the waste of public money; but volunteers who might be willing to work for a few hours are quite prepared to do it for very small remuneration, if any at all. I have mentioned the Civil Defence Service, and I did not know whether or not I should declare an interest, but I was a member of it during the 'sixties and I was one of many who were bitterly disappointed when it had to go into abeyance. I recall particularly the comradeship and the sense that we were doing a useful job for the community.

If I had the time and opportunity, I should enjoy volunteering for working in a UFO information centre, if that might be a suggested name for the organisation that would be required. I shall be interested to hear the summings up in this debate. I can give no explanation why there should be these phenomena concentrated within particularly the past 32 years as was confirmed by the noble Earl, Lord Clancarty, and these flying saucers in the year 1947 when the phrase was coined; but I would just accentuate what has been said before and add that if they are man-made or some astronomical feature, and provided there is no risk of any security breach, then the public have a right to know about them.

9.20 p.m.

The Earl of HALSBURY: My Lords, in common with everyone else who has spoken, I should like to thank the noble Earl, Lord Clancarty, for giving us an opportunity to have, as it were, a scamper over the course and exchange views on this very interesting and controversial topic. At the same time, I should like to congratulate the noble Viscount on his maiden speech, which was obviously a very well thought out and well assemble attention to the increasing number of sightings and landings on a world wide scale of UFOs, and to the need for an intra-governmental study of UFOs.' He wound up his speech by calling upon the government to reveal what they knew about the phenomenon and asked the Minister of Defence, Fred Mulley, to give a national TV broadcast on the issue in the same way his French counterpart, Robert Galley, had done in 1974.[17]

'The almost total lack of primary radar observations of unnatural phenomena leads us to be sceptical of Lord Clancarty's claims, although we would not wish to state categorically that "UFOs" do not exist'

More than a dozen peers, including two eminent retired scientists, made contributions to the debate. Lord Hewlett was briefed by Sir Bernard Lovell, director of the Jodrell Bank radio telescope in Cheshire, which had searched the skies 24 hours every day for the past 30 years. Jodrell was the first to detect the Russian satellite *Sputnik* in 1957 and 'has observed thousands of possible subjects for identification as UFOs, but not a single one has proved other than natural phenomena.' He added: 'Of the thousands of reports of sightings that have been made, whenever it has been possible to make an investigation they have been found to be natural phenomena or in some instances, I regret to say, pure myth.'

Several peers reported their own sightings, including Lord Gainford who described seeing the New Year's Eve rocket re-entry 'a bright white ball with a touch of red followed by a white cone' over the Scottish hills.

'It was heading eastwards and seemed rather low in the sky, passing over the hills between Loch Sweyne and Loch Fyne [and] as the ball disappeared into the distance it seemed to divide into two parts.'

The Earl of Halsbury recalled his own sightings during the First World War when he was an eight-year-old boy:

'I used to go out after dark into the garden of the house where we lived and come back reporting the number of Zeppelins I had seen. What I had seen … was a large illuminated cigar-shaped object. In fact, what I was looking at was the lenticular shape that the perspective of a searchlight thrown onto a cloud base makes, and I was interpreting it as a Zeppelin and I was telling my parents how many I had seen.'

Other peers referred to the link between belief in UFOs and religious faith. Lord Davies of Leek compared UFOs with belief in angels: 'Do noble Lords believe in angels?' he asked. 'The answer from some will be yes and yet they have never seen one … but if I said I had seen a flying saucer they would not believe me. What is the difference?' In his contribution, the Bishop of Norwich said he was concerned the UFO mystery 'is in danger of producing a 20th century superstition in our modern and scientific days which is not unlike the superstition of past years.'

The Government's reply to Lord Clancarty's motion was delivered in elegant language by Lord Strabolgi. Drawing upon the Ministry of Defence's long experience he did his best to pour cold water on the idea of UFOs as alien spacecraft. He also dismissed claims by Liberal peer Lord Kimberley that the government was involved in a 'conspiracy of silence' about UFOs, with the comment 'there is nothing to have a conspiracy of silence about … the idea belongs, I suggest, to the world of James Bond.'

As Patrick Stevens and his advisors watched from the spectator's box Strabolgi declared there were ten of thousands of unusual things to be seen in the sky. 'It is the custom to call such phenomena "UFOs", and to transpose this easily into "alien space craft",' he said. '[But] often the appearance is too fleeting and the description too imprecise for a particular cause to be attributed. What we can say is that there is a great variety of plain explanations. There is no need … for the far-fetched hypothesis of alien space craft.'

Strabolgi then outlined the colossal distances that would make visits from outer space unlikely. Referring to Clancarty's claim that evidence existed of thousands of such visits he said 'there is nothing to convince the Government that there has ever been a single visit by an alien spacecraft.' And he rounded off his presentation with a direct response to Lord Clancarty's call for the government to reveal what it knew. 'As for telling the public the truth about UFOs, the truth is simple,' he said.

'There really are many strange phenomena in the sky, and these are invariably reported by rational people. But there is a wide range of natural explanations to account for such phenomena. There is nothing to suggest to Her Majesty's Government that such phenomena are alien spacecraft.' Plainly the MoD hoped the Lords debate would draw a line under their involvement in the subject once and for all, but within a short time they would be permanently drawn back into the debate by one of the most sensational UFO incidents reported on British soil.

CROP CIRCLES AND ALIEN ABDUCTIONS

D URING CHRISTMAS WEEK 1980 the music of John Lennon, murdered in New York, filled the airwaves on both sides of the Atlantic and *Hangar 18,* a sci-fi movie based on the Roswell incident, was on release in British cinemas. The movie poster proclaimed:

'On October 25th a large metallic object crashed in the Arizona desert. The government is concealing a UFO and the bodies of alien astronauts. Why won't they tell us?'

That same week Fylingdales, the RAF's early warning station in North Yorkshire, tracked 12 satellites as they decayed from their orbits. Of these, one was a particularly large object, part of the rocket that launched the Soviet spy satellite *Cosmos 749,* which re-entered earth's atmosphere shortly after 9.00 pm on Christmas Day. In a replay of the events on New Year's Eve two years earlier (see p.95) the rocket broke into several pieces as it did so, creating a spectacular firework display in the night sky over northwest Europe. To complete the heavenly spectacle, astronomers recorded three fireball meteors burning up in the atmosphere, the largest and brightest of which was seen at 3.00 am on 26 December 1980.

On that night police stations, coastguards and the RAF received hundreds of calls reporting between four and five 'comet-like objects leaving bright trails'. The next day excitable newspaper headlines spoke of fireballs, lights moving in convoys and even 'a giant spaceship spurting out smaller craft'. But while the explanation for these events was soon revealed, that for others has proved more elusive. For unknown to the outside world, a series of weird events was unfolding in a quiet corner of the Suffolk coastline. What is known today as the Rendlesham Forest incident has been described as 'the world's first officially observed, and officially confirmed, UFO landing'—Britain's equivalent of Roswell. And as the witnesses were all military personnel, their accounts have naturally been regarded as being highly reliable and credible.

Britain's Roswell

In 1980 RAF Woodbridge and RAF Bentwaters were part of a giant United States Air Force complex hidden within the thick pine plantations of Rendlesham Forest, near the Suffolk coast 8 miles from Ipswich. All was quiet during the Christmas holiday and military activity was minimal. Then at 3 am on 26 December, the time the brightest of the fireballs was visible over southern England, a security patrol saw unusual lights that appeared to fall into Rendlesham Forest a mile beyond the east gate of the base's runway. Fearing an aircraft had crash-landed, three unarmed USAF patrolmen obtained permission to go into the forest beyond RAF Woodbridge to investigate.

A dramatic account of what followed is described in an official United States Air Force memo; written by a senior officer, Lieutenant Colonel Charles Halt, it has become one of the most famous documents in UFO history. Halt described how 'the individuals reported seeing a strange glowing object in the forest … metallic in appearance and triangular in shape', 2–3 m long and 2 m high. This UFO

> 'illuminated the entire forest with a white light [and] had a pulsing red light on top and a bank of blue lights underneath. The object was hovering or on legs. As the patrolmen approached the object, it manoeuvred through the trees and disappeared. At this time the animals on a nearby farm went into a frenzy.' (DEFE 24/1512 and DEFE 24/1948/1)

The airmen were convinced that something had landed in the forest and, responding to their radio messages, RAF Woodbridge's security desk phoned Suffolk police to report: 'a sighting of some unusual lights in the sky, we have sent some unarmed troops to investigate; we are terming it a UFO at present.' Two British police officers visited the forest and reported back: 'Air Traffic Control checked. No knowledge of aircraft. Reports received of aerial phenomena over southern England during the night. Only lights visible in this area was from Orford light house. Search made of area—negative.'[1]

This was far from the end of the mystery as two nights later the lights were back. This time RAF Bentwaters deputy base commander, Lieutenant Colonel Charles Halt, was attending a party when the news arrived. Arming himself with a Geiger counter and hand-held tape recorder, he took a small team of hand-picked men into the woods determined, as he said later,

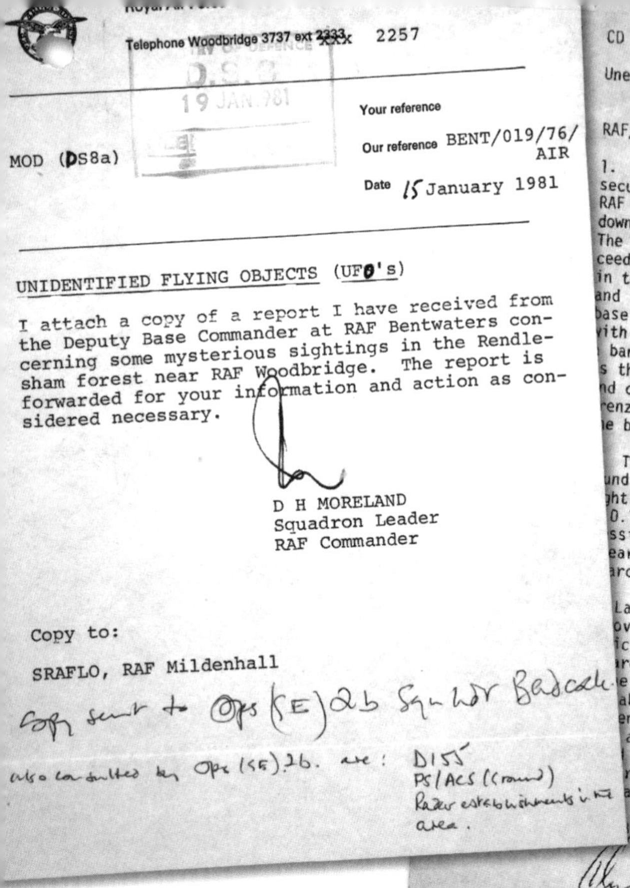

D.S.8
19 JAN 1981

MOD (DS8a)

Your reference

Our reference BENT/019/76/
AIR

Date 15 January 1981

UNIDENTIFIED FLYING OBJECTS (UFO's)

I attach a copy of a report I have received from
the Deputy Base Commander at RAF Bentwaters concerning some mysterious sightings in the Rendlesham forest near RAF Woodbridge. The report is
forwarded for your information and action as considered necessary.

D H MORELAND
Squadron Leader
RAF Commander

Copy to:

SRAFLO, RAF Mildenhall

Copy sent to Ops (E) 2b Sqn Ldr Badcock
also consulted by Ops (SS) 2b. are: DIS5
PS/ACS (round)
Radar establishments in the area.

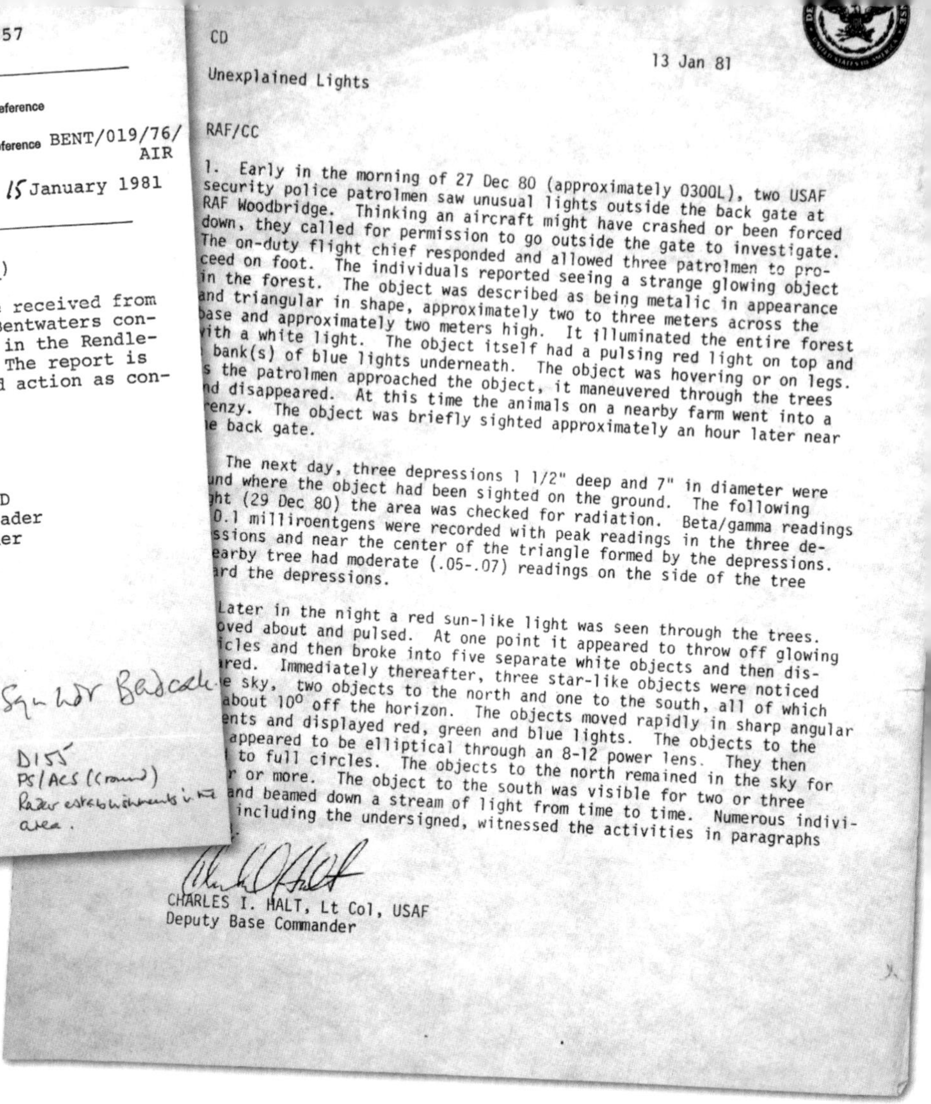

CD

Unexplained Lights

13 Jan 81

RAF/CC

1. Early in the morning of 27 Dec 80 (approximately 0300L), two USAF
security police patrolmen saw unusual lights outside the back gate at
RAF Woodbridge. Thinking an aircraft might have crashed or been forced
down, they called for permission to go outside the gate to investigate.
The on-duty flight chief responded and allowed three patrolmen to pro-
ceed on foot. The individuals reported seeing a strange glowing object
in the forest. The object was described as being metalic in appearance
and triangular in shape, approximately two to three meters across the
base and approximately two meters high. It illuminated the entire forest
with a white light. The object itself had a pulsing red light on top and
a bank(s) of blue lights underneath. The object was hovering or on legs.
As the patrolmen approached the object, it maneuvered through the trees
and disappeared. At this time the animals on a nearby farm went into a
frenzy. The object was briefly sighted approximately an hour later near
the back gate.

2. The next day, three depressions 1 1/2" deep and 7" in diameter were
found where the object had been sighted on the ground. The following
night (29 Dec 80) the area was checked for radiation. Beta/gamma readings
of 0.1 milliroentgens were recorded with peak readings in the three depressions and near the center of the triangle formed by the depressions.
A nearby tree had moderate (.05-.07) readings on the side of the tree
toward the depressions.

3. Later in the night a red sun-like light was seen through the trees.
It moved about and pulsed. At one point it appeared to throw off glowing
particles and then broke into five separate white objects and then disappeared. Immediately thereafter, three star-like objects were noticed
in the sky, two objects to the north and one to the south, all of which
were about 10° off the horizon. The objects moved rapidly in sharp angular
movements and displayed red, green and blue lights. The objects to the
south appeared to be elliptical through an 8-12 power lens. They then
turned to full circles. The objects to the north remained in the sky for
an hour or more. The object to the south was visible for two or three
hours and beamed down a stream of light from time to time. Numerous individuals, including the undersigned, witnessed the activities in paragraphs

CHARLES I. HALT, Lt Col, USAF
Deputy Base Commander

FIG. 39 (LEFT) The
cover note sent to the
MoD's UFO desk by
Squadron Leader Don-
ald Moreland, the British
base commander at RAF
Woodbridge, reporting
'mysterious sightings in
the Rendlesham forest'.
DEFE 24/1512

FIG. 40 (RIGHT)
The famous memo by
Lt Col Charles Halt that
describes UFOs sighted
by United States Air
Force personnel outside
RAF Woodbridge in
December 1980.
DEFE 24/1512

to debunk the UFO stories. In fact he was soon to undergo his own close
encounter that transformed this case into one of the most perplexing UFO
mysteries recorded in the National Archives files.

Halt's experience began as his team visited the scene of the first UFO
landing in the forest. Here they found evidence of damage to trees and
detected higher than expected levels of radiation, both on the trees and in
three shallow holes in the ground. These 'depressions' formed a triangular
pattern that appeared to fit the description of the UFO given by the airmen
on the first night. During the expedition Halt recorded a running timed
commentary of events on his hand-held tape recorder. A copy of this tape
was released in 1984 and it contains this dramatic section:

HALT: 01.48 [am] We're hearing very strange sounds out of the farmer's
barnyard animals. They're very, very active making an awful lot of
noise… You just saw a light? Where? Wait a minute. Slow down.
Where?

VOICE: Right on this position here. Straight ahead. In between the trees
— there it is again. Watch, straight ahead, off my flashlight there, sir.
There it is.

HALT: I see it too. What is it?

VOICE: We don't know, sir.

HALT: It's a strange, small red light, looks to be maybe a quarter to a half
mile, maybe further out…

At that point the noise from animals is replaced by 'deathly calm' and tension in the small team increases when Halt announces the flashing light is moving towards them. With his voice reflecting surprise and amazement Halt cries out: 'It's coming this way. It is definitely coming this way … pieces are shooting off. There is no doubt about it. This is *weird*!'[2]

In his memo Halt describes this UFO as 'a red sun-like light' that moved through the trees, pulsated, then 'appeared to throw off glowing particles and then broke into five separate white objects and then disappeared.' He has since described it as oval in shape with a black centre, resembling a blinking eye.[3] The tape-recording continues as Halt and his men move out of the forest into an open field where they saw 'three star-like objects' hovering about 10 degrees off the horizon, two in the northern sky and another in the south.

These lights remained visible for over an hour, and the one in the south appeared to send down beams of light to the ground from time to time. While these sightings were going on Lieutenant Colonel Halt called Eastern Radar at RAF Watton, but nothing was seen on their screens.

'Curious but sceptical'

Lieutenant Colonel (later Colonel) Charles Halt is a central figure in the Rendlesham UFO mystery. Halt took statements from the airmen involved in the initial UFO incident on 26 December 1980 and his tape-recording of the second night's events was played to his superiors including a visiting general, Charles Gabriel. As, from the closure of Project Blue Book onwards, the United States Air Force had no official interest in UFOs and as these sightings took place outside the perimeter fence, Halt was instructed to report them to the British authorities.

Halt waited for the RAF base commander, Squadron Leader Don Moreland, to return from his Christmas holiday before asking his advice. It was Moreland who advised Halt to write the famous memo summarizing the events, which he sent with a covering note to the UFO desk at Whitehall. Both men expected the MoD would contact them and were surprised when nothing happened.

Halt's memo, titled 'Unexplained Lights', dated 13 January 1981, reached the UFO desk officer Simon Weeden almost three weeks after the sightings.

Weeden immediately circulated details to a number of other MoD departments asking for their advice. The contents of these internal discussions
first emerged in 2001 when the contents of the Rendlesham file were released
under the Code of Practice for Access to Government Information, a precursor to the British Freedom of Information Act (FOIA). They reveal the
Defence Intelligence Staff were unable to explain the sightings, but offered
to follow up the unusual radiation readings described by Halt. According to
Weeden, the RAF air defence staff who scrutinized Halt's report were 'curious but sceptical'. The documents reveal their inquiries relied upon the
accuracy of the dates and times supplied by Halt's memo as the basis for
their checks with air defence radars. These found no evidence that anything
unusual had been detected. As a result MoD decided that 'US nightime
military movements', the beam from the Orford Ness lighthouse or even
lights used by poachers were more likely explanations than an alien landing.[4]

Rumours about a UFO landing at the base had by that time leaked out
to civilian UFOlogists, along with a story that an unidentified object had
been tracked by RAF radars shortly before the drama in the forest. During
1982 when the protest against American Cruise missiles at RAF Greenham
Common was underway, the MoD began to receive letters asking if the
UFO story had been spread to conceal a military accident involving a missile or aircraft. After issuing denials of these rumours one official noted sar-
castically: 'I hope that Bentwaters does not become East Anglia's answer to
Warminster.'[5]

Despite increasing pressure the MoD refused to discuss Halt's report
until 1983 when the contents of his memo, released under the American
Freedom of Information Act, were splashed across page one of the *News of
the World* under the headline: 'UFO LANDS IN SUFFOLK—AND THAT'S
OFFICIAL'.

By that time sensational stories had begun to emerge from United States
Air Force personnel who claimed they were present at a second UFO landing in the forest, when contact had taken place between senior American
officers and the occupants of the UFO. It was claimed that threats had been
made against airmen who witnessed these events and that a cover-up was
underway. The public stance of the MoD remained that Halt's report had
been scrutinized by air defence staff who decided Halt's report had 'no
defence significance', but they refused to be drawn on the nature of their
investigation. This apparent stonewalling by the MoD led two retired officials, Ralph Noyes and Admiral Lord Peter Hill-Norton—a former Chief of
Defence staff—to accuse the British Government of a cover-up, the latter
stating:

'If the [USAF] report … is accurate, there is evidence that British airspace and territory are vulnerable to unwarranted intrusion to a disturb-

ing degree. If, on the other hand, [Halt's report] must be dismissed, then we have evidence—no less disturbing, I suggest—that a sizeable number of USAF personnel at an important base in British territory are capable of serious misperception, the consequences of which might be grave in military terms.'[6]

Lighthouse or UFO?

One of the earliest investigations of the Rendlesham UFO mystery was carried out by journalist and astronomer Ian Ridpath. The MoD's file on the incident, released by the National Archives in 2009, reveals how Ridpath discovered an important fact from the Suffolk police log of the incident. According to this, officers were called to the scene of the initial incident at RAF Woodbridge in the early hours of 26 December 1980. In his memo to the MoD, Halt stated this sighting took place on 27 December. This error is significant because, as noted above, a bright fireball meteor was seen over southern England shortly before 3 am on 26 December, at the same time the United States Air Force security guards reported seeing lights falling into the forest. Then it emerged that Halt was also wrong about the date of his own sighting. In his memo he suggests this occurred on 29 December 1980, when in fact it occurred in the early hours of 28 December.

Further blows to the credibility of the story emerged when Ridpath contacted Vince Thurkettle, a young forester who lived in the forest when the sightings occurred. Thurkettle had plotted on a map the route taken by Halt's team and found they were looking directly at the flashing beam of the Orford Ness lighthouse, 6 miles away on the coast. After visiting the forest to record an interview for *BBC Breakfast News*, Ridpath wrote:

> 'Sure enough the lighthouse beam seemed to hover a few feet above ground level, because Rendlesham Forest is higher than the coastline. The light seemed to move around as we moved. And it looked close— only a few hundred yards away among the trees.'[7]

This explanation gained further weight in 1998 when the original statements made by the airmen involved in the earlier 26 December incident were released by an American UFO group. These revealed how, after responding to the report of lights falling into the forest, three airmen had seen various coloured lights apparently within the trees. They drove into the forest to investigate, then left their vehicle and continued on foot. Eventually they emerged from the trees following a group of red and blue lights that disappeared. In his statement, airman 1st class John Burroughs says: 'Once we reached the farmer's house we could see a beacon going around so we went towards it. We followed it for about two miles before we could see it was coming from a lighthouse.' In the statements only one of the three-man team, Sergeant Jim Penniston, claimed the lights they saw in the forest were attached to a structured object that was 'definitely mechanical in nature'.

Other elements of the story have been questioned too. One of the easiest to dismiss is the claim that the UFO was seen on radar. While the MoD file reveals that checks were carried out on incorrect dates and times provided by Halt's memo, it clearly states that no unusual targets were detected by any RAF radars during the Christmas/New Year period of 1980. This was confirmed by Squadron Leader Derek Coumbe who was duty commander at RAF Watton, the air traffic control centre for the region during the incident. When I spoke to him in 2001 he recalled receiving a call from RAF Bentwaters whilst Halt's team were in the forest during the early hours of 28 December 1980. 'They were very jumpy and panicky on the phone,' he said, 'but I personally checked the radar picture and there was absolutely nothing to be seen. They kept coming back and implying there should be something but we kept a watch on it through the whole period and nothing was seen.'[8]

Equally significant are the criticisms levelled at two other key elements of the story: the ground traces and radiation that Halt claimed were discovered in the forest. British police officers who examined the alleged landing site after the first UFO sighting said the three holes found at the landing site 'were of no depth and could have been made by an animal'. Vince Thurkettle, who had visited the scene soon after, was equally unimpressed by what he saw.

The holes, he thought, resembled those produced by burrowing animals such as rabbits, while the damage on nearby trees looked to him like the axe marks used to identify sections of forest earmarked for felling. And as for the radiation, three independent scientific experts, including the makers of the Geiger counter, have since stated there was nothing unusual in the levels recorded by Halt's team in the forest. The manufacturers later announced these were 'of little or no significance'.

> The MoD's reluctance to reveal what little it knew about the UFO incidents encouraged the mystery to grow and provided fuel for allegations of cover-ups

So what conclusions can be drawn about the UFO incident that is widely known today as Britain's Roswell? Can all the weird sightings really be explained by a fireball, the lighthouse and bright stars as Ian Ridpath has concluded or did a genuine unidentified flying object visit Suffolk as the airmen continue to believe?

What is clear from the Rendlesham file is the MoD's reluctance to reveal what little it knew about the UFO incidents encouraged the mystery to grow and provided fuel for allegations of cover-ups. Two decades passed before the full contents of their file on the Rendlesham incident were revealed. Early in 2001, with Britain's own Freedom of Information Act pending, the MoD finally released the papers they held on the incident after I applied to see them. They did not contain the 'smoking gun' anticipated by UFOlogists who had speculated about the contents for 20 years. Instead the file revealed a half-hearted investigation by disinterested officials. Most surprising of all, the papers revealed the MoD did not feel it was necessary to interview Halt or any of the airmen involved in the original sightings.

To this day Colonel Halt and the other airmen remain convinced the lights they saw on the two nights were genuinely unidentified. At a press conference in Washington DC in 2007 he said: 'I have no idea what we saw but do know whatever we saw was under intelligent control.'

The MoD's final assessment of Halt's report was not revealed until further papers were opened at the National Archives in 2008. In a private briefing given to Lord Hill-Norton during 1985, defence minister Lord David Trefgarne said:

> 'it is highly unlikely that any violation of UK airspace would be heralded by such a display of lights. I think it equally unlikely that any reconnaissance or spying activity would be announced in this way. We believe that the fact Col Halt did not report these occurrences to MoD for almost two weeks after the event, together with the low key manner in which he handled the matter are indicative of the degree of importance in defence terms which should be attached to the incident.' (DEFE 24/1924/1)

As was the case with the original Roswell incident, there is a great difference between the few certain facts that can be established from contemporary records and the elaborate legend that has grown up around the Rendlesham UFOs. The legend has been nurtured by tabloid headlines and sensational TV documentaries and today is so well known that the Forestry Commission have set up a 'UFO trail' in the forest for pilgrims who wish to relive the story in their imagination. As the decades pass attempts to separate fact from fiction become increasingly difficult. All that can be said with certainty is that it is unlikely we will ever know what *really* happened in Rendlesham forest in December 1980.

Mysterious marks on the ground

Eyewitness testimony, even that from the most credible witnesses such as pilots and airmen, can fall short of convincing evidence as it is open to many different interpretations. In addition, photographs and movie footage can be faked and radar traces can prove equally misleading. Hard physical evidence, such as the ground traces reported at Rendlesham, if it could have been identified by scientific examination as having an origin other than terrestrial, offers the promise of proof and is understandably the most keenly sought. If such hard evidence were found it could solve the UFO mystery once and for all.

The search for this kind of conclusive explanation has had a long history, featuring in the earliest UFO files at the National Archives. One example dates from July 1963 when farmer Roy Blanchard found a huge 8-foot deep crater in a barley and potato field at Charlton in Wiltshire. Charlton was just 15 miles from the town of Warminster that became a focus for UFO sightings later in the 1960s (see p.90). The hole was described as having zig-zag markings emanating from its centre and 'looked as though it had been scooped out by an enormous spoon.' It was discovered shortly after a farm worker heard a loud explosion similar to a lightning strike.

Mr Blanchard was convinced a UFO was responsible for the crater and he contacted the police who in turn called out the Army's bomb disposal squad. They cordoned off the field believing the crater might contain the remains of a wartime bomb or fragments of a meteorite. The national media preferred to speculate about flying saucers and excitement grew when the Army's instruments detected a metal object deep within the crater. After almost a week spent excavating the bomb squad located the mysterious relic. This was identified by the British Museum as a lump of ironstone, a sedimentary rock with a high iron content.

The excitement which followed the discovery led to questions in the House of Commons. In response to a Parliamentary question on 29 July 1963 the Secretary of State for War, Joseph Godber, said 'the [object] initially thought to be a meteorite appears in fact to have been a piece of local rock and was not the cause of the crater.' Then a spokesman for the Army's Southern Command told the media: 'It is not a bomb so it has nothing to do with us. The cause of the hole ... is unexplained, but it is no part of the Army's task to unravel such mysteries.'[9]

Strange circles in the corn

Some 20 years later the fields of Wiltshire would, of course, play host to that great late twentieth-century mystery—crop circles. Unusual swirled circles have appeared in fields of crops across southern England for centuries. Until the last two decades of the twentieth century no one seriously suggested they could be the work of aliens, though the sudden and uncanny appearance of swirled rings overnight in the middle of virgin crops have always led some to suggest the intervention of some supernatural agency.

A tantalizing example is provided by a pamphlet titled 'The Mowing Devil', published in 1678, which features a woodcut depicting a horned devil cutting a field of oats with a scythe to produce a flattened circle within the crop. The text describes how a farmer argued with a workman over the cost of mowing his field, swearing 'that the Devil should mow it rather than He'. That same night 'the crop of oats showed as if it had been all of a flame ... [and] next morning [it] appeared so neatly mowed by the Devil.' The pamphlet then describes what could easily be an example of a modern crop circle, telling how the Devil 'cut them in round circles, and placed every straw with the exactness that it would have taken above an Age for any Man to perform what he did that one night.'[10]

'The Mowing Devil' pamphlet was intended as a moral lesson. The writer warned his audience not to make angry invocations to evil spirits that they might live to regret. Nevertheless, it is tempting to imagine that it could have been inspired by the appearance of unusual crop formations in seventeenth-century England.

The modern circles mystery can be traced to August 1980 when farmer John Scull discovered rough circular swathes of flattened oats in his fields below the Westbury White Horse on the edge of the Bratton Downs in Wiltshire. As in the case of the Charlton crater, the media immediately linked these to flying saucers as Westbury is close to the UFO-haunted town of Warminster. But the first crop circles to achieve prominence in the national media appeared during the summer of the following year when a formation of three appeared in a natural amphitheatre known appropriately as The Devil's Punchbowl at Cheesefoot Head near Winchester. The central circle was 55 ft in diameter and two smaller circles, half its size, were arranged perfectly on either side.

The prominent positioning of the circles, below a road running through a popular beauty spot in one of England's most popular tourist areas, guaranteed a wide audience of bemused motorists. Inevitably, a string of curious visitors soon began to arrive among whom was the late engineer and UFOlogist, Pat Delgado. He examined the field and was struck by the sharply defined edges of the circles and the manner in which the corn stalks had been flattened in a clockwise swirl. Writing in the magazine *Flying Saucer Review* Delgado said there was no other evidence of damage to the crops. If human vandals were responsible, how did they enter and leave the field without leaving traces? It seemed to him that 'the rings could only have been made by something descending onto the field'. In the introduction to *Circular Evidence*, the book he co-authored in 1989, Delgado said the discovery at Cheesefoot Head had a 'profound' impact upon him.

Later Delgado and another enthusiast, Colin Andrews, began collecting information about other crop circles and both were quoted in the media as experts on the circles mystery. In *Circular Evidence* the two authors, whilst not directly attributing the crop circles to UFOs, said they believed '[they] are created by an unknown force field manipulated by an unknown intelligence.'

Meanwhile a physicist, Dr Terence Meaden, began to formulate another theory after visiting some of the early circles discovered in Wiltshire and Hampshire. Writing in *The Journal of Meteorology*, he expressed his opinion that a rare type of spinning air vortex—a mini whirlwind—was a more likely natural cause for the strange crop circles.

Official Interest

By the summer of 1983 what had begun as a minor local mystery became the focus for international media attention when a new formation of five circles appeared at Westbury. Naturally, further links were made with 'the famous Warminster triangle' although no reliable reports of UFOs had so far been made in the area where the circles had been found. Fortuitously, this story broke in the wake of publicity surrounding the release of the Spielberg movie *E.T.* and the *Daily Express* published a dramatic aerial photograph of the Westbury circles alongside a picture of the loveable alien character from the film. The headline read: 'ET—phone the *Express*'.

FIG.41 Various attempts were made to explain the crop circles that appeared across Wiltshire and Hampshire. The author of this letter suspected 'vertical takeoff and landing aircraft'—but who was to blame? DEFE 24/1517

As the files at the National Archives show, the MoD had now begun to receive letters from concerned members of the public. A man from Lancashire wrote to the UFO desk to say he believed it was unlikely that ordinary humans could flatten the corn in such a precise way. In his opinion they had been 'made by a vertical-landing and takeoff aircraft' equipped with tripod landing gear similar to that used by NASA's lunar module. The writer asked if a foreign power had developed a version that was being used for 'some nefarious purpose'. UFO desk officer Pam Titchmarsh responded on 26 July 1983:

'in the case of the marks in the cornfield there have, to [our] knowledge, been no reports of UFOs in the area and no study has therefore been undertaken by the Ministry. I understand, however, that common opinion in the media puts the marks down to a whirlwind.' (DEFE 24/1517).

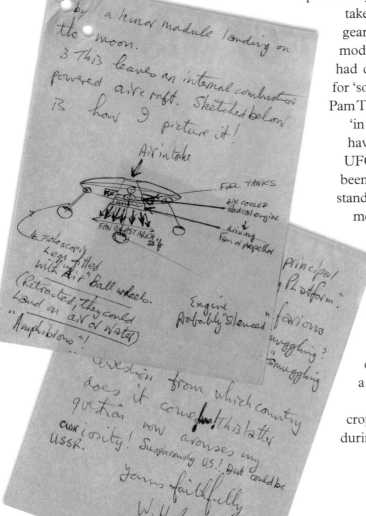

Other explanations at the time included rutting hedgehogs, giant hailstones and the apparently more sensible idea of hovering military helicopters, but this was quickly disproved. Downwash from helicopter rotor-blades damages crops by swirling them around in a random fashion in all directions.

It was because of this last theory that crop circles reappeared in the MoD's in-tray during August 1985, when a farmer near the

Army Air Corps station at Middle Wallop in Hampshire discovered some strange depressions in a field of ripe wheat. According to a report sent to the MoD, the farmer called the base demanding to know what on earth Army helicopters were doing in his fields. An Army team, led by Lieutenant Colonel G.J.B. Edgecombe, visited the field and found 'an exactly circular hole in the wheat [which had] been laid flat in a clockwise twist 40 ft in diameter (as if a plank had been put with one end at the centre and swept round in a complete circle).' This central circle was surrounded by four smaller circles. None of the soldiers could explain the circles and they returned to take aerial photographs of the field from a helicopter.

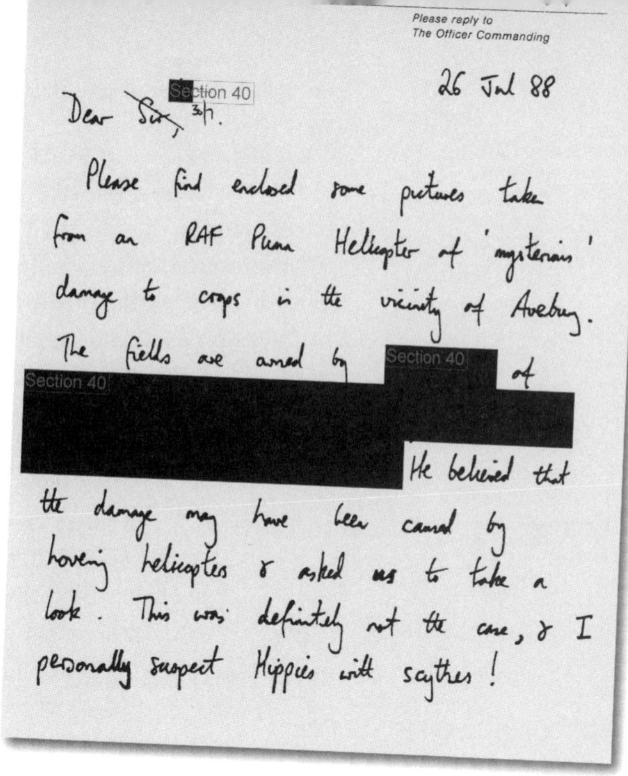

Lieutenant Colonel Edgecombe's report and photographs were sent to the UFO desk and then on to the Defence Intelligence Staff branch DI55 with the comment 'although I don't think this can properly be regarded as a UFO sighting, there might conceivably be defence interest and [we] would therefore be grateful for your expert comments on the photographs.'

On 12 December 1985 DI55 replied, saying it was clear something unusual had occurred but 'just what remains a mystery'. As there had been no 'unusual sightings' reported in the area prior to the discovery of the circles, DI55 was inclined, like Dr Meaden, to suspect the cause was 'some kind of natural phenomena such as mini-tornadoes bouncing off the ground.'[11]

FIG.42 Some officials were fairly sure who was to blame for the crop circle mystery as this July 1988 note from RAF Odiham shows. DEFE 24/1931.

Government conspiracy?

As the files at the National Archives show, MoD interest in crop circles continued for a number of years. In July 1988 a Puma helicopter was sent from RAF Odiham to photograph a crop circle formation in fields close to Silbury Hill, near Avebury in Wiltshire, after another complaint from a farmer. He was told the damage

> 'was definitely not caused by helicopters [and] it would seem that the circles have been man-made and deliberately sited to line up and form a pattern with Silbury Hill, although we can't understand why.'

However these investigations were to have an unforseen and unfortunate consequence: news of military helicopters hovering over fields and photographs taken by service personnel began to reach crop circle enthusiasts and led to rumours of a secret government investigation.

With questions in Parliament and rumours of Royal interest, officials tried to discourage military helicopter crews visiting or taking photographs of crop circles during their routine training over the West Country. In a 1991 memo circulated to the armed services, UFO desk officer Owen Hartop said this practice put the branch in a 'difficult position' as publicly the MoD was on record as saying it did not investigate unexplained phenomena unless they had any 'defence significance'. His circular added: 'for the [Army Air Corps] to involve themselves in this way erodes this position, as the UFO lobby will see this as active investigation of UFO-related activity (as they view corn circles)—something that we have categorically and publicly stated that we do not do'.[12] This advice appears to have been ignored.

By the 1990s the numbers of crop circles had increased dramatically along with their size and complexity. In 1990 alone an incredible 700 new examples were discovered along with giant formations the size of football pitches. Smaller circles began to develop outside the main rings to form doubles, triples and multiple rings. In addition, complex new design elements began to appear such as hieroglyphs, symbols such as the Celtic cross and spectacular 'pictograms' based upon complex mathematical formulae.

Employing just wooden planks, string and old-fashioned guile to avoid leaving evidence behind them, the two friends set out to fool the world...

While some people believed these could be messages from an 'unknown intelligence', others suspected they were created by human beings. Then on 9 September 1991 the national newspaper *Today* revealed how two Hampshire-based watercolour artists, Doug Bower and Dave Chorley, had confessed they had been secretly creating the circles for 15 years. Mr Bower claimed he had always been interested in UFOs and got the idea whilst in Australia during the 1960s when swirled circles found in reedbeds in Queensland were called 'flying saucer nests.'

On returning to England he began to meet his friend Dave Chorley on Friday evenings for a drink at a public house near Cheesefoot Head. They created their first crop circle in 1976: 'There was a lot of interest in UFOs at the time so I suggested we should flatten some corn to make it look like something had landed during the night.' Employing just wooden planks, string and old-fashioned guile to avoid leaving evidence behind them, the two friends set out to fool the world. Four years passed before their creations reached the newspapers and another three before the prank took off. 'We wanted the papers to catch on so we could have a good laugh about it,' Doug told reporter Graham Brough. 'We started doing them in the Punchbowl at Cheesefoot Head so people could look down on them from the road. Then all of a sudden we saw an article in the local paper and then articles in the national papers and we knew we had done it.' He added: 'The first publicity made it even more exciting [and] once the papers started saying a UFO had landed we started to go down to Warminster, where there had been a lot of UFO sightings, and do the circles there to create a bit of a stir.'

Doug and Dave's revelations dampened interest in crop circles for a short while and their confessions marked their retirement from the field. As their activities came to an end a second generation of circle-makers, led by teams such as London-based Rod Dickinson and John Lundberg, began to produce ever more elaborate designs. While Doug and Dave's motivation was simply to create the impression of a UFO landing, other circle-makers regard their more elaborate designs as works of art. More recently, a number of sophisticated formations have been commissioned by advertisers selling everything from breakfast cereals to holidays.

Despite the bursting of the crop circle bubble many crop circle enthusiasts, or 'cereologists' as they became known, continue to believe that it is possible to distinguish hoax crop circles from genuine examples that remain unexplained. Indeed, a few even feared a cover-up, believing the MoD was trying to hide the truth about their origins. When Doug and Dave's confession was first published, rumours spread that their claims were part of a cunning plan by the authorities. The files at the National Archives show that shortly after their story was published by *Today*, a UFOlogist wrote to the MoD asking for confirmation that they had organized a 'secret meeting' with officials from the Ministry of Agriculture, Fisheries and Food (MAFF) and the Department of the Environment to discuss crop circles. The rumour alleged the Government was so alarmed by the phenomenon that it had discussed spreading disinformation to mislead the public. This included the employment of crop circles hoaxers and the creation of a 'bogus news agency … to spread this untrue story to the public.'[13]

Alien encounters

During the first two decades of the modern UFO era the phenomenon was largely restricted to accounts of anomalous disc- and cigar-shaped objects, or lights in the night sky. For those who believed that flying saucers existed and were piloted by intelligent beings it was only a matter of time before someone made contact with them. During the twentieth century popular ideas about what extraterrestrials might look like were drawn mainly from science fiction films and magazines, where aliens tended to originate from nearby planets in our solar system such as Mars and Venus. Their appearance reflected their motives, from the hideous monsters described by H.G. Wells in his *The War of the Worlds* (1898) to the benevolent, angel-like creatures with wings pictured by Fenton Ash in his 1909 novel *Trip to Mars*.

In the immediate aftermath of the Second World War it was perhaps inevitable that depictions of aliens in Hollywood movies tended to emphasize their hostility. Films such as *The Thing from Another World* (1951), *Invaders from Mars* (1953) and *Invasion of the Body Snatchers* (1956) fed upon the early saucer panics to portray aliens as belligerent creatures bent upon invading Earth. More complex motives were displayed by the alien Klaatu, played by Michael Rennie in the seminal 1951 movie *The Day the Earth Stood Still*, who came in peace but nonetheless threatened humankind with extinction if his message was not heeded. In Britain monstrous, hostile aliens featured in *The Quatermass Experiment*, first shown on BBC TV in 1953.

Throughout the Cold War the threat of nuclear annihilation continued to preoccupy both film-makers and those who claimed to have made contact with occupants of flying saucers. The most notorious of these 'contactees', as they became known, was a Polish-American émigré, George Adamski, who ran a hamburger stall on the slopes of the Mount Palomar observatory in California. His 1953 book, co-written with British author Desmond Leslie, *Flying Saucers Have Landed*, sold more than a million copies worldwide and was translated into 50 languages.

Adamski described his meeting in the Mojave Desert with a tall, blond angelic being from Venus, the planet of love, who emerged from a flying saucer scout craft. The being indicated his peaceful intent by means of telepathy and, as Klaatu had, warned Earthlings of the danger posed by atomic bombs. Adamski's sensational story immediately polarized opinion both in the newly-founded UFO community and the wider world. While his tome was welcomed by many who believed flying saucers were here to save mankind, it was denounced by scientists and astronomers who dismissed Adamski's claims as 'preposterous'. The book also contained photographs of Venusian spacecraft taken by Adamski from his Californian home. These were panned by critics such as Arthur C. Clarke as obvious and crude fakes.

The book's sequel, *Inside the Spaceships* (1956), described the author's visits to inhabited parts of the Moon, Venus and Saturn. Adamski attracted a small cult following, but his claims were wildly improbable even before the first space probes reached our neighbouring planets. These confirmed what scientists had already suspected: beyond Earth our solar system appeared to be pretty devoid of life. Today controversy continues to surround the possibility that micro-organisms might exist below the Martian surface, but we know there are no canals as some astronomers once believed. Venus has a furnace-like surface temperature and atmospheric pressure nearly 100 times that of the Earth, with sulphuric acid clouds floating on a blanket of dense carbon dioxide. Adamski's blond, peace-loving Venusians are unlikely inhabitants of this fiery hell.

> Adamski described his meeting in the Mojave Desert with a tall, blond angelic being from Venus, the planet of love, who emerged from a flying saucer scout craft

From this point accounts of contacts with the crews of UFOs underwent subtle changes and the friendly, Nordic-looking aliens who befriended George Adamski were replaced by colder, ambivalent creatures whose motives and purpose appeared more inscrutable and sinister than anything Hollywood had previously imagined.

Missing time

The seminal story that sparked the modern obsession with 'alien abductions' was told by Betty and Barney Hill, a couple from New Hampshire in the USA. Their experience began late one night in September 1961 as they returned home from a holiday in Canada. Whilst driving through the deserted White Mountains they saw a brightly lit UFO that appeared to follow them. At one stage Barney, who was driving, stopped the car and watched the object through binoculars. Behind a row of windows he saw a group of humanoid figures watching him and, believing they were about to be captured, he drove off in panic.

Soon afterwards the couple were confronted by the landed UFO and its occupants who were now blocking the road. The next thing the Hills consciously recalled was an odd beeping noise. Suddenly they were aware of being on a road 35 miles further south and when they returned home they realized the journey had taken two hours longer than expected. Betty subsequently experienced a series of disturbing dreams where the crew of the UFO took her onto the craft against her will.

FIG.43 Drawing of a flying saucer seen by a member of the public beside the Basingstoke Canal near Aldershot in 1983. According to the account in the MoD files, he was taken on board by small green-clad aliens who scanned his body and announced: 'You can go. You are too old and infirm for our purpose.'
DEFE 24/1925/1

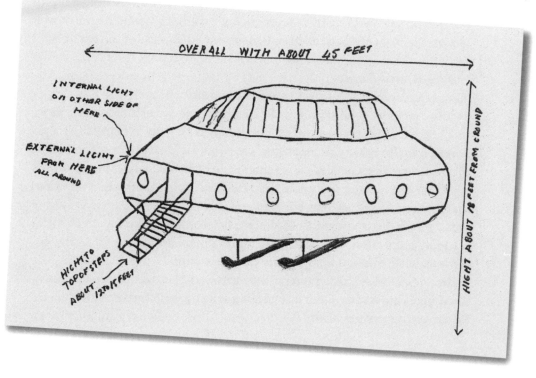

In 1964 the Hills were hypnotically regressed by a Boston psychiatrist, Dr Benjamin Simon, and their stories recorded. Their separate accounts of what transpired during the period of missing time appeared to match Betty's dreams in significant places. Details emerged of a medical examination, a tour around the spacecraft and a lengthy conversation between Betty and the leader of the alien crew. She described her captors as shorter than her husband with grey skin and dark eyes and prominent noses. They were human in appearance, wore jackets, trousers and caps similar to military uniforms and behaved in 'a professional way ... there was no haste, no waste of time.'[14]

When their tale was published by journalist John Fuller in the bestselling book *The Interrupted Journey* (1966), the Hills became overnight celebrities. Their incredible story, with its key motifs of 'missing time' and medical examination, went on to become the template for all future alien abduction stories.

> [the Hills'] incredible story, with its key motifs of 'missing time' and medical examination, went on to become the template for all future alien abduction stories

Sightings of and contact with UFO occupants were few and far between in Britain before the Hills' story was serialized by the London *Daily Mirror* in October 1966. Two years later the couple appeared in the BBC documentary *Flying Saucers and the People Who See Them*. In stark contrast to the reaction received by Adamski and other contactees during the 1950s, on this occasion more people were prepared to suspend disbelief in the existence of aliens. It seemed that now the space age had become reality, people were willing to accept stories describing encounters with extraterrestrials. The path was open for others to come forward with accounts of alien abductions from Britain and other parts of the world.

Aliens visit Devon

In Britain, despite the protestations of sincere witnesses such as Angus Brooks (see p.75), officials remained largely unmoved by reports of 'close encounters'. This term was originally coined in 1972 by Dr J. Allen Hynek, Project Blue Book's consultant astronomer, to classify types of UFO experiences. A close encounter of the first kind (CE1) involved the close approach of a UFO, while a CE2 left permanent evidence either on the witness or the environment. Close encounters of the third kind, used by Steven Spielberg as the title of his 1978 blockbuster film, involved the observation of UFO occupants. The Hills' story falls into a further category, with a CE4 involving contact with or abduction by the alien occupants.

The MoD's scientists pointed out that stories in this category usually relied upon the testimony of a single witness and were rarely supported by independent evidence. They felt that 'some must be hoaxes; in other cases we would be prepared to accept that the people concerned believe they have seen something; but we are convinced that they were victims of some form of hallucination.'[15]

Perhaps the first account of a CE3 in the files at the National Archives that the MoD took seriously enough to warrant an investigation comes from 1968. This was reported by a lorry driver, Andrew Perry, who arrived at a police station in Devon on the night of 27 February to report a bizarre and terrifying experience. In a police statement Mr Perry described how he was driving his articulated lorry on the road from Bideford to Cullompton at 6.55 pm when he saw a bright light appear at the crest of a hill. As he got closer he could see the light came from a mushroom-shaped object.

> 'I drove a bit further down the road until I was abreast of the object, and I would think by then it was about 300 yards distant. I stopped the lorry and climbed out of my cab, leaving the engine running. I climbed onto the trailer to get a better view, and saw also what appeared to be five or six figures about 4 ft in height, they were a dozen or so yards from the object and were spread out around it...' (AIR 20/11894)

Suddenly these figures scrambled towards the UFO and disappeared inside. Then it climbed vertically and emitted a very high-pitched whirring noise that caused his lorry to vibrate. By this time fear had replaced curiosity and he jumped back into the cab.

> 'I put the engine in gear, and started to go down the road as fast as I could go. The object had risen to about 200 ft and I travelled about a dozen yards, the noise from the object was so intense I couldn't hear my engine running—as it passed overhead. Suddenly, for no apparent reason my engine cut out. I braked, stopped and cradled my head in my arms as I thought this object was coming right down on top of me. A few seconds passed, the noise went and when I looked up it was about the size of a football and was going away into the sun at a really fantastic speed. I pulled myself together after a moment or so and automatically pressed the starter button. The engine started and I went as fast as ever I could to the nearest police station.' (AIR 20/11894)

Mr Perry's report was circulated to a number of MoD branches and checks were made on air defence radar without success. Officials attempted to apply a sensible explanation and suspected that a low-flying helicopter was involved, but checks with RAF and Navy bases ruled out this possibility. Unable to reach a conclusion, the MoD categorized Perry's report under 'miscellaneous' and decided to take no further action.

From the late 1970s the number of stories describing UFO landings and sightings of occupants reported to the Ministry began to increase. Desk officers continued to file these alongside the far more frequent reports of shapes and lights in the sky. For example, during a UFO flap in the

Midlands during February 1988 a woman contacted RAF Cosford, near Wolverhampton, to report a square-shaped UFO with a dome on top that was illuminated by red and green lights. The UFO was silent at first until it 'moved as though [it was] going to crash into her house' but stopped just a few yards away. As it moved towards her a row of partitioned windows became visible behind which she saw, in a lighted cabin, 'three people, two sitting and one standing; all appeared to be wearing white suits.' Terrified, she ran inside the house and, looking through the window, watched as the object disappeared.[16]

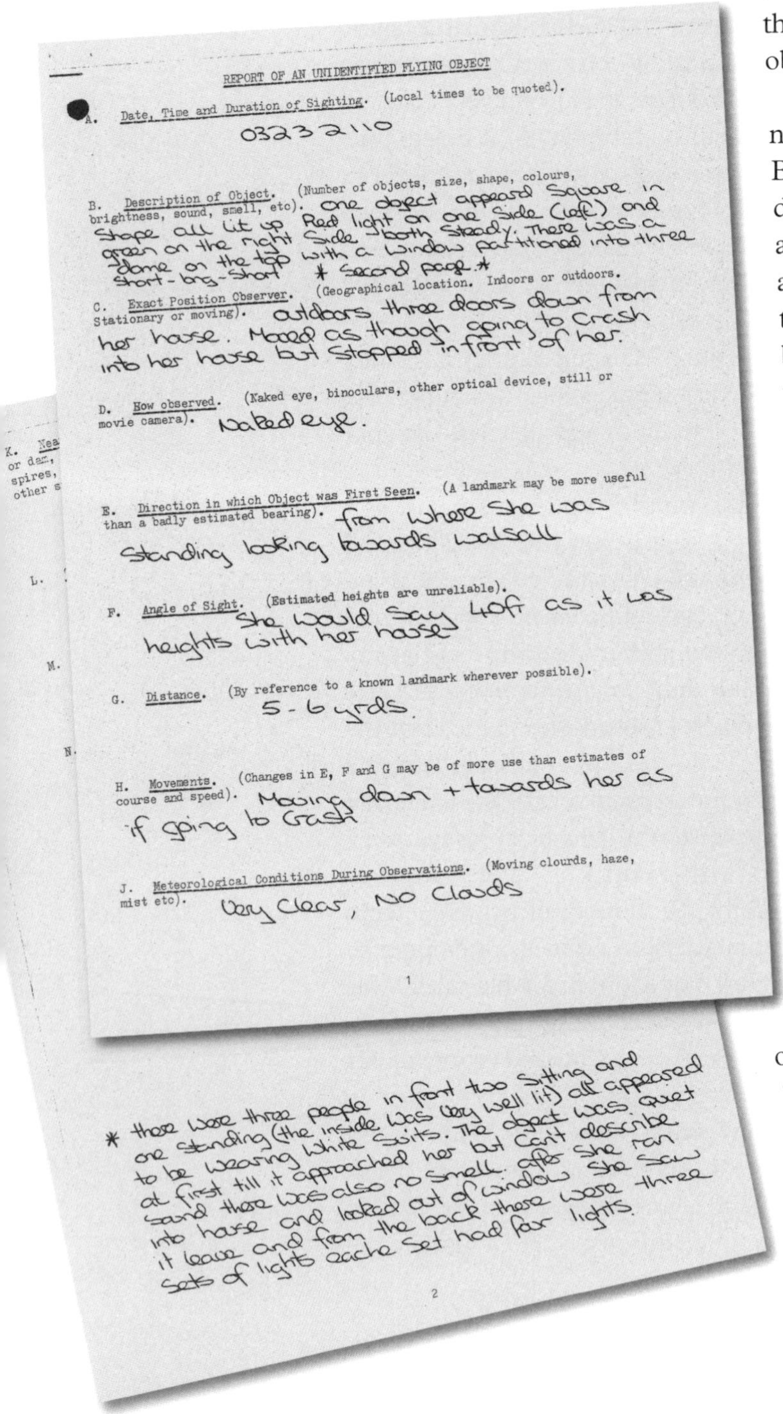

REPORT OF AN UNIDENTIFIED FLYING OBJECT

A. Date, Time and Duration of Sighting. (Local times to be quoted).
0323 2110

B. Description of Object. (Number of objects, size, shape, colours, brightness, sound, smell, etc). one object appeared Square in shape all lit up Red light on one Side (left) and green on the right Side both Steady. There was a dome on the top with a window partitioned into three short-long-short * second page.*

C. Exact Position Observer. (Geographical location. Indoors or outdoors. Stationary or moving). outdoors three doors down from her house. Moved as though going to crash into her house but stopped in front of her.

D. How observed. (Naked eye, binoculars, other optical device, still or movie camera). Naked eye.

E. Direction in which Object was First Seen. (A landmark may be more useful than a badly estimated bearing). from where she was standing looking towards walsall

F. Angle of Sight. (Estimated heights are unreliable). She would say 40ft as it was heights with her house

G. Distance. (By reference to a known landmark wherever possible). 5-6 yrds.

H. Movements. (Changes in E, F and G may be of more use than estimates of course and speed). Moving down + towards her as if going to crash

J. Meteorological Conditions During Observations. (Moving clouds, haze, mist etc). Very Clear, No Clouds

1

* there were three people in front two sitting and one standing (the inside was very well lit) all appeared to be wearing White Suits. The object was quiet at first till it approached her but can't describe sound there was also no smell. after she ran into house and looked out of window she saw it leave and from the back there were three sets of lights eache set had four lights.

2

FIG. 44 A completed UFO report form from the MoD files, recording a sighting from the West Midlands in 1988 of a object containing 'three people … wearing white suits.' DEFE 24/1928/1

A similar report was made one night in November 1992 when a Brighton man phoned the RAF to describe a brightly-lit UFO shaped like a 'squashed rugby ball' that hovered above his house. Through windows in the side he saw two men wearing beige uniforms standing in front of what looked like machinery. When one of the crew members appeared to notice him the lights went out and the UFO disappeared out towards the English Channel. A RAF note on the report reads:

> 'Caller sounded genuine enough and his main concern seemed to be that he didn't want to talk too much about the craft if it was "one of ours that we wanted to keep secret".' (DEFE 24/1954/1)

One of the most bizarre examples of an 'alien encounter' in the MoD files was described in a report from RAF Wattisham, Suffolk on 21 November 1989. This described how the RAF community liaison officer at the base received a call from 'a distressed female' who refused to divulge her name and address. After he reassured her she revealed how at 10.30 pm the previous night she had been walking her dog on a sports field not far from her home in Norwich. She was approached by a man with fair hair and a Scandinavian accent who wore a light brown garment similar to a flying suit.

> 'He asked her if she was aware of stories about [crop circles], and then went on to explain that he was from another planet similar to earth and that the circles had been caused by others like him who had travelled to earth. He went on to explain that the purpose of their visits were [sic] friendly but that they were told not to have contact with the people of earth for fear that they might be treated as a potential threat. He had spoken to her because he felt it was important for contact between the two people to occur. The caller said that she was completely terrified while this was taking place and couldn't remember much else about the conversation. After about ten minutes the man left her and she ran towards home until she heard a loud buzzing noise behind her and turned to see a large spherical object, glowing orange-white, rising vertically from behind some trees, which rose steadily until out of sight.' (DEFE 24/1938/1)

The RAF Wattisham report ended with the following comment: '[our] conversation with the lady lasted about one hour followed by another ten minutes when she rang again. I could not get her to divulge her name or address but I believe that this was a genuine call.'

A matter for the civil police

Public fascination with stories of alien abductions spread across the world following the publication in 1981 of a book by American artist and UFOlogist Budd Hopkins, *Missing Time*. This was followed in 1987 by science fiction author Whitley Strieber's personal account of encounters with small creatures he called 'the visitors'. *Communion* went on to become an international bestseller and its striking cover image of an alien face ensured that everyone in the western world was aware what these mysterious creatures looked like. The inverted, pear-shaped head and the black slanting eyes soon became the trademark of the grey aliens. In the aftermath of these books and the tabloid stories that accompanied them, the number of letters received by the Ministry of Defence describing contacts with aliens began to grow.

In 1992 a new UFO desk officer, Nick Pope, opened a file titled 'Unidentified Flying Objects (UFOs): Close encounter reports, Alien entities, abductions'. Unlike most of his predecessors he had developed a personal interest in the subject. Displaying a spirit of openness rarely seen before in the MoD, Pope collected accounts of alien contacts recorded in files dating back to 1985 and was willing to make copies of these available to UFOlogists. In a covering letter sent to a number of UFO organizations in 1992 he wrote:

'In my time here I have not received a single report of any close encounters but we have, in the past, received a very small number of letters that might fall into the category of a close encounter of the third or fourth kind.'

He added:

'As we receive so few, and recognizing their value to researchers, I agreed that these reports could be released ... I draw no conclusions from this material, and remain open-minded as to what may have prompted these reports.' (DEFE 24/1943/1)

This file contains five letters dated between 1985 and 1992 from people who wished to tell the MoD about their contacts with alien beings, including one account dated January 1985 by a Cheshire man who wished to reveal details of his 'physical and psychic contacts' with green aliens that began in his childhood. One of these, a being called Algar, was killed in 1981 by another race of beings who wanted to stop him making contact with the MoD. The writer claimed he had visited their secret bases and described how he and his wife saw one of their craft shot down by rival aliens over Wallasey Town Hall. A contemporary MoD note on the letter simply reads: 'No reply sent.'

One account in particular from the file stands out as eerily similar to the stories described in the books by John Fuller and Budd Hopkins. The Lancashire woman who sent it had clearly thought long and hard before writing to the Ministry with a story she realized sounded unbelievable. Her letter described how one night in October 1982 she and her mother were returning to a town near Manchester from visiting a sick relative. Whilst driving on the normally busy East Lancashire Road, they spotted a strange light in the sky that appeared to pace their car. When she tried to accelerate, the car was inexplicably slowed by the appearance of 'an odd-looking black type 1930s car that was in front of ours ... the driver was tall, stocky and wearing a strange German-type hat.' Even though the car in front was dangerously close, this odd-looking driver did not appear to show any sign of movement and as their car came to a standstill, with the electric system going haywire, she decided to open her window and look out.

The writer claimed he had visited [the aliens'] secret bases and described how he and his wife saw one of their craft shot down by rival aliens over Wallasey Town Hall

'To my horror, above my car was an unusually shaped craft of some kind, about 30 feet above us. The lights on this object were huge and very dazzling; the size of the thing was roughly about the size of a double decker bus on its side ... the strangest thing though was that ... we both felt as though time had stood still and it was very frightening indeed.' (DEFE 24/1943/1)

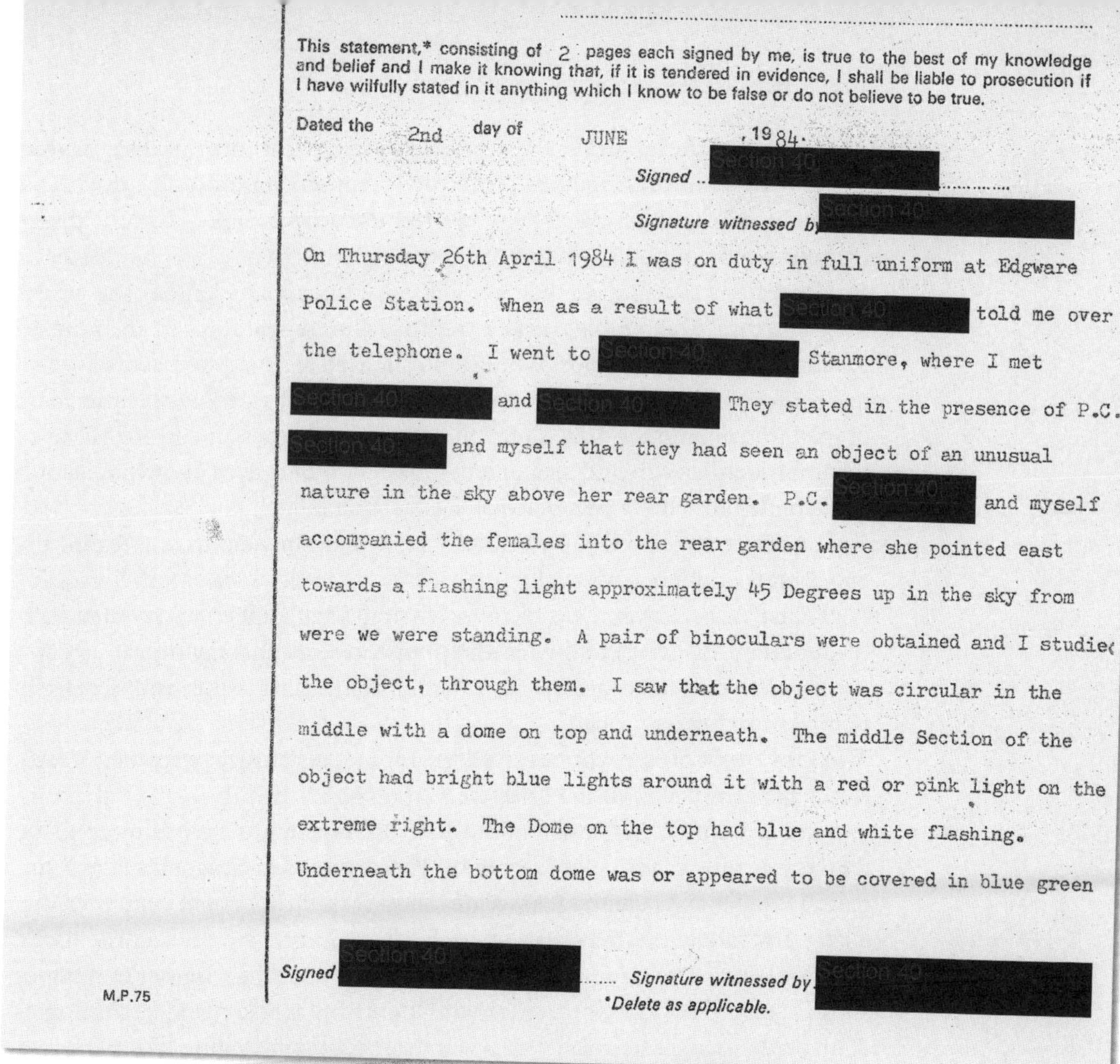

This statement,* consisting of 2 pages each signed by me, is true to the best of my knowledge and belief and I make it knowing that, if it is tendered in evidence, I shall be liable to prosecution if I have wilfully stated in it anything which I know to be false or do not believe to be true.

Dated the 2nd day of JUNE , 1984.

Signed ....██████ Section 40 ██████........

Signature witnessed by ██████ Section 40 ██████

On Thursday 26th April 1984 I was on duty in full uniform at Edgware Police Station. When as a result of what ██ Section 40 ██ told me over the telephone. I went to ██ Section 40 ██ Stanmore, where I met ██ Section 40 ██ and ██ Section 40 ██ They stated in the presence of P.C. ██ Section 40 ██ and myself that they had seen an object of an unusual nature in the sky above her rear garden. P.C. ██ Section 40 ██ and myself accompanied the females into the rear garden where she pointed east towards a flashing light approximately 45 Degrees up in the sky from were we were standing. A pair of binoculars were obtained and I studied the object, through them. I saw that the object was circular in the middle with a dome on top and underneath. The middle Section of the object had bright blue lights around it with a red or pink light on the extreme right. The Dome on the top had blue and white flashing. Underneath the bottom dome was or appeared to be covered in blue green

Signed ██ Section 40 ██ Signature witnessed by ██ Section 40 ██

*Delete as applicable.

M.P.75

Unidentified object as seen by PC ██████ and PC ██████ through binoculars at approximately 11pm dated 26th April 1984.

Blue and white lights

red light

Blue lights

White Blue, Green Pink/Red lights

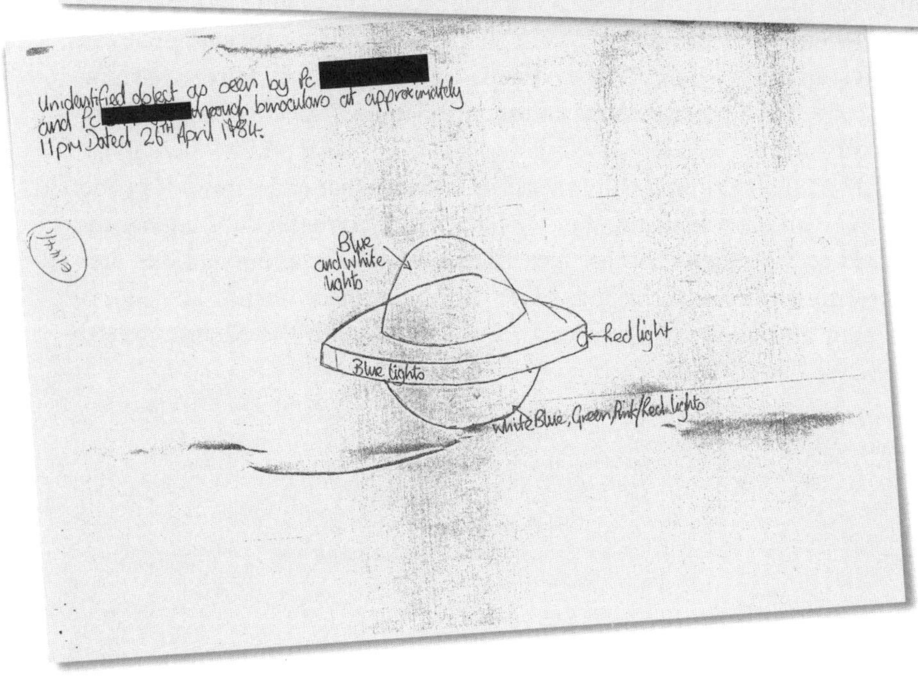

FIG. 45 (ABOVE) Part of a statement by a police officer called to witness a UFO seen by members of the public in Edgware, North London, during April 1984.
DEFE 24/1925/1

FIG. 46 (LEFT) A police officer's drawing of the Edgware UFO.
DEFE 24/1923/1

After this bizarre interlude she screamed and the car in front disappeared, along with the hovering UFO. The two women immediately drove to a nearby petrol station where they spotted the object again before it disappeared into the night sky. When the letter writer arrived home her husband was distraught, fearing she had been involved in an accident, as she was so long overdue. The couple worked out that almost one hour of the journey could not be accounted for. Worse still, she was alarmed to discover bruising on her legs and suffered sickness and 'terrible dreams' in the aftermath of the UFO encounter. Like Betty and Barney Hill, these involved visions of being inside the craft and seeing a tall man with blue eyes and white shoulder-length hair who wore a one-piece silver suit.

Her letter to the Ministry ended with a plea for help as she feared the experience might be repeated:

'Please … could you help me to solve or at least explain to me what happened on that road and why it happened to me and my mum… I can't talk to anyone about this because I don't think most people would believe. But I swear it happened.'

The UFO desk officer who received the report was clearly perplexed by this lady's detailed account and struggled to respond with the standard explanations of weather balloons and aircraft lights. He was forced to concede that some rare cases, such as hers, 'where rational explanations are not readily available … can be very disturbing'. The MoD could not, however, justify any follow-up investigation, 'unless a clear threat to the security of the UK had been identified.' The best he could do was to advise her to contact a UFO society or consult a doctor who 'may not be able to explain the incidents, but … might be able to help you to stop worrying about them.'[17]

In 1996 another 'abductee' challenged the MoD to justify its policy of disinterest in cases where British citizens claimed to have suffered harm as a result of actions by occupants of unidentified craft in UK airspace. The reply stated firmly:

'Abduction is a criminal offence and as such is a matter for the civil police. As the MoD is not aware of any evidence which might substantiate the existence of extraterrestrial activity, the matter of abduction by alien lifeforms is a non-issue as far as [we] are concerned.'[18]

TURN OF THE CENTURY UFOs

THE QUESTION 'Do UFOs exist?' is no longer an issue for David Hastings, a veteran pilot with 40 years flying experience that began with service in the RAF. Like many civilian pilots and some military aircrew, a dramatic personal sighting left him in no doubt the answer to that question is an emphatic 'Yes!' The event that convinced Hastings happened on the final leg of an epic trans-American trip. On the afternoon of 9 September 1985 he and his experienced co-pilot had just left the Grand Canyon behind them in their twin-engined Cessna Skymaster. As they approached restricted airspace at 10,500 ft above the Mojave Desert ground radar reported: 'no conflicting traffic'.

Hastings recently described what happened next, saying:

'You can imagine our surprise when a small dot appeared at our same altitude and in our 12 o'clock which rapidly grew in size. We were both convinced that we were about to have a head-on mid-air collision with a high speed military jet aircraft and both pushed hard down on the control columns, expecting a tremendous bang and the end of our flight.'[1]

At that point a huge black shadow passed over the cockpit. It vanished without making a sound and left no turbulence behind it. The two shaken pilots turned and asked each other: 'What the hell was that?' A check with ground control told them that still nothing was showing on radar but as minutes passed and tension grew both men were gripped by the feeling that *something* was flying in formation alongside them. Hastings then remembered his camera in the back of the plane. Unstrapping himself, he grabbed

FIG. 47 Two photographs taken by pilot David Hastings during a near-miss over the Mojave Desert near the mysterious 'Area 51' on 9 September 1985. The second shows a mysterious elongated object. UFO or experimental aircraft?

it, taking two shots from the port windows before the feeling passed, leaving them 'shaken and puzzled'.

When the film was developed the pair were staggered by the results. While the first snap showed just the Cessna's port wing and the mountains below, the second showed a dark, elongated object with what appears to be some form of heat or exhaust emerging from its underside. Later in the trans-American trip a friend in the US Navy asked to borrow the photograph. All he would say on returning it was 'no comment'.

This reaction is given another dimension when you consider where the sighting occurred. The two men's trip had taken them past restricted military airspace and close to Edwards Air Force Base and the secret Nevada Test and Training Range that contains Groom Lake. Both of these fall within the mysterious region known as 'Area 51' and both have, over the years, been home to a number of 'black project' programmes such as the Stealth fighter and the B-2 flying wing. Could it be that Hastings' near-miss had been with some advanced top secret military aircraft? Hastings for one remains unconvinced by this idea and certain the object he saw that day was not man-made. 'Having flown for over 40 years like most pilots I have always accepted UFOs,' he told me. 'You only have to look up at the sky at night to realize that we cannot be the only planet that supports life.'

UFOs and pilots

In retirement David Hastings felt confident writing and talking about his experience. For a pilot this is actually quite unusual. Flying aircraft is a responsible job and, quite understandably, few wish to be known as 'the one who sees flying saucers', however sure they might be of what they have seen. The late Graham Sheppard, a British Airways pilot who made two sightings of his own and famously spoke out on the issue, estimated that some 10 per cent of aircrew had some form of UFO experience during their career. In 1999 he said: 'I must have spoken to 20 pilots who have had sightings but all are adamant they do not want publicity.'[2]

One of the earliest sightings from the modern era remains one of the most unusual. It was reported by the crew and passengers of a BOAC Stratocruiser during a flight from New York to London in June 1954. The captain, James Howard, was interviewed live by BBC news on landing and his story was widely reported by national newspapers who treated it as a reliable report from a credible witness. Captain Howard described how he and co-pilot Lee Boyd watched a group of strange objects for 18 minutes as they cruised at 19,000 ft above Goose Bay in Labrador. When first spotted, shortly after 9 pm, the sun was low on the horizon and six small dark objects were visible below the port beam. As they climbed the crew saw these were arranged on either side of a large 'jellyfish-shaped' object that was constantly changing form. Howard contacted Goose Bay by radio and an F-94 fighter was diverted to intercept them, but before it reached the scene, 'the small objects seemed to enter the larger [UFO], and then the big one shrank'.

Howard's report was investigated by Project Blue Book, who decided it was possible the UFOs were a mirage of a bright planet created by unusual weather conditions. However, when pressed by the BBC, Captain Howard said there was 'no question that this was not an illusion … and that it was being intelligently handled.'[3]

UFO reports from aircrew are regarded as particularly persuasive evidence, as pilots are trained observers who often have many years of flying experience. Captain Howard's sighting was the first of many by civilian pilots to receive wide publicity in Britain, but until 1968 there was no formal procedure whereby aircrew could file their reports directly with the Ministry of Defence. As a result news of some incidents never reached the MoD or arrived so late that investigation was impossible as vital evidence, such as radar tapes, had been lost. But as a direct result of the UFO flap of 1967 (see p.73), the MoD was forced to improve the system whereby they received UFO reports from a range of official sources such as the police and airports.

From January 1968 all air traffic control centres were instructed to report any unusual sightings directly to RAF West Drayton so they could be investigated quickly. These instructions now form part of the Manual of Air Traffic Control, the service's reference book. In addition, the Civil Aviation Authority has, since 1976, kept a record of UFO incidents reported by British aircrew alongside a range of other more commonplace hazards. These range from other aircraft that stray from their flight plan to microlites, gliders and hot-air balloons. In those cases where crews report a near-miss with another aircraft, an independent team of experts is called in to investigate. The task of the Joint Airmiss Working Group, which is made up of both military and civilian aviation specialists, is to assess the possibility of a collision and, where possible, take steps to reduce future risks.

During a frank exchange of views within the MoD, an intelligence officer said reports of UFOs in the busy air lanes over the English Channel raised 'flight safety questions'

But when a near-miss is reported as having involved a UFO the team has found it difficult to reach any conclusions as such incidents cannot be neatly pigeonholed into any tangible hazard category. As a result, the potential risks posed by UFOs—as in something real but unknown—have tended to be downplayed by both the MoD and the Joint Airmiss Working Group, which have dealt with unexplained incidents on a case-by-case basis.

The MoD's informal policy of down-playing potential hazards to aircraft posed by UFOs is illustrated by files at the National Archives that cover a 1977 review of policy. During a frank exchange of views within the MoD, an intelligence officer said reports of UFOs in the busy air lanes over the English Channel raised 'flight safety questions'. Responding to his concerns, Wing Commander D.B. Hamley of the RAF's Inspectorate of Flight Safety admitted the MoD's attitude to UFOs was 'ostrich-like', adding: 'If we do not look, it will go away. If it does not officially exist, I cannot get terribly worked up if someone sees one, in the "busy air lanes over the Channel" or anywhere else.'[4]

DATE AND TIME OF INCIDENT IN GMT | M | REPORTED BY RADIO TO LON 127.1 AFIS· TWR· APP· ACC· FIC * AT 04/21/91 ~ 2000 /Z

In cloud/rain/snow. sleet/fog/haze
Flying into/out of sun
Reported/estimated flight visibility — 30 Km/NM*
— Km/NM*

SECTION 2 - DETAILED INFORMATION.

DESCRIPTION OF OTHER AIRCRAFT, IF RELEVANT:
Type, high/low wing, N. of engines
Radio call sign, registration
Markings, colour, lighting
Other available details | N |

OBJECT SIMILAR MISSILE - WITHOUT EXHAUST FLAME -
UNKNOWN
LIGHT BROWN - SIMILAR DESERT COLOUR
ABOUT 3 METERS LENGTH - ROUND SHAPE -

DESCRIPTION OF INCIDENT:
If desired add comment or suggestion, including your opinion on the probable cause of the incident.
(In case of near-collision give information on respective flight paths, estimated vertical and horizontal sighting and miss distances between aircraft and avoiding action taken by either o/c) | O |

DURING DESCENT, AT FL 222 I SAW FOR A-
BOUT 3-4 SECONDS A FLYING OBJECT, VERY
SIMILAR TO A MISSILE, LIGHT BROWN COLOU-
RED, WITH A TRACK OPPOSITE THEN MINE
WHICH WAS 320° - IT WAS HIGHER THAN
US ABOUT 1000 ft -

AT ONCE I SAID " LOOK OUT - LOOK OUT" TO MY
COPILOT WHO LOOKED OUT AND SAW WHAT I HAD
SEEN - AS SOON AS THE OBJECT CROSSED US I ASKED TO
THE ACC/OPERATOR IF HE SAW SOMETHING ON HIS SCREEN
AND HE ANSWERED " I SEE AN UNKNOWN TARGET 10 N.M.
BEHIND YOU" -

DATE 04/22/91 TIME 8 P.M.
PLACE LONDON
OF COMPLETION OF FORM | Mod. (6924) NAV UNI A4 |

FUNCTION AND SIGNATURE CPT
OF PERSON — Section 40
REPORT | FUNCTION AND SIGNATURE OF PERSON RECEIVING REPORT

SECTION 3 - SUPPLEMENTARY INFORMATION
by ATS unit concerned (not for pilot's use)

HOW REPORT RECEIVED | P | RADIO/ TELEPHONE/ TELEPRINTER* AT ARO/ AFIS/ TWR/ APP/ ACC/ FIC *
DETAILS OF ATS ACTION:
Clearance, incident observed on radar, warning given, result of local enquiry, etc. | Q |

* Delete as appropriate

SIGNATURE OF ATS OFFICER _____ DATE/ TIME GMT _____
ICAO - PANS RAC (DOC 4444 - RAC/ 501/ 10

On collision course!

This 'ostrich-like' official attitude towards reports of near-misses between aircraft and UFOs continued into the 1990s when a spate of disturbing incidents occurred over the British Isles. Although many of these were reported by the media at the time, full details of the official investigations and their findings did not emerge until the relevant MoD files were opened by the National Archives in 2008.

The most surprising fact to emerge was that the most dramatic encounter recorded in the files was never subject to a full 'airmiss' inquiry. The files reveal that this report was investigated internally by the MoD, although the captain reported it officially as a near collision with an unidentified flying object. On 21 April 1991, the pilot of Alitalia Flight AZ 284, carrying a total of 57 passengers en route from Milan, was on his final descent into Heathrow airport. The jet had crossed the Channel coast and was around 6 miles west of Lydd in Kent and under London Air Traffic Control. It was around 8 pm and still light when, according to the captain's handwritten report:

'during descent, at [22,200 ft] I saw for about 3–4 seconds a flying object, very similar to a missile, light brown coloured … with a track opposite than mine… It was higher than us, about 1000 ft. At once I said: "*Look Out! Look Out!*" to my co-pilot who looked out and saw what I had seen. As soon as the object crossed us I asked [Heathrow] if he saw

FIG. 48 The 'near collision' report made by the pilot of Alitalia Flight AZ 284 C to the Civil Aviation Authority following his close encounter with a missile-shaped UFO over Lydd, Kent, in April 1991.
DEFE 24/1923/1

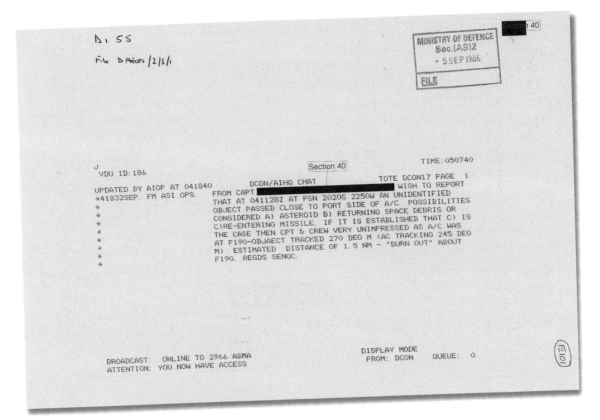

```
J
  VDU ID:186                          Section 40              TIME: 050740

  UPDATED BY AIOP AT 041840      DCON/AIHQ CHAT          TOTE DCON17 PAGE  1
  *41832SEP. FM ASI OPS.    FROM CAPT                         WISH TO REPORT
                            THAT AT 041128Z AT PSN 2020S 2250W AN UNIDENTIFIED
  *                         OBJECT PASSED CLOSE TO PORT SIDE OF A/C. POSSIBILITIES
  *                         CONSIDERED A) ASTEROID B) RETURNING SPACE DEBRIS OR
  *                         C)RE-ENTERING MISSILE. IF IT IS ESTABLISHED THAT C) IS
  *                         THE CASE THEN CPT & CREW VERY UNIMPRESSED AS A/C WAS
  *                         AT F190-OBJAECT TRACKED 270 DEG M (AC TRACKING 245 DEG
  *                         M) ESTIMATED DISTANCE OF 1.5 NM — "BURN OUT" ABOUT
  *                         F190. REGDS SENOC.



  BROADCAST:  ONLINE TO 2966 ASMA               DISPLAY MODE
  ATTENTION: YOU NOW HAVE ACCESS                  FROM: DCON    QUEUE:  0
```

FIG.49 One of many reports by civilian aircrew of near-misses with UFOs; this example was reported to the MoD by the captain of an airliner flying over the South Atlantic on 5 September 1986. DEFE 24/1924/1

something on his screen and he answered "I see an unknown target 10 [nautical miles] behind you." (DEFE 24/1953/1)

The air traffic controller's report, a few pages further on in the same National Archives file, confirmed that 'at the time of the incident a primary response was observed behind [the aircraft] tracking northeast', but checks with coastguards, police and the army failed to identify it. A replay of the radar tapes revealed the track of the 'primary contact' had been recorded on film and scribbled on one of the sheets are the words: 'Possible slow-moving target—Cruise Missile?'

The *Sunday Times* reported the outcome of inquiries that had been made by the MoD to trace the origin of the mysterious 'missile' and quoted an aviation expert who said it was possible the object could have been a stray military target or 'drone' used for air defence practice. Initially, it certainly seemed possible that whatever the captain had seen came from the nearby army ranges at Lydd or from a ship at sea. However, the file on the incident makes it clear that the MoD soon ruled this out.

Their investigation ended two months later when it became apparent they would be unable to explain the incident. The MoD's bland conclusion simply read:

'In the absence of any clear evidence which could be used to identify the object it is our intention to treat this sighting like that of any other Unidentified Flying Object and therefore we will not be able to undertake any further investigation into the sighting.' (DEFE 24/1953/1)

This incident was just the tip of a small iceberg. During the summer of 1991 there were a further six UFO reports made by airline crews and passengers but only one of these was subject to a detailed investigation by the 'airmiss' working group.

On 15 July the crew of a Britannia Airways Boeing 737 returning from Greece and descending into Gatwick under London control at 14,000 ft saw 'a small black lozenge-shaped object' zoom past at high speed just 100 yds off the port side of the aircraft. Gatwick confirmed a 'primary contact' was visible on radar 10 nautical miles behind the 737 moving at a speed estimated at 120 mph. Immediately air traffic control warned a following aircraft which made 'avoiding turns to the left to avoid the [UFO], which had appeared to change heading towards it, but its pilot reported seeing nothing.' This incident could not be ignored and a formal 'airmiss' investigation was opened. In their report, completed in April 1992, the working group said they 'were unsure what damage could have occurred had the object struck the 737; the general opinion was that there had been a possible risk of collision.'[5]

The working group admitted they could not explain the incident but suggested the 'unidentified object' that came so close to the 737 might have been an escaped balloon. Shortly after their report was completed, the Civil Aviation Authority's in-house magazine, *Airways*, published a photograph of a toy balloon called the 'UFO Solar'. Manufactured in Europe and costing just 99p, when inflated the balloon was 10 ft in length, black, lozenge-shaped and—according to the makers—capable of reaching 'extraordinary altitudes' up to 30,000 ft. It cannot be doubted the appearance of this balloon fits some aspects of the crew's story, but as in so many UFO incidents it is never possible to say conclusively: 'case closed'.

> The 737 was cruising just above the clouds and visibility was at least 10 miles when, without warning, a glowing wedge-shaped object appeared following a course directly towards the plane

Balloons are unlikely to have been responsible for another airmiss incident reported by a British Airways crew, this time near Manchester airport. At 6.45 pm on 6 January 1995 their Boeing 737, carrying 60 passengers from Milan, had descended to 4,000 ft above the Peak District hills in preparation for landing. The 737 was cruising just above the clouds and visibility was at least 10 miles when, without warning, a glowing wedge-shaped object appeared following a course directly towards the plane.

The captain had this exchange with air traffic controllers:

B-737 (6.48 pm): ...we just had something go down the [right hand side] just above us very fast.

MANCHESTER: Well there's nothing on radar. Was it ... an aircraft?

B-737: Well, it had lights, it went down the starboard side very quick.

MANCHESTER: And above you?

B737: ... just slightly above us, yeah. [6]

The 737's captain told the working group this UFO was in sight for just two seconds and created no noise or air displacement as it whizzed past. He said it was illuminated with a number of small lights making it look like a Christmas tree. The first officer said he instinctively ducked when he saw 'a dark object pass down the right hand side of the aircraft at high speed; it was wedge-shaped with what could have been a black stripe down the side ... he felt sure that what he saw was a solid object—not a bird, balloon or kite.'

The investigation was unable to trace any civilian or military aircraft and ruled out a stray hang-glider or night-flying microlite as being 'extremely unlikely'. But although they could not identify the object the working group pointed out that almost all unusual sightings of this kind 'can be explained by a range of known natural phenomena.'

One possibility independently proposed by astronomer Ian Ridpath and UFOlogist Jenny Randles was a fireball meteor. They pointed out that it was not unusual for experienced pilots to misidentify such bright fireballs as they tend to appear and disappear suddenly, without warning. In darkness, with no reference points, it would be easy to conclude an object was alarmingly close to their aircraft when in fact it was many miles away, burning up in the upper atmosphere.

Nevertheless, the airmiss working group commended the two pilots for their courage in submitting their report. They noted that sightings by aircrew 'are often the object of derision, but the Group hopes that this example will encourage pilots who experience unusual sightings to report them without fear of ridicule.' Their report, published in February 1996, decided there was no doubt that both

'saw an object ... that was of sufficient significance to prompt an airmiss report. Unfortunately the nature and identity of this object remains unknown. To speculate about extraterrestrial activity, fascinating though it may be, is not within the Group's remit and must be left to those whose interest lies in this field.' [7]

UFO or black project?

Near collisions with unidentified objects, such as those reported by pilots like David Hastings and the captain of Alitalia flight AZ 284, highlight the frequent links between the UFO phenomenon and military secrets. The most recent MoD files released by the National Archives contain many hints that certain types of experimental military aircraft have been seen and reported as UFOs in recent years.

One possible example occurred late on the night of 22 September 1987 when the Goodwin family were returning to their home in Staffordshire from a visit to Walsall illuminations. In his account, Dominic Goodwin, then 21 years old, said they had just passed through Baggots Wood when his father, who was driving, shouted: 'What on earth is that?' Dominic, who I subsequently interviewed, continued: 'when I looked up I saw the underneath of what seemed to be a triangular-shaped craft. [The UFO] was moving very slowly, almost stationary. I wound down my window and there was no noise at all.' Mr Goodwin senior added:

> 'I thought it was a plane about to crash, but all of a sudden it stopped and hovered before us. I have never seen anything like it ever before. It was just like something out of a Steven Spielberg movie; I was petrified. The object was huge, about 50–100 feet long, triangular in shape surrounded by about 30 different brightly-coloured lights flashing around it in sequence. It was only about 100 feet above us and its light lit up the ground...' (DEFE 24/1930/1)

The Goodwins felt sure this was no ordinary aeroplane. In fact their story was just one of many similar sightings of silent, triangular-shaped UFOs that were reported from many parts of Britain and Europe during the decade that followed. In 1990 sightings became so frequent in Belgium that on one occasion the Belgian air force scrambled F-16 fighters to investigate. Officials later admitted their pilots had detected something on radar that remained unexplained. Were these nocturnal craft, as many suspected at the time, a new American stealth aircraft operating secretly from RAF bases in Britain, or were they a UK-designed prototype developed using cutting edge stealth technology?

The Cold War came to an end with the fall of the Berlin Wall in November 1989, but mutual suspicions continued on both sides of the former Iron Curtain. Old habits die hard and during the decade that followed even former allies began to suspect each other of using high performance aircraft to spy upon their territory. At the same time, there was a natural temptation on behalf of some aviation journalists and their sources in the defence industry to attribute impressive UFO sightings to advanced 'black projects'. In many cases, the truth often turned out to be more mundane.

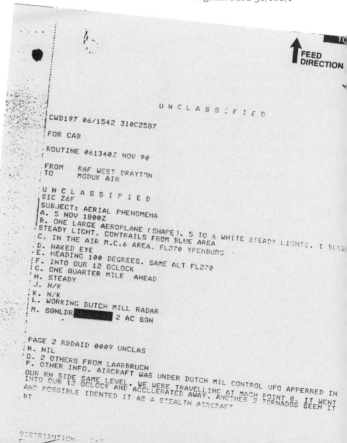

FIG. 50 The report received by the MoD from the pilots of a group of RAF Tornadoes who were overtaken by a UFO whilst on exercise over Germany in November 1990. They suspected it was the then-secret United States Air Force Stealth Fighter. DEFE 31/180/1

In 1990 the crews of six RAF Tornado jets were taking part in an exercise at 27,000 ft over Germany on the evening of 5 November under the control of Dutch military radar. As darkness fell at 6 pm their aircraft were suddenly overtaken by a large flying object. In a military signal to RAF West Drayton the RAF flight commander described how the UFO 'went into our 12 o'clock [position] and accelerated away.' He described seeing an object surrounded by 'five to six white steady lights [and] one blue steady light [with] contrails from [the] blue area.' The crews discussed their experience and decided the UFO could have been the American Stealth fighter.

Although still a military secret, this aircraft was frequently in the news after photographs showing its distinctive triangular profile were declassified. Commenting upon their report, an intelligence officer wrote: 'Clearly the incident happened and clearly the pilots saw what they believe (with hindsight) to be a stealth aircraft [but] I doubt very much if the USAF or even the Soviet Air Force (if they were flying) would admit to anything.'[8]

A file opened by the National Archives in 2009 reveals the MoD did not investigate the Tornado crews' report because it occurred outside UK airspace, but officials evidently suspected some type of 'black project' aircraft was involved. If they had made further inquiries they would have discovered other sightings had been made by aircrews elsewhere in Europe at the same date and time, some of which described loud bangs as the formation of lights moved through the sky. Space tracking stations identified these

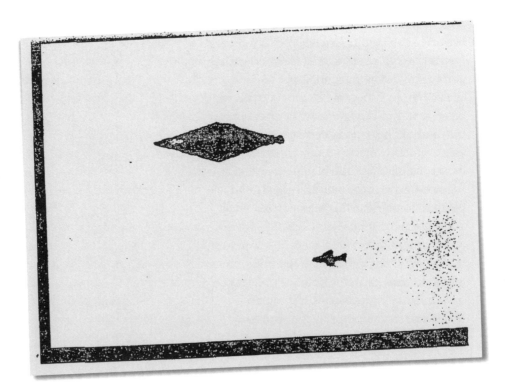

FIG. 51 A photocopy of an original colour print showing a strange diamond-shaped UFO accompanied by a Harrier jet, seen over Calvine in Scotland in daylight one afternoon in August 1990. The MoD's Defence Intelligence Staff were unable to explain the object depicted in the photograph. DEFE 31/180/1

lights as the debris from a Soviet rocket which had earlier launched the *Gorizont 21* communications satellite into orbit.

In hindsight there can be no doubt this is what the Tornado pilots saw, but at the time the MoD filed this report away as 'unexplained'.

The Cosford incident

Alongside this can be placed the events that occurred in the early hours of 30/31 March 1993 when another UFO flap flopped onto the MoD's doorstep. Recently released files show the MoD alone received more than 30 separate sightings that were made on this night, including reports from police officers in Devon and Cornwall and others from military personnel at RAF Cosford, near Wolverhampton. Most of these witnesses described seeing a formation of two or three white lights with vapour trails moving swiftly across the sky in a southeasterly direction, some claiming the lights appeared in a triangular formation.

The MoD's UFO desk officer, Nick Pope, was so concerned by this flap he asked the RAF to examine radar tapes from the night in question, but nothing unusual could be seen. It later emerged that most of these sightings could be traced to the decay into Earth's atmosphere of a Russian rocket used to launch the *Cosmos 2238* spy satellite into orbit. This explanation was confirmed by similar sightings from Ireland and France that were made on the same evening. UK astronomer Gary Anthony and NASA space debris expert Dr Nick Johnson have produced a computer simulation of the trajectory followed by the debris that neatly explains the majority of sightings reported that night.

But before full details of this explanation had emerged, some MoD officials appear to have convinced themselves that the March 1993 flap was caused by a genuine UFO. On 22 April the head of the UFO desk took matters a step further by sending a memo to the Assistant Chief of Air Staff, Sir Anthony Bagnall, that claimed: 'there would seem to be some evidence ... that an unidentified object (or objects) of unknown origin was operating over the UK'. He added: 'If there has been some activity of US origins which is known to a limited circle in MoD and is not being acknowledged it is difficult to investigate further.'[9]

Back in the First World War, when reports of phantom Zeppelins flooded into the War Office, some officials were prepared to believe at least some of these UFOs really *were* airships, until it became obvious this was not possible. Likewise, during the 1990s their successors at the MoD suspected that advanced spy planes or even aliens might be responsible for some UFO flaps. For a time the UFO desk adopted a slogan that would become the catchphrase for the popular TV series *The X-Files*: 'I want to believe.'

Aurora — the plane that never existed

During the 1980s a detachment of SR-71 spy planes was based at RAF Mildenhall, Suffolk, headquarters of the US 3rd Air Force in the UK, until shortly after the fall of the Berlin Wall. During this period rumours spread that Mildenhall and other United States Air Force bases in England were being used by other black project aircraft, particularly during the period of NATO operations in the former Yugoslavia where the F-117 fighter saw action. This coincided with a dramatic rise in the number of sightings of large triangular UFOs such as those described by Dominic Goodwin. They were often called 'Silent Vulcans' owing to their sleek delta-winged shape, huge size and apparently noiseless flight. Despite their unconventional shape these UFOs often displayed the flashing white strobes and rotating red and green beacons that are the standard aircraft lighting systems used for night-flying.

Stealth technology has advanced in leaps and bounds since the F-117 and the B-2 bomber were removed from the secret list, and speculation has continued to grow about what might constitute the next generation of 'black project' aircraft. From the late 1980s rumours spread that the United States Department of Defense was testing a highly advanced hypersonic aircraft as a replacement for the ageing SR-71. The mystery began in 1985 when a Pentagon budget report listed a project called 'Aurora' alongside the SR-71, apparently by mistake. The United States Air Force later explained the error by claiming the name was used in the document to conceal the existence of another then-secret project, the B-2 Stealth bomber. But by then it was impossible to put the genie back inside the bottle.

Although Secretary of the Air Force, Donald Rice, went on record to flatly deny such a project existed, throughout the 1990s sightings of the Aurora frequently made headlines in UFO magazines and specialist aviation journals such as *Jane's Defence*. The Aurora was said to be capable of incredible feats, such as high altitude flight at Mach 8 at a top speed of 5,300 mph. In 1992 *The Scotsman* published a story that claimed an anonymous air traffic controller had seen a fast-moving blip 'emerge from the area of the joint NATO–RAF station at RAF Machrihanish at approximately three times the speed of sound.' Puzzled by the experience, he called up the remote airfield on the tip of the Kintyre peninsula but was told to forget what he had seen.[10]

This story prompted Scottish MPs to ask in Parliament if permission had been given to the Americans for secret flights through British airspace. Privately, the MoD advised Defence Secretary Tom King on 2 March 1992 that the last SR-71 left the UK from RAF Mildenhall in 1990 and added: 'There may or may not be an Aurora project. There is no knowledge in the MoD of a "black" programme of this nature, although it would not surprise the relevant desk officers in the Air Staff and DIS if it did exist.'[11]

Despite denials, the Aurora story refused to die. When in December 1992 *Jane's Defence Weekly* published a statement from an impressive eye-witness, relations between the US and UK were put under further strain. Chris Gibson's account was the most credible to emerge from the welter of rumours that preceded it. He was a member of the Royal Observer Corps and an expert in aircraft identification, so his account of what he saw flying low over the North Sea one afternoon in August 1989 carries the weight of experience. Gibson was working on an oil rig at Galveston Key, about 100 miles northeast of Great Yarmouth, at the time. His attention was attracted by a colleague who returned from the deck calling out:

I looked up, saw a KC-135 tanker and two [USAF] F-111s, but was amazed to see the triangle. I'm trained in instant recognition, but this triangle had me stopped dead

> '"Have a look at this": I looked up, saw a KC-135 tanker and two [USAF] F-111s, but was amazed to see the triangle. I am trained in instant recognition, but this triangle had me stopped dead. My first thought was that it was another F-111, but … it was too long and it didn't look like one. My next thought was that it was an F-117, as the highly swept platform of the [Stealth fighter] had just been made public. Again the triangle was too long and had no gaps.'[12]

Gibson was left struggling for ideas and as the formation passed by he realized the two men had seen something that did not officially exist. On checking his aircraft recognition manual, he found nothing matched and immediately sat down to sketch what he had seen. Publication of his drawings prompted the British Air Attaché in Washington to write to the Air Staff in London for advice on what he should tell the Americans. His letter, dated 22 December 1992, read:

> '[The US] Secretary of the Air Force, the Honorable Donald B. Rice, was to say the least incensed by the renewed speculation, and the implied suggestion that he had lied to Congress by stating that Aurora did not exist … the whole affair is causing considerable irritation within HQ [US Air Force] and any helpful comments we can make to defuse the situation would be appreciated.'[13]

To date, no convincing explanation for the North Sea sighting has been provided by the MoD and the United States has never confirmed the existence of the mysterious Aurora. Writing in 1997 Gibson concluded: 'Whether this aircraft was Aurora is debatable [and] my background precludes jumping to conclusions based on a single piece of evidence. I don't know what it was, but it was the only aircraft I have ever seen that I could not identify.'[14]

Open skies?

Public fascination with UFOs, alien abductions and crop circles peaked in the mid-1990s, partly as a result of the popularity of the hit US TV series *The X-Files*. The fictional plot embraced UFO conspiracy theories and series creator Chris Carter's storyline appeared to reflect widespread suspicion that governments were hiding facts about UFOs and aliens from the public.

Shortly after the fictional series aired on British TV a serving MoD official went public with what the press began to call 'Britain's real X-files'. In 1996 Nick Pope published a personal account of his tour of duty on the UFO desk, which resulted in his conversion to a believer in UFOs. The cover blurb for his book *Open Skies, Closed Minds* proclaimed the three years he spent researching the subject at the MoD (1991–4) had changed his life: 'from starting out as a sceptic, he became a firm believer in the reality of UFOs.' Drawing upon cases that impressed him as evidential, such as the Rendlesham incident and the March 1993 UFO flap, he concluded that 'extraterrestrial spacecraft are visiting Earth and that something should be done about it urgently.'

This public declaration, from a former UFO desk officer, went much further than any previous statement from more senior officials such as Ralph Noyes. In fact Pope's statements in his book, as well as in a series of TV and radio programmes, directly contradicted his own department's long-standing policy, repeated in all correspondence with the public. For if UFOs were of 'no defence significance', here was someone who had been responsible for implementing this policy who clearly did not believe it. According to Pope's own account, some former colleagues were unhappy with the content of his book and attempts were made to block its publication. Fortunately, the risks of censorship in a new era of open government overcame these objections.

Files released by the MoD in 2007 under the Freedom of Information Act have revealed that other defence officials privately shared Nick Pope's belief that some UFOs could be spacecraft piloted by extraterrestrials. The evidence suggests this was not because, as some believe, they had privileged access to hard evidence that was being concealed from the public. Rather, they reached their conclusions by reading and watching the same books and TV programmes that were widely available to everyone else. From the 1950s onwards, some have been inclined to believe the 'Extra Terrestrial Hypothesis' (ETH), while others dismissed the subject as being irrelevant.

Early in the 1990s it seems the faction who wanted to believe began to gain some small influence on the MoD's UFO policy. During August 1993 a RAF Wing Commander working for the Defence Intelligence Staff lobbied MoD officials at a Whitehall briefing on the need for a properly funded study of UFOs. He opened his case by stating:

'I am well aware that anyone who talks about UFOs is treated with a certain degree of suspicion. I am briefing on the topic because DI55 have a UFO responsibility, not because I talk to little green men every night!'[15]

This official, his name blacked out as with all others in the most recent documents released by the MoD, continued: 'the national security implications [of UFOs] are considerable. We have many reports of strange objects in the skies and we have never investigated them.' He said if the sightings were caused by American stealth aircraft then these would not constitute a threat, 'although it would be most alarming if the craft were using UK airspace without authority.' If on the other hand they were of Russian or even Chinese origin, there *would* be a clear threat and '[MoD would] urgently need to establish the nature of the craft and its capabilities.' He then turned to the subject of extraterrestrials:

'If the sightings are of devices not of the earth then their purpose needs to be established as a matter of priority. There has been no apparently hostile intent and other possibilities are: (1) military reconnaissance, (2) scientific, (3) tourism.'

The Wing Commander said the key priority for the MoD was 'Technology Transfer', which he explained in this way:

'if the reports are taken at face value then devices exist that do not use conventional reaction propulsion systems, they have a very wide range of speeds and are stealthy. I suggest we could use this technology, if it exists.'

Against this background, intelligence officers argued that the MoD could be placed in a vulnerable position if they were ever questioned in Parliament on the basis for their public stance that UFOs were 'of no defence significance'. This internal debate came to a head in 1995 when MoD documents released under the 30-year rule by the National Archives in its previous incarnation as the Public Records Office, revealed that UFO reports had been routinely copied to Defence Intelligence branches since the 1950s. When officials realized these documents were now in the public domain an exasperated intelligence officer wrote to the UFO desk:

'If the sightings are of devices not of the earth then their purpose needs to be established as a matter of priority'

'I see no reason for continuing to deny that [Defence Intelligence] has an interest in UFOs. However, if the association is formally made public, then the MoD will no doubt be pressurised to state what the intelligence role/interest is. This could lead to disbelief and embarrassment since few people are likely to believe the truth that lack of funds and higher priorities have prevented any study of the thousands of reports received.'[16]

In the margin of this sentence a UFO desk official scribbled: 'Ouch!'

Project Condign

The problem for the MoD was that if no official study had ever been carried out, how could they honestly claim that UFOs posed no threat to the defence of the realm? The existence of this Achilles heel troubled senior intelligence officers throughout the 1990s until finally, after years of internal wrangling, they reluctantly agreed to earmark £50,000 of public money from an existing defence contract for a UFO study. This was a momentous moment. After 50 years and thousands of reports this was the first time that a detailed study had been commissioned by the MoD to investigate whether UFOs were a real phenomenon that might pose a threat to the defence of the UK.

The person selected to conduct the study was a contractor from the aerospace industry who had previously acted as a special advisor to the MoD on UFOs. His identity has been withheld due to the sensitive nature of his other work for the Defence Intelligence Staff. In 1996 he was asked to carry out a study that included, as part of its remit, an assessment of any possible flight safety risks posed by what intelligence officers now routinely referred to as 'unidentified aerial phenomena' (UAP). This acronym was chosen because it was seen as avoiding both the implication of an extraterrestrial origin and the presence of some form of piloted craft. It followed that those incidents that could not be explained by the MoD remained 'unidentified' rather than 'extraterrestrial'.

The UFO study was hidden by the codename 'Project Condign', a word the Oxford English Dictionary defines as 'severe and well deserved (usually of punishment)'. Its terms of reference were 'to determine the potential value, if any, of UAP sighting reports to Defence Intelligence'. In addition, 'the available data [was to be] studied principally to ascertain whether there is any evidence of a threat to the UK and ... to identify any potential military technologies of interest.'

Its foundation stone was a sample of UFO sightings taken from reports held in defence intelligence files. By the completion of the project in February 2000 details of more than 3,000 sightings covering a 10-year period ending in 1997 had been manually entered into a computer database.

The nameless official who produced the report was faced with a number of problems. Firstly, as the study was conducted in secret on a strict 'need-to-know' basis, he could not contact witnesses or consult independent experts. Secondly, the raw data upon which he relied for the study was of very poor quality. An earlier Air Ministry report in 1955 had found around 90 per cent of UFO reports could be explained if they were investigated thoroughly before the scent went cold (see p.60). In contrast, most of the sightings received by the MoD between 1987 and 1997 had simply been glanced at and then filed away.

Inevitably, the flawed methodology that underpinned Project Condign led to conclusions that were ultimately questionable. For example, the project's author concluded that, despite hundreds of UFO reports made from the ground, 'there is no firm evidence … that a RAF crew has ever encountered or evaded a low altitude UAP event.' This conclusion cannot in my view be regarded as definitive given the limited information available to the author: elsewhere he notes that he was unable to access the contents of intelligence files on UFOs before 1975 that would have contained detailed reports from RAF aircrew such as Michael Swiney (see p.48). These had been destroyed years earlier when someone in the MoD decided they contained nothing of defence or historical interest.

Other sections of the study are based upon more reliable information including UFO reports made by civilian aircrew. In his discussion of this

FIG. 52 The UFO desk warns MoD branches to expect sightings of a bright cigar-shaped UFO over London in the spring of 1993. DEFE 31/181/1 and DEFE 24/1954/1

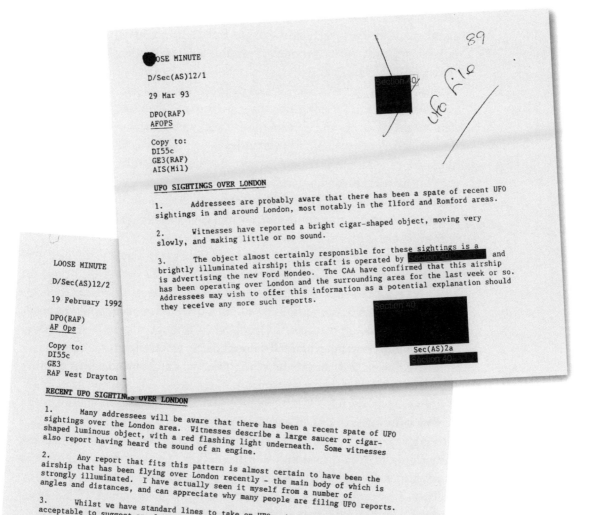

LOOSE MINUTE

D/Sec(AS)12/1

29 Mar 93

DPO(RAF)
AFOPS

Copy to:
DI55c
GE3(RAF)
AIS(Mil)

UFO SIGHTINGS OVER LONDON

1.   Addressees are probably aware that there has been a spate of recent UFO sightings in and around London, most notably in the Ilford and Romford areas.

2.   Witnesses have reported a bright cigar-shaped object, moving very slowly, and making little or no sound.

3.   The object almost certainly responsible for these sightings is a brightly illuminated airship; this craft is operated by ██████ and is advertising the new Ford Mondeo. The CAA have confirmed that this airship has been operating over London and the surrounding area for the last week or so. Addressees may wish to offer this information as a potential explanation should they receive any more such reports.

Sec(AS)2a

LOOSE MINUTE

D/Sec(AS)12/2

19 February 1992

DPO(RAF)
AF Ops

Copy to:
DI55c
GE3
RAF West Drayton

RECENT UFO SIGHTINGS OVER LONDON

1.   Many addressees will be aware that there has been a recent spate of UFO sightings over the London area. Witnesses describe a large saucer or cigar-shaped luminous object, with a red flashing light underneath. Some witnesses also report having heard the sound of an engine.

2.   Any report that fits this pattern is almost certain to have been the airship that has been flying over London recently – the main body of which is strongly illuminated. I have actually seen it myself from a number of angles and distances, and can appreciate why many people are filing UFO reports.

3.   Whilst we have standard lines to take on UFOs, it is perfectly acceptable to suggest any logical explanation for a sighting to a caller, and in this instance I suspect it might put a few people's minds at rest to suggest that – if the details fit – the object that they saw was this airship.

4.   I hope this is helpful.

topic the author wrote:

> 'It is clear that unexplained air misses are discussed among crews... It is believed that many more civil events due to UAP remain unreported. This is because ... the airline crews have most probably decided that the UAP are benign, secondly they are concerned about their individual reputations as professionals and finally the effect any publicity might have on airline business.'[17]

For this section of the study the author was forced to rely upon details of just seven 'unexplained' incidents reported to the airmiss working group between 1988 and 1996. Of these, all but one occurred below 20,000 ft in good visibility and all were witnessed by at least two members of the flight crew. Like David Hastings, the objects they reported were 'always extremely close and closing fast' when first sighted, but the experience was so fleeting that 'no evasive action could be taken in the time available and no damage, other than a fright to the crew has occurred.' Some crews described close sightings of 'black objects' the size of small fighter aircraft. Three involved radar trackings, but just one of these was coincident with the visual sighting.

Despite the restrictions he faced, the author of the Condign report boldly stated in his conclusions that 'the possibility exists that a fatal accident might have occurred in the past' as a result of aircrew taking sudden evasive action to avoid a UFO when flying fast and low. This statement was made after the author scrutinized more than one hundred unexplained fatal accident reports involving RAF aircraft during a period of 30 years. Whilst none of these contained any evidence linking them with UFOs, he did find anecdotal evidence that some aircrew had lost their lives as a result of close encounters in the former Soviet Union.

The study recommended that military aircrew should be advised that 'no attempt should be made to out-manoeuvre a UAP during interception'. The author's advice to civilian aircrews was: 'although UAP appear to be benign to civil air-traffic, pilots should be advised not to manoeuvre, other than to place the object astern, if possible.' Although the possibility of aircrew actually encountering a UFO remained very low and the level of risk from a collision was judged as being lower than a bird strike, the study decided this could not be ruled out.

The official word: UFOs exist!

Although classified secret at the time, a copy of the Condign report was released under the Freedom of Information Act in 2006. The papers revealed that work on the UFO database began in 1997 as Tony Blair's government swept to power, ushering in an era of 'open government'. Although the MoD did not anticipate it at that time, the clock was ticking towards a

point when they would have to find a way of making their entire back catalogue of UFO reports available to the public.

In the meantime a restricted group of senior officials received the conclusions of the report, 'the first UK detailed and authoritative report which
has been produced since the 1950s'. The executive summary contained the
following stunning admission:

> 'That [UFOs] exist is indisputable. Credited with the ability to hover,
> land, take-off, accelerate to exceptional velocities and vanish, they can
> reportedly alter their direction of flight suddenly and
> clearly can exhibit aerodynamic characteristics well
> beyond those of any known aircraft or missile—either
> manned or unmanned.'[18]

This short summary covered a hefty four-volume report,
465 pages in length. The 'summary of findings' led the
author to conclude that although UFOs, or 'UAPs' certainly existed, they posed no threat to defence. He found
no evidence among the 30 years of reports on file that
UFOs 'are incursions by air objects of any intelligent
(extraterrestrial or foreign) origin'. Furthermore, 'no
artefacts of unknown or unexplained origin have been
reported or handed to the UK authorities, despite thousands of UAP reports.'

Although the MoD did not anticipate it at that time, the clock was ticking towards a point when they would have to find a way of making their entire back catalogue of UFO reports available to the public

In addition, the report's author had found nothing about UFOs in classified signals intelligence or from information gathered by electronic eaves-
dropping. Apart from a few ambiguous, blurred photographs and videos
there was little useful imagery showing UFOs and no reliable radiation
measurements, even from supposedly evidential cases such as Rendlesham.

The Condign study did not attempt to investigate any specific sightings
in depth and confined its scrutiny to individual UFO flaps that were sub-
jected to statistical analysis using its computer database. Although flawed in
its methodology, the study found many could be explained as the misidentifications of man-made aircraft, natural phenomena and 'relatively rare and
not completely understood phenomena'.

It was this final category that contained the most controversial claim made
by the Condign report. The author identified more than 20 natural phenomena that have undoubtedly generated UFO sightings in the past. Some
less familiar phenomena listed included new types of lightning called red
sprites and blue jets that appear high above thunderclouds. These were identified and photographed in recent years and may explain some of the UFO
sightings made by aircrew. Alongside these are noctilucent clouds, auroral
displays, sun dogs and other poorly-understood aerial phenomena such as
'earthquake lights', ball lightning (see p.19) and atmospheric plasmas.

Plasma is the most common form taken by matter. Atmospheric plasmas are clusters of electrically charged particles that can take the form of gaseous clouds and beams that respond to electromagnetic fields. It follows that many unexplained atmospheric phenomena such as ball lightning and the Will-o'-the-Wisp described in Chapter 1, along with 'earthquake lights' produced by movements in the earth's crust, are also types of plasma observed in the lower atmosphere.

The study concluded there was 'strong evidence' that a residue of un-identified sightings, particularly those reported by aircrew, were caused by these atmospheric plasmas. The report lists examples of ball lightning flying ahead or behind aircraft that resemble the 'foo-fighters' reported by aircrew during the Second World War (see p.22). On other occasions aircrew have reported lightning balls entering the fuselage of aircraft during thunderstorms.

FIG. 53 An example of an 'Identified Flying Object', in this case caused by laser lights from a Tina Turner concert. DEFE 24/1939/1

Although witnesses often perceive UFOs as solid objects, the report's author concluded the plasma explanation was more likely. But he had to admit that 'the conditions and method of formation of the electrically-charged plasmas and the scientific rationale for sustaining them for significant periods is incomplete and not fully understood.'

Despite the lack of scientific evidence for these mysterious plasmas occurring naturally in the lower atmosphere, the author ventured further into speculative territory, applying his theory to explain 'close encounter' stories. Drawing upon experimental research carried out by a Canadian neuroscientist, Dr Michael Persinger, he pondered the idea that plasmas and 'earthquake lights' might explain a range of alien abduction experiences. His report toyed with the improbable-sounding idea that on rare occasions exposure to atmospheric plasmas may cause responses in the temporal-lobe area of the brain, leading those affected to experience periods of 'missing time' and elaborate hallucinations that might be interpreted as supernatural experiences or contact with alien

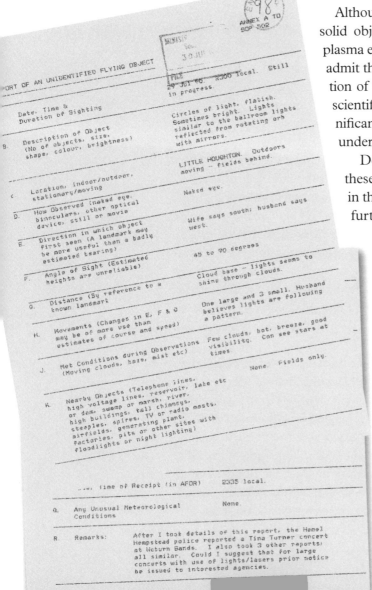

beings. This, the report's author suggested, may be 'a key factor in influencing the more extreme reports [that] are clearly believed by the victims.'

Leaving aside such far-out speculation, the Condign report's key recommendation was that UFOs had no intelligence value and that the Defence Intelligence Staff should cease to receive the reports that had been routinely copied to them by the MoD's UFO desk since 1967.

The report's conclusions and recommendations were circulated within the MoD during December 2000, classified as 'Secret: UK Eyes Only'. The covering letter made it clear that officials believed it was too early, at this stage, to release the results of the study to the public:

> 'Although we intend to carry out no further work on the subject ... we hardly need remind addressees of the media interest in this subject and consequently the sensitivity of the report. Please protect this subject accordingly, and discuss the report only with those who have a need to know.'[19]

In fact, this memo and the report it covered remained secret for just over five years before I obtained a copy of it using the Freedom of Information Act. In 2000, when the report was completed, government files on UFOs were still being routinely withheld for up to half a century, and in other cases had been destroyed long before the arrival of open government. Today, however, the Freedom of Information Act has opened this secret world to unprecedented scrutiny and allowed everyone access to thousands of pages of official documentation on the UFO mystery.

UFOs: no defence significance?

The completion of the Condign report in 2000 brought to an end half a century of intelligence interest in UFOs that began officially in 1950 when Sir Henry Tizard asked the MoD to set up a Flying Saucer Working Party (see p.41). The Condign study concluded that UFOs existed, but were natural phenomena that did not pose a threat to the defence of the UK.

But was this the end of official interest in UFOs? The answer is a definite no. UFOs will simply not go away. During the 1950s officials were sceptical but felt UFOs could not be ignored as there remained a small risk that some could be enemy aircraft from behind the Iron Curtain. But as that danger ebbed new ones have emerged in the aftermath of the 9/11 attacks on New York and Washington. On at least two occasions since 2001 false alarms have led the United States to scramble aircraft in response to mysterious blips seen on radar approaching Washington DC. On the first occasion, in November 2003, White House staff were evacuated until the objects were identified. On both these occasions, as had happened years earlier, these UFOs were found to be 'false radar targets' created by atmospheric conditions and even flocks of birds.

In Britain the MoD's UFO desk continues to receive sightings and every year a small number are sent to the Directorate of Counter Terrorism and UK Operations for expert scrutiny. Today it is this branch that is responsible for the air defence of the UK, and their responsibility to decide if any UFO report should be investigated further. To date the MoD says that none have been assessed as a risk to defence—but they continue to watch the skies just in case.

One of the most impressive UFO reports examined by the MoD in recent years was that made by the pilots of two aircraft above the English Channel on 23 April 2007. The story came to light when Ray Bowyer, the captain of one of the aircraft, saw two strange objects in the sky in daylight during a flight from Southampton to the island of Alderney, in the Channel Islands. News of this experience spread across the globe when Captain Bowyer landed at Alderney airport to file an official report.

> As excitement spread passengers on the small propeller-driven aircraft began watching the lights through the cabin windows. At least nine passengers seated immediately behind the pilot saw the UFOs.

Details were passed both to the MoD and to the French Space Agency's UFO project, as the sighting occurred in French airspace. In the past full details of the incident could have remained secret for at least 30 years, but using the Freedom of Information Act UFOlogists were quickly able to obtain a copy of the MoD's file on the incident that contained Mr Bowyer's report to the Civil Aviation Authority. This revealed his Trislander was approaching Alderney at 4,000 ft shortly after 2 pm when he spotted 'a bright light ahead which I thought was the reflection from the sun off glass in Guernsey.' Scrutinizing the light through binoculars he was amazed to see a 'sparkling yellow' object shaped like a long thin cigar suspended horizontally on the horizon. The object had 'very sharply defined' edges and two thirds from the left end was a narrow patch, dark grey in colour. Bowyer's initial impression was that the object was the size of a 737 airliner or larger, hovering over the sea at around 2,000 ft just 15 miles away from his small aircraft.

The recording of his conversation with air traffic controller Paul Kelly was also released. According to this, after Bowyer had explained what he had seen, Kelly stated he could now see 'a very faint primary contact' on his radar, 4 miles from the aircraft, though he concluded this was caused by weather returns. As Bowyer continued his approach to the airport he then saw a second UFO: 'It was exactly the same but looked smaller because it was further away.'

As excitement spread passengers on the small propeller-driven aircraft began watching the lights through the cabin windows. At least nine passengers seated immediately behind the pilot saw the UFOs. One of these was Kate Russell, who was sitting with her husband, John, four rows back.

When I interviewed her about the incident she said: 'At first I thought it was the sun reflecting off glass but what I was looking at was a very bright light over the sea below us. There were two lights and I saw them on two separate occasions.' She added:

'I don't believe in little green men but this was something quite extraordinary, something we don't have an explanation for at the present time.

Ray Bowyer, our pilot, is a sound rational man but he was quite shaken.'[20] With the objects still visible to the captain and passengers, controller Paul Kelly used his radio to alert other aircrew in the Channel and asked if they could see anything. One of these was the pilot of a Jetstream aircraft en route to Jersey from the Isle of Man. The captain, Patrick Patterson, said he 'was able to see something fitting the description, yellow/beige in colour, in my eight o'clock position, slightly to the north-west of Alderney at what I estimated to be 2,000 feet below.' Visibility was fairly poor but he could see the object for about one minute.

Meanwhile, Captain Bowyer was preparing his aircraft for landing and as he descended he saw the two UFOs change their positions so they appeared to line up, one directly above the other. When he reached a layer of haze at 2,000 ft the UFOs vanished. They were visible for 12 minutes in total, during which his sighting had been corroborated both by passengers and the captain of a second aircraft.

Despite good evidence that *something* unusual had been seen, the MoD decided that because the sighting occurred in French airspace these UFOs posed no threat to the UK. Thus, as has happened so many times before over the years, while a potential defence significance can lead to official interest, lack of the same means the vast majority are overlooked—whatever the possible explanation. In this case a group of scientists and others with an interest in UFOs, of whom I was one, attempted to investigate further. After a year's work we were able to eliminate many of the usual explanations such as sun dogs, mirages and reflections. Our work revealed that media stories describing enormous UFOs up to a mile wide and detected by radar were based on speculation and misunderstanding. Nevertheless, we concluded this was a genuine example of an 'unidentified aerial phenomena' and one deserving further scientific study.

Ray Bowyer's final word on the subject was equally open-minded:

'I can't explain it. I'm not saying it was from another world. All I'm saying is I've never seen anything like it in all my years flying.'[21]

AFTERWORD

I N THIS BOOK I have selected the most impressive UFO stories from the British Ministry of Defence's files on UFOs and examined the results of the occasional government investigations during the twentieth century. After more than 60 years of sightings—more than one hundred if you factor in the phantom Zeppelins and foo-fighters of the First and Second World Wars—what conclusions can be reached about this puzzling and persistent mystery?

In 1968 Professor R. V. Jones concluded that, if pushed to give his opinion one way or the other on the existence of UFOs, he would have based his decision on the assumption that they were either straight fantasy or the incorrect identification of a 'rare and unrecognised phenomenon'.[1] Just over a decade later, Lord Strabolgi expressed a similar point of view during the House of Lords UFO debate, stating 'there really are many strange phenomena in the sky, and these are invariably reported by reliable people, [but] there is a wide range of natural explanations to account for such phenomena.'[2]

As the many stories collected for this book have shown, it seems likely that a rational explanation, whether mundane or extraordinary, lurks behind almost every UFO report. A wide variety of different things ultimately cause UFO sightings, including bright stars and planets, advertising blimps and balloons, hoaxes, concert lights, meteors and space junk burning up in the atmosphere. Together these UFOs become Identified Flying Objects, but often only after detailed investigation. It is amongst all of this background noise that any genuine UFOs, such as some form of alien craft, would be found if they truly existed.

It is true that in some cases, such as those UFOs reported by test pilots over Farnborough in 1950 (Chapter 2) or the phenomena seen by radars at RAF Lakenheath-Bentwaters in 1956 (Chapter 3), rational explanations are hard to come by. But at the same time it is also true that we lack the one thing that would settle the debate once and for all: tangible evidence, such as wreckage from a crash or an artefact of unquestionable extraterrestrial origin.

'I want to believe'

This links to one of the most enduring popular beliefs that plays a major role in the modern UFO mystery—the government cover up. Could that be the reason why concrete proof of the existence of UFOs has proved so elusive? Addressing this subject during the 1979 House of Lords debate, Lord Strabogli expressed the view that the idea of an international conspiracy to hide evidence of aliens belonged to the world of James Bond. Throughout modern history, governments have failed to agree on almost every subject; it seems improbable that they could all, successfully and successively, have colluded to hide evidence of alien visitations, both from the public and the scientific community, for more than half a century.

But despite recent moves by the British and other governments to be more open about their limited interest in UFOs, official statements on this subject continue to be widely disbelieved. In July 2008, for example, just two months after the National Archives began releasing the most recent of the Ministry of Defence's UFO files, a survey for the *Sun* newspaper found that 50 per cent of the respondents said they believed the government might be, or definitely was, concealing evidence from the public. Faced with such a deeply-rooted will to believe, attempts by the MoD and others to demystify the subject and educate the public to identify common sources of UFOs are doomed to failure.

The available evidence backs the idea that government interest in UFOs was always purely pragmatic, motivated by fears over what first Germany and later Russia might be up to. In 2002 when the MoD last published a policy statement on UFOs it stated that their sole interest in the subject was to establish whether any particular incident had any 'defence significance', namely whether UK airspace had been invaded by hostile or unauthorized aircraft. As for visitors from other worlds, the ministry says it remains 'totally open-minded', but to date 'knows of no evidence which substantiates the existence of these alleged phenomena'. Personally, I have no doubt this is the truth.

Two lamps in a darkened hall

Today British intelligence agencies have washed their hands of UFOs while the MoD approaches the subject as more of a public relations than a defence problem. Meanwhile, the UFO desk itself continues to receive reports from the public, and their contact details can be found in the resources section of this book. Since 2005 basic details of the UFO reports they receive are entered into a spreadsheet and these are released each year on the MoD's FOIA website. During 2008 a total of 285 individual sightings were logged by the Directorate of Air Staff, to which the UFO desk now belongs. This is the highest total since the last peak of public interest in 1996–7.

During my research for this book I interviewed a retired MoD scientist who was responsible for checking UFO reports received by the Defence Intelligence Staff. He admitted that a number could not be explained, but said that, given Earth's status as a rather ordinary little planet, one of the things he had found 'strange about the whole business' was the sheer volume of reports received, saying: 'I seem to remember at least half a dozen or more every day. Surely there could not have been that number of aliens?'[3]

In fact the MoD has received more than 11,000 UFO reports since 1959, a figure that will be only a tiny proportion of the actual total number of sightings, as very few people decide to make an official report. Across the world the total since 1947 must run to millions. This by itself makes a rather strong case for a rational explanation for most UFO sightings, because, put simply, there are just too many UFOs for them all to be alien visitors. What then are the chances that the Earth might be visited today, or even within the short window of time in which human civilization has existed?

Following the opening of the latest UFO files at The National Archives in 2008, Lord Martin Rees, Astronomer Royal and President of the Royal Society, suggested the question of extraterrestrial visits does not, as some believe, rely upon whether other planets capable of hosting life exist in other solar systems. Intelligent humans exist today as the result of a mind-boggling series of accidents and coincidences that may just be unique to our planet. In an article published by *The Times*, Lord Rees pointed out we may not even recognize a truly alien intelligence if they had developed an unfamiliar technology or method of communication.[4] This raises questions that are more to do with biology than astronomy. For example, what are the odds that intelligent life that we could recognize would have evolved in a similar fashion elsewhere in the universe, with a completely different throw of cosmic dice? And even if it had, what is the likelihood that two advanced civilizations could exist simultaneously in separate planetary systems close enough for communication or travel to be possible?

The astronomer Patrick Moore has illustrated this problem by comparing it to a darkened hall in which two lamps are installed. If each lamp was programmed to switch on at random for 10 seconds each day, the chances of them both being illuminated at the same time is similar to the likelihood of two civilizations existing at the same time in adjacent solar systems. When you consider the vast distances separating solar systems even within the Milky Way, those odds lengthen still further.

With our present knowledge of the universe, it is impossible at the present time to be absolutely certain. Whether we believe or not, for the time being we must be content with mystery. Indeed, at some level, perhaps that is what we all want, for mystery is a necessary ingredient in our lives. As American astronaut, Neil Armstrong, said in his address to the US Congress following the moon landings of 1969,

'Mystery creates wonder, and wonder is the basis for man's desire to understand. Who knows what mysteries will be solved in our lifetime, and what new riddles will become the challenge of the new generations?'

FIG.54 Sketch of an alien creature involved in a galactic war, from a MoD file with the title: 'close encounter reports, alien entities, abductions, etc', opened in 1992. DEFE 24/1943/1

NOTES ON THE TEXT

ONE
STRANGE LIGHTS IN THE SKY

1 *Cardiff Evening Express and Evening Mail*, 19 May 1909
2 Hansard (Written Answers, Commons) 21 November, 1912
3 Ibid.
4 C. Cole and E.F. Cheeseman, *The Air Defence of Great Britain, 1914–1918* (Bodley Head, 1969)
5 TNA ADM 131/119
6 *Meteorological Magazine*, vol. 56, no. 667, August 1921
7 *Meteorological Magazine*, vol. 56, no. 668, September 1921
8 Extract from personal communication, 19 May 1987
9 Churchill Archives, University of Cambridge, R.V. Jones papers, DI42
10 Ibid.
11 *Fortean Times* 64, August/September 1992
12 TNA AVIA 7/1070
13 Extract from personal communication, 28 November 2001

14 NARA record group 331 – US National Archives
15 Ibid.
16 Robertson Panel report, January 1953, CIA archive
17 Ibid.
18 Extract from personal communication, 20 March 2003

TWO
THE FLYING SAUCER AGE

1 See TNA FO 371/56988 and FO 371/56951
2 R.V. Jones, *Most Secret War* (Hamish Hamilton, 1978)
3 See TNA AIR 29/1370 and AIR 29/1597
4 *Daily Mail*, 29 April 1947
5 US National Archives, Project Blue Book records, T-1206
6 Mass Observation Archive, University of Sussex, M-DA DI22
7 H. Evans and D. Stacy (eds.), *UFO 1947–97: Fifty Years of Flying Saucers* (John Brown, 1997)
8 R. Durant, 'Public Opinion Polls and UFOs', in Evans and Stacy, ibid.
9 K. Pflock, *Roswell: Inconvenient facts and the will to believe* (Prometheus, 2001)
10 C. Berlitz and W.L. Moore, *The Roswell Incident* (Grosset & Dunlap, 1980)
11 Col. R. Weaver and 1st Lt James McAndrews, *The Roswell Report: Fact Versus Fiction in the New Mexico Desert* (HQ USAF, 1995)
12 US National Archives, Project Blue Book records, T-1206.
13 E. Ruppelt, *The Report on Unidentified Flying Objects* (Doubleday, 1956)
14 *Daily Herald*, 16 April 1950
15 Broadlands Archive, University of Southampton, BAI 172
16 TNA DEFE 19/9
17 Extract from interview with S. Hubbard, 18 April 2002

18 *New York Times*, quoted in *The Times*, 30 July 1952
19 Churchill Archives, University of Cambridge, Lord Duncan-Sandys papers, DSND 15/4
20 Extract from interview with Michael Swiney, 13 March 2002
21 Extract from interview with David Crofts, 26 February 2002
22 TNA AIR 29/2310
23 J. Gough, *Watching the Skies* (HMSO 1993)
24 RAF Radar Museum newsletter no. 35–36, April–July 2003
25 TNA AIR 16/1485
26 TNA CAB 157/27

THREE
COLD WAR UFOs

1 Extract from RAF report prepared by Flight Lieutenant J.R. Salandin, 604 Squadron, Royal Auxiliary Air Force, 28 November 1954
2 *Lancashire Evening Post*, 18 February 1954
3 G. Haines, 'A Die-hard issue: CIA's role in the study of UFOs, 1947–90', *Studies in Intelligence* 1 (1997)
4 Ibid.
5 TNA AIR 20/9994
6 University of Hull, Patrick Wall papers, DPW/82/1
7 TNA AIR 40/2769
8 B.D. Gildenberg, 'The Cold War's classified Skyhook Program', *Skeptical Inquirer*, May 2004
9 See TNA AIR 2/17902–4
10 TNA AIR 27/2775
11 J. Oberg, 'Close Encounters of a Fabricated Kind', *New Scientist*, 24/31 December 1981
12 Extract from interview with Freddie Wimbledon, 25 March 2001
13 Extract from interview with John Brady, 11 February 2001
14 Extract from interview with Ralph Noyes, May 1989

15 *The Scientific Study of UFOs* (University of Colorado, 1969)
16 TNA AIR 2/18564
17 TNA DEFE 31/118
18 Extract from interview with David West, 29 April 2007
19 *Exeter Express & Echo*, 24 October 1967
20 Ibid.
21 TNA AIR 20/11890
22 TNA AIR 2/17983
23 TNA AIE 2/17983

FOUR
CLOSE ENCOUNTERS

1   TNA DEFE 31/119
2   TNA AIR 20/12550
3   R. Musson, 'The Enigmatic Bala Earthquake of 1974', *Astronomy & Geophysics* vol. 47 (October 2006); A. Roberts, 'The Berwyn Mountains UFO Crash', *Fortean Times* 252 (August 2009)
4   TNA AIR 2/19083
5   TNA AIR 2/18874
6   TNA DEFE 24/978
7   TNA DEFE 71/34
8   TNA DEFE 24/1535
9   TNA DEFE 24/1535
10 *Western Mail*, 27 January 1996
11 TNA DEFE 24/1210
12 TNA DEFE 24/1212
13 *Daily Mirror*, 2 January 1979
14 TNA FCO 55/1403
15 TNA DEFE 31/164
16 TNA AIR 20/12966
17 Hansard (Parliamentary debates, House of Lords), 18 January 1979

FIVE
CROP CIRCLES AND ALIEN ABDUCTIONS

1   Suffolk police log released under FOIA, 2005: *http://tinyurl.com/204vp51*
2   *www.ianridpath.com/ufo/halttape.htm*

3   Statement by Charles Halt at Coalition for Freedom of Information press conference, Washington DC, 12 November 2007: *www.freedomofinfo.org/national_press_07/halt_statement.pdf*
4   Extract from personal communication, August 2005
5   TNA DEFE 24/1948/1
6   TNA DEFE 24/1970/1
7   *Guardian*, 5 January 1985
8   Extract from personal communication, June 2001
9   TNA AIR 2/17318
10 *The Mowing Devil: or, Strange News out of Hartfordshire* (1678) —the original pamphlet can be found at The British Library
11 TNA DEFE 24/1925/1
12 TNA DEFE 24/1955/1
13 TNA DEFE 24/1956/1
14 John Fuller, *The Interrupted Journey* (Dial Press, 1966)
15 TNA AIR 2/18117
16 TNA DEFE 24/1928/1
17 TNA DEFE 24/1929/1
18 MoD letter dated 1996, reproduced in Nick Pope, *The Uninvited* (Simon & Schuster, 1997)

SIX
TURN OF THE CENTURY UFOs

1   Extract from personal communication, April 2009
2   *Daily Express*, 8 February 1999
3   BBC News online, 23 July 1999: *http://news.bbc.co.uk/1/hi/sci/tech/392451.stm*
4   TNA DEFE 71/33
5   TNA DEFE 24/1956/1
6   Airmiss report No. 2/95 (published by the Civil Aviation Authority); copy included in Sec(AS)12/1 Part A—UFO Policy, 1985–1995, released under FOIA
7   Ibid.
8   TNA DEFE 31/180/1

9   TNA DEFE 24/2086/1
10 *The Scotsman*, 18 February 1992
11 Sec(AS)12/1 Pt A—UFO Policy, released under FOIA
12 Extract from personal communication, March 1997; *Jane's Defence Weekly*, 12 December 1992
13 BDS/RAF/303 dated 22 December 1992, released under FOIA
14 Extract from personal communication, March 1997
15 DI55 UFO policy file, 1971–1996, released under FOIA
16 Ibid.
17 *UAPs in the UK Air Defence Region*, volume 3: *http://tinyurl.com/kqll2*
18 *UAPs in the UK Air Defence Region*, executive summary: *http://tinyurl.com/kqll2*
19 'UAP—DI55 report' DIST letter dated 4 December 2000 and covering UAP report, released under FOIA
20 Extract from interview with Kate Russell, 28 June 2007
21 J. F. Baure, et. al., 'Unusual atmospheric phenomena observed near Channel Islands, UK, 23 April 2007,' *Journal of Scientific Exploration*, vol. 22:3, August 2008

AFTERWORD

1   R. V. Jones, 'The Natural Philosophy of Flying Saucers', *Physics Bulletin* 19 (July 1968)
2   Hansard (Parliamentary debates, House of Lords), 18 January 1979
3   Extract from personal communication, June 2005
4   *The Times*, 21 October 2008

RESOURCES

• The Ministry of Defence operates a UFO hotline on (01494) 496254 for members of the public who wish to report sightings. You can also report sightings by email to ufodesk@mod.uk or by letter to RAF Business Secretariat 13, Room 2E03, Spitfire Block, HQ Air Command, RAF High Wycombe HP14 4UE.

SELECTED ONLINE RESOURCES

THE UNITED KINGDOM

THE NATIONAL ARCHIVES.
The UFO page contains an online archive of Ministry of Defence files released by the National Archives. These can be downloaded as PDF files at *http://www.nationalarchives.gov.uk/ufos.* The site also contains a research guide and a collection of podcasts and video-casts that provide context to the files. Earlier files featured in this book can be found by searching the National Archives catalogue at *http://www.nationalarchives.gov.uk /catalogue/* and ordered and viewed onsite.

THE MINISTRY OF DEFENCE.
A selection of UFO files can be found via the Ministry of Defence's Publication Scheme. These include PDF copies of the Defence Intelligence Staff (DIS) 'UAPs in the UK Air Defence Region' (see Chapter 6) and a tabulated list of UFO sightings reported to Secretariat Air Staff, Sec(AS), and later Directorate of Air Staff (DAS), between 1997 and 2007. Just type the search term UFO at the following link: *http://www.mod.uk/DefenceInternet/FreedomOf Information/PublicationScheme/SearchPublication Scheme.htm.*

THE UNITED STATES OF AMERICA

THE NATIONAL ARCHIVES AND RECORDS ADMINISTRATION.
This has a UFO page at *http://www.archives.gov/foia /ufos.html* and holds the Project Blue Book archive. It also holds copies of *The Roswell Report: Fact vs Fiction in the New Mexico desert* (HQ USAF, 1994) and *The Roswell Report: Case Closed* (Washington DC, 1997). The latter two documents can be viewed online via the Galvin Library of the Illinois Institute of Technology at *http://contrails.iit.edu/history/roswell,* while samples of Project Blue Book documents are available via the privately-run Project Blue Book Archive at *http://www.bluebookarchive.org/.*

THE OFFICE OF THE SECRETARY OF DEFENSE AND JOINT STAFF.
Documents and links relating to UFOs can be found at *http://www.dod.mil/pubs/foi/ufo/.*

THE CENTRAL INTELLIGENCE AGENCY.
See *http://www.foia.cia.gov/ufo.asp,* which has a link to historian Gerald Haines' article, 'A Die-Hard Issue: CIA's Role in the Study of UFOs, 1947–1990', originally published in *Studies in Intelligence* (1997).

NATIONAL SECURITY AGENCY.
http://www.nsa.gov/public_info/declass/ufo/index.shtml.

ELSEWHERE IN THE WORLD

THE NATIONAL LIBRARY AND ARCHIVES OF CANADA.
This holds 9,500 documents relating to UFOs from 1947 until the early 1980s at *http://www.collections canada.gc.ca/databases/ufo/index-e.html.*

CENTRE NATIONAL D'ETUDIES SPATIALS.
GEIPAN, the French Space Agency unit responsible for research and investigations of 'Unidentified Aerospace Phenomena' (UAPs), placed its archives online in March 2007 at *http://www.cnes-geipan.fr /geipan/ipn.html.*

EJÉRCITO DEL AIRE.
The Spanish Air Force declassified its UFO files in 1992. Their contents are described in an article by private researcher, Vicente-Juan Ballester Olmos, at *http://www.anomalia.org/declass.htm.*

THE NATIONAL ARCHIVES OF AUSTRALIA.
Royal Australian Air Force UFO files can be accessed via *http://www.naa.gov.au/*. The RAAF first opened their files in 1982 to researcher Bill Chalker of the Australian UFO Research Network. He describes their content at *http://www.auforn.com/MilitaryFiles .html*.

ARCHIVES FOR UFO RESEARCH.
This Swedish site can be found at *http://www.afu .info/*.

THE ITALIAN CENTRE FOR UFO STUDIES.
See *http://www.arpnet.it/ufo/english.htm*.

SELECTED PRINT RESOURCES

P. BROOKESMITH, *UFO – The Government Files* (Blandford, 1996)

K. CHESTER, *Strange Company: Military Encounters with UFOs in World War Two* (Anomalist Books, 2007)

D. CLARKE and A. ROBERTS, *Flying Saucerers: A Social History of UFOlogy* (Heart of Albion, 2007)

D. GILLMOR (ed.), *The Scientific Study of Unidentified Flying Objects* (Vision, 1970)

T. GOOD, *Above Top Secret* (Sidgwick & Jackson, 1987)

R. V. JONES, *Most Secret War* (Hamish Hamilton, 1979)

N. POPE, *Open Skies, Closed Minds* (Simon & Schuster, 1996)

J. RANDLES, *The UFO Conspiracy* (Blandford, 1987)

J. RANDLES, *UFO Crash Landing?* (Blandford, 1998)

J. RANDLES, *Something in the Air* (Robert Hale, 1998)

N. REDFERN, *A Covert Agenda: The British Government's UFO Top Secrets Exposed* (Simon & Schuster, 1997)

E. RUPPELT, *The Report on Unidentified Flying Objects* (Doubleday, 1956)

N. WATSON, *The Scareship Mystery: A Survey of Phantom Airship Scares 1909–1918* (Domra, 2000)

INDEX

Numbers in *italic* refer to plate numbers.

A

Ackhurst, Leslie 75, 77
Adair, Lieutenant W. 15
Adamski, George 116; *Flying Saucers Have Landed* 116; *Inside the Spaceships* 116
Air Historical Branch files 14, 15
Air Ministry 32; abolition of 70; attempt to control spread of information about UFOs 58; destroying of UFO records 68; drawing up of UFO report form 60; foo-fighter enquiries 24, 25; investigations into UFO reports 49–50, 51; offloading of public correspondence on UFOs to UFO desk 69; yearly reports on UFOs 60–1, *66*
Air Ministry Secret Intelligence Summary (AMSIS) 60
Air Miss Working Group 131, 132, 142
air misses 128, 129–32, 142
Air Technical Intelligence Center 46
air traffic control centres 128

aircraft: design based on flying saucers 61; link between UFO sightings and experimental military 132–4, 136–7
aircrew, civilian: UFO reports made by 127–8, *130*, 132, 134, 141–2
airships 12–13 *see also* 'phantom airship' sightings
Airways 131
alien abductions 117–24; explanations for 144–5; and the Hills 117–18; public fascination with 121
aliens: depiction of 115–16; encounters with 116–17, 119–24, *120*, *123*; popular image of 121
Alitalia Flight AZ (284) 129–30, *129*
Allied Air Intelligence 25
Alvarez, Dr Luis 57
American National Academy of Sciences 81
Andrews, Colin 111
Anthony, Gary 135
Ape, SS 15
Apollo programme 80
'Area 51' 127
Armstrong, Neil 151
Arnold, Kenneth 34–6, *35*
Ash, Fenton: *Trip to Mars* 115
atmospheric plasmas 143–4
Aurora project 136–7
'Avro-cars' 61

B

B-2 Stealth bomber 127, 136
Bagnall, Sir Anthony 135
Baker, Annie 20–1
ball lightning 19–22, 29, 80, 82–3, 143, 144
balloons: Mogul project 38, 62; and air miss incidents 131; and Skyhook programme 39–40, 61–2; UFO sightings put down to 15, 34, 37, 38, 46, 58, 61–2, 64, 74, 78, 82; UFO Solar 131
BBC 80
Becke, Major 14–15
Bedell Smith, Walter 57
Bentine, Michael 25, 28
Bentwaters, RAF 64, 103, 108
Berkner, Dr Lloyd 57

Berlitz, Charles 91
Berlitz, Charles and Moore, William: *The Roswell Incident* 37–8
Bermuda Triangle 91
Birch, Alex 70, *71*
Birch, Nigel 58, 62
birds: and radar incidents 51–2
'black projects' 133–4, 136
Blanchard, Roy 110
Blériot, Louis 13
Blount, Bertie 42
Blue Book project *see* Project Blue Book
Boulmer, RAF 88–9
Bower, Doug 80, 114–15
Bowyer, Ray 146–7
Boyd, Lee 127
Brady, Squadron Leader John 65
Brawdy, RAF 91, 92
Brewyn Mountains incident (1974) 86–8
Broad Haven Primary School 90, 93
Brooks, Angus 75–7, *76*, 118
Burroughs, John 107

C

Cabell, Major General Charles P. 46
Carruthers, Jim 74
Carter, Chris 138
Carter, Jimmy 75
Cassie, Alex 75, *76*–7
Cave-Penny, Mrs 18
Chadwell, Dr Harris Marshall 42, 57
Chain Home radar stations 26, 33
Chapman, Robert 77
Charlton crater 110, 111
Cherwell, Lord (Frederick Lindemann) 46, 47
Chinese lanterns 15
Chorley, Dave 114–15
Churchill, Winston 13, *13*, 14, 46, *47*
CIA 40, 42; convening of panel to investigate UFO sightings (1953) 57–8
Civil Aviation Authority 128, 131
Clancarty, Lord 96–8, 100
Claridge, Ronald 30–1
Clarke, Arthur C. 116

close encounters: explanations for 144–5; reports on 116–17, 118; term of 118; *see also* alien abductions

Close Encounters of the Third Kind 94–5, 118

Cochrane, Sir Ralph 51

Code of Practice for Access to Government Information 106

Coe, Phillis 20

Cold War 39, 54, 116, 133

Cold War UFOs 56–78

Colin, Group Captain Neil 98

Condign Report (2000) 140–5

Condon Report (1969) 80–1

Contact International 96

Contact UK 55

corn circles *see* crop circles

Cosford, RAF 120, 135

Cosmos 749 (Soviet spy satellite) 102

Cosmos 1068 95

Cosmos 2238 135

Coumbe, Squadron Leader Derek 108

Cowan, Squadron Leader J.A. 92

Cox, Eric 73

Crofts, Lieutenant David 48, 50, 51

crop circles 90, 110–15, *112*, 121

D

Daily Express 58, 94, 112

Dartmoor: reports of mysterious lights over 17–19

Davies, Lord 100

Davis, Colin *94, 95*

Davis, Squadron Leader Tony 65

Day the Earth Stood Still, The 116

DDI (Tech) 51, 60

Defence Intelligence Staff 70, 75, 81, 93, 106, 113, *134*, 138, 140, 145

see also DI55

Delgado, Pat 111

Devil's Punchbowl, The 111

Devonport 17–18

DI55 70, 74, 77, 84, 88, 90, 97, 113, 139

Dickinson, Rod 115

Dickison, Dr John 74, 75

Directorate of Counter Terrorism and UK Operations 146

Directorate of Scientific Intelligence/Joint Technical Intelligence Committee (DSI/JTIC) 41

Drury, Lieutenant-Colonel W.P. 18

DSI/JTIC Report No 7 Unidentified Flying Objects 42, 43, 45

E

Eade, Charles 41

earthquake lights 144

Eastchurch 13–14

Edgecombe, Colonel G.J.B. 113

Eisenhower, General Dwight D. 27

Elliott, Lieutenant Montague 17

Essen raid (1944) 22

E.T. 112

Evans, Hilary 36

experimental military aircraft: links with UFOs 132–4

Extra Terrestrial Hypothesis (ETH) 138

F

F-117 136, 137

Farnborough: flying saucers over (1950) 43–5, 148

Fennessy, Sir Edward 26, 27

Fighter Command 26, 33, 48, 52, 60

fireball meteors 86, 102, 107, 132

First World War 14, 25; 'phantom airship' sightings 11–17, *12, 17*, 25, 135;

reports of mysterious lights over Dartmoor 17–19

'flying cross' incidents (1967) 73–6

Flying Saucer Review (magazine) 96, 111

Flying Saucer Working Party 40–2, 43, 44, 45, 61, 145; report (1951) 42, 61

flying saucers: aircraft designs based on 61; and Arnold 34–6, *35*; books on 41; first opinion poll on 36; first sightings of over North America 33–4; origin of term 35; *see also* UFOs

Flying Saucers and the People Who See Them (tv documentary) 80, 118

foo-fighters 22–5, *24*, 27–9, 57, 96, 144

Formby, Wing Commander Myles 45

Freedom of Information Act (2006) 108, 138, 142, 145

Frost, John 61

Frow, Air Commodore Brian 30

Fuller, John 122; *The Interrupted Journey* 118

Fylingdales, RAF 95, 102

G

Gabriel, General Charles 105

Gainford, Lord *99*, 100

Gairy, Sir Eric 97

Galley, Robert 100

General Accounting Office (GAO) 38

'ghost plane' flap (1947) 33–4, 51

ghost rocket scares (1946) 32–3, 36

Gibson, Chris 137

Gildenberg, Duke 62

Godber, Joseph 110

Goldsmit, Dr Samuel 57

Goodwin, Dominic 133, 136

Gorizont 21 satellite 134–5

Gough, Jack: *Watching the Skies* 51

Greene, Francis 78

Greenham Common, RAF 106

Grigg Committee (1957) 9

H

Halsbury, Earl of 100

Halt, Lieutenant Colonel Charles 103–6, *104*, 107, 108, 109

Hamley, Wing Commander D.B. 128

Hangar 18 (film) 102

Harrison, Fred 11–12

Hartop, Owen 114

Hastings, David 125–6, *126*, 127, 132, 142

Haut, Lieutenant Walter 37

Hendry, Arthur 79–80

Hewlett, Lord 100

Hill, Betty and Barney 117–18

Hill-Norton, Admiral Lord Peter 106, 109

Hopkins, Budd: *Missing Time* 121, 122

Hopkins, Group Captain E.D.M. 27

Horton, Flight Lieutenant Arthur 22–3

House of Lords: UFO debate 96–101, *98, 99*, 148, 149
Howard, Captain James 127, 128
Hubbard, Stan 43–5, *43*
Huddart, Barry 52
Hynek, Dr J. Allen 73, 94, 118

I

Invaders from Mars 116
Invasion of the Body Snatchers 116

J

Jane's Defence Weekly 136, 137
Jeffreys, Harold 21–2
Johnson, Dr Nick 135
Joint Air miss Working Group 128, 131, 134, 142
Jones, Professor Reginald Victor 24, 25, *25*, 28, 29, 32, 33, 74, 148
Journal of Meteorology 111

K

Kelly, Paul 146
Keyhoe, Donald: *The Flying Saucers are Real* 41
Kilburn, Flight Lieutenant John 48
Kimberley, Lord 101
King, Tom 136

L

Lack, David 52
Lakenheath-Bentwaters incident (1956) 64–6, 69, 148
Leslie, Desmond 116
Lever, Captain 29, 30
lightning 143 *see also* ball lightning
Little Rissington, RAF: UFO sighting (1952) 48–50, *50*
London: 'phantom airship' sightings over (1916) 16–17
Lott, Alan 84–5, *85*
Lovell, Sir Bernard 100
Lundberg, John 115

M

McClelland, Flight Sub-Lieutenant H. 17
McDonald, Air Vice Marshal Bill 54
Machrihanish, RAF 136
Manston, RAF 67
Mantell, Captain Thomas 39, 62, 91

Marcel, Major Jesse 37–8
marks on the ground 109–10
marsh gas 19
Meaden, Dr Terence 111–12
'Men in Black' 70–1
Mercer, Flight Lieutenant M.J. 72, 77
Meteorological Magazine, The 21
Meteorological Office 19–20, *21*, 22, 29, 58, 80, 88
Middle Wallop, RAF 113
Mildenhall, RAF 136
military secrets: links with UFOs 36, 40, 132–4
Mills, Dr Alan 19
missing time 117–18, 144
MoD (Ministry of Defence) 149; and alien abductions 118–19, 124; believing of UFOs by some officials within 138; commissioning of UFO study (Condign Report) 140–5; creation of unified (1964) 70; and crop circles 112–13, 115; dealing with and investigating of UFO reports 8, 72, 73, 75, 76, 77, 81, 84, 119, 150; discontinuing of annual statistical analysis of UFO reports 81; downplaying of potential risks posed by UFOs in near-miss incidents 128, 129, 130–1; explanations for UFOs 83, 93; internal debate on UFOs 138–9; policy towards UFOs 80; public stance that UFOs were of 'no defence significance' 106, 139; releasing of files to National Archives 89; and Rendlesham incident 106, 107, 108–9; standard letter in reply to UFO reported sightings *81*, 82, 84; statistical analysis of UFO reports 80
Mogul project 38, 62
moon landings 80
Moore, Patrick 151
Moreland, Squadron Leader Donald *104*, 105
Morgan, Flight Sub-Lieutenant Eric 16
Morris, Captain Joseph: *The German Air Raids on Great Britain* 16

Mountbatten, Lord 41, 47
'Mowing Devil, The' 110–11
Mulley, Fred 100

N

NASA 80
National Archives UFO page 8
natural phenomena: as explanation for UFO sightings 46, 51, 53, 80, 97, 100, 101, 132, 143-4, 145; *see also* ball lightning
near-misses: between UFOs and aircraft 128, 129–32, *129, 130*
Neatishead, RAF 64
New York Times 46
New Zealand: UFO sightings 96, 97
News of the World 70
Newton, Irving *38*
Newton Stewart 54
9/11 145
North Sea: UFO sightings over 88–9
Norwich, Bishop of 100
Noyes, Ralph 51, 54–5, 66, 69, 106, 138

O

Odiham, RAF 113, *113*
Oldfield, Joan and Tom 77–8
Operation Charlie incidents 40
Operation Mainbrace 47, 51
Orford Ness lighthouse 107

P

Paget, Peter: *The Welsh Triangle* 91
Patterson, Patrick 147
Peck, Robin 79
Peduzie, J.A. 92–3
Penniston, Sergeant Jim 107–8
Perks, Colin 71–3, *72*
Perry, Andrew 119
Persinger, Dr Michael 144
Petrozavodsk (Soviet Union) 64
'phantom airship' sightings 11–17, *12, 17, 25*, 135; (1909) 11–12, 15; above London (1916) 16–17; first year of First World War (1914) 14–15; Sheerness incident (1912) 13–14; Vickers shipyard sighting 14–15

pilots, military: large object sightings over Alps 29–30; sighting of foo-fighters 23–5, 27–8; UFO sightings by 43–4, 56–7, 58, 62, 64–7, 89–90, *89*, 125, 127–8

pilots, civilian: and near miss incidents 129–32; and UFO sightings 125, 127–8

plasmas, atmospheric 143–4

Pope, Nick 121–2, 135, 138; *Open Skies, Closed Minds* 138

Project Blue Book 46, 51, 57, 60, 61, 63, 66, 74, 81, 127

Project Condign *see* Condign Report

Project Grudge 40, 42, 46

Project Sign 39–40

Project Y 61, *61*

Provost & Security Service (P&SS) 92

Pugh, Randall Jones 90–1

Punchbowl (Cheesefoot Head) 114

Q

Quartermass Experiment, The 116

R

radar angels 25–6, 27, 51–2

radar incidents 25–6, *27*, 33–4, 46, 51–4, 58, *59*, 64–6, 68–9, 145

Ramey, Brigadier Roger 37

Randles, Jenny 132

Rees, Lord Martin 150

Rees, Merlyn 74

Rendlesham Forest incident (1980) 103–9, *104*, 138

Rennie, Michael 116

Rice, Donald 136

Ridpath, Ian 107, 108, 132

Roberts, Andy 24

Robertson, Dr Bob 27–8, 29, 57, 60

Robinson, Douglas 15

rockets, ghost 32–3, 36

Roswell Files report (1994/5) 38–9

Roswell incident (1947) 36–9, *37*, *38*, 62, 87, 102

Rothnie, A.K. 83–4

Royal New Zealand Air Force 97

Ruppelt, Captain Edward 40, 46, 51

Russell, Kate 146–7

S

St Mawgan, RAF 83

Salandin, Flight Lieutenant James 56

Samford, Major General John 46

Sandys, Duncan 41, 47

Scarborough Daily Post 17

Schiff, Steven 38

schoolchildren: UFO sightings by 90, 93

Schulgen, Brigadier General George 39

Scientific Study of Unidentified Flying Objects (1969) 81

Scotsman, The 136

Scull, John 111

Second World War 22, 25; foo-fighter sightings by aircraft pilots 22–5, *24*, 27–9, 57, 96, 144; large object sightings over the Alps 29–30; radar incidents 25–6, 27; spotting of UFO during raid on southern France 30–1, *31*

'secret weapon' hypothesis 36, 40 *see also* 'black projects'

Sheerness incident (1912) 13–14

Sheppard, Graham 127

Shuttlewood, Arthur 90

Silbury Hill, crop circles 113

'Silent Vulcans' 136

Simon, Dr Benjamin 118

Skyhook programme 39–40, 61–2

Soviet Union 40, 61–2; denouncement of UFOs 64

Spielberg, Steven 94, 112

Sputnik 100

spy planes: and UFO sightings 62–4

SR-71 Blackbird 63, 64, 136

Startup, Bill 96

stealth aircraft 127, 133, *133*, 134, 136, 139

Stevens, Patrick 97, 98, 101

Strabolgi, Lord (David Kenworthy) 98, 101, 148, 149

Strieber, Whitley: *Communion* 121

Sueter, Murray F. 13–14

'sun dogs' 83

Sunday Dispatch 41

Supreme Headquarters Allied Expeditionary Force (SHAEF) 27

Sweden: and ghost rocket scare 32–3

Swiney, Air Commodore Michael 48–50, 51, 141

T

Taylor, Anne 82

Thayer, Gordon 66

Thing from Another World, The 116

Thomas, Dafyd Ellis 87–8

Thurkettle, Vince 107, 108

Titchmarsh, Pam 112

Tizard, Sir Henry 41, 42, 145

Today 114, 115

Tomorrow's World 78

Topcliffe incident (1952) 47–8, *49*

Tornado crew, UFO report (1990) 134

Torres, Lieutenant Milton 67–8

Trefgarne, Lord David 109

Trimingham, RAF 52

Truman, President Harry 46

Tudor, Rear-Admiral F.C.T. 17

Turnbull, Hugh 91

Turney, G.L. 42

Twining, General Nathan F. 39

U

U2 spy plane 62–3, 64

UFO cover up 38, 39, 70, 94, 106–7, 108, 115, 149

UFO database 142

UFO Desk 69–70, 81, 90, 113, 135, 138, 145, 146, 149–50

UFO flaps: (1952) 46–7; (1967) 73–5, 80, 128; and Condign study 143; February (1988) 120; March (1993) 135, 138; Washington (1952) 46, 57; Welsh (1977) 90–1, 93

UFO hotspots 90–1

UFO Register, The 55

'UFO Solar' 131

UFOs (unidentified flying objects): attempts to control spread of information about sightings 57–8, 60; balloons as explanation for sightings 15, 34, 37, 38, 46, 58, 61–2, 64, 74, 78, 82; debate in House of Lords on 96–7, 148, 149; destruction of reports 9, 50, 68; difficulties faced by official investigations 78; ending of

intelligence interest in 145;
filming of 77–8, *78*, 96; naural
phenomena and sightings 46, 51,
53, 80, 97, 100, 101, 132, 143–4,
145; near collision between
aircraft and 128, 129–32, *129,
130*; official explanations for
82–3, 93, 143, 148; ordering of
pilot to shoot down (1956) 67–8;
photographs taken by public 70,
71; pilot sightings *see* pilots,
civilian; pilots, military; public
belief and fascination in 69, 94;
public sightings and reports
40–1, 56–7, 71–2, 75–6, 79–80,
82–4,   84–6, *85*, 94–5; radar
incidents 25–6, *27*, 33–4, 46,
51–4, 58, *59*, 64–6, 68–9, 145;
recent sightings (2007/08) 146–7,
150; reduction in official interest
81–2; and 'secret weapon'
hypothesis 36, 40; spy planes and
sightings of 62–4; types of *55*;
Venus mistaken for 75
unidentified aerial phenomena
(UAP) 140
United Nations 97
United States Air Force *see* USAF
United States Army Air Force
(USAAF) 24, 25, 34
Upton Primary Junior School 93,
93
USAF (United States Air Force)

25, 40, 42, 63, 105, 136; closing
down Project Blue Book 81, 105;
formation 39; and Project Blue
Book *see* Project Blue Book;
sightings by personnel 39, 64, 65,
69, 106, 107; and UFO reports
46, 63
USAF Missile Development
Center 62

V
Vandenberg, General Hoyt 40
Venus 74, 75, 97, 116
Vickers shipyard (Barrow-in-
Furness): airship sightings 14–15
Vulcan crew: UFO encounter by
89–90, *89*

W
Waddington, RAF 89
Wales: UFO sightings in West 90–3
Wall, Major Patrick 60
War Office 32
War of the Worlds radio broadcast
(1938) 41
Ward, George 60–1, 66, 68–9
Warminster triangle 90, 110, 111,
112
Washington DC: UFO panic
(1952) 46, 57
Wattisham, RAF 120–1
Watton, RAF 108
Waycott, Clifford 73

Weeden, Simon 105–6
Wells, H, G.: *The War of the Worlds*
115
West, David 69–70
West Drayton, RAF 128
West Freugh, RAF: UFO sightings
at (1957) 53–4, 55, 64
West Malling incident (1953) 62
Westbury: crop circles at 112
Whitworth, Wing Commander
Peter 53
Widdecombe-in-the-Moor
(Dartmoor) 19
Will-o'-the-Wisp 19, 144
Willey, Roger 73
Wiltshire: crop circles 90, 110,
111–12, 113; moving lights
incident 86, 90
Wimbledon, Flight Lieutenant
Freddie 64
'winter of discontent' 95
Wood, Flight Lieutenant 88
Woodbridge, RAF 103, 107

X
X-Files, The 135, 138

Y
Yeager, Chuck 33

Z
Zeppelin, Count 14
Zeppelins 12, 13–14, *14*, 16

ACKNOWLEDGMENTS
Special thanks to friends and fellow researchers who
have provided assistance and material during the
writing of this book (in no particular order): Keith
Chester, Peter Hassall, Joe McGonagle, Gary Anthony,
Andy Roberts, Nick Redfern, Martin Shough,
Nigel Watson, Ian Ridpath, Joel Carpenter, Paul Fuller,
Mark Pilkington, John Rimmer, John Keeling and
Peter Brookesmith.
     For access to archive material, special thanks are due
to DAS4 staff and Records Management staff at the
Ministry of Defence and Andrew Riley at the Churchill

Archive, University of Cambridge. Thanks are also
given to the staff of the British Library (St Pancras
and Newspaper Library, Colindale); the BBC Written
Archive; the Broadlands Archive at the University of
Southampton; the Mass Observation Archive at the
University of Sussex; and the Hull University Archives
for the Patrick Wall papers.
     I wish to thank my colleagues at the National
Archives whose hospitality, patience and attention
to detail are much appreciated, in particular
Tom Wharton, Catherine Bradley and everyone in
the PR team.